Praise for
Code That Fits in Your Head

"We progress in software by standing ho came
before us. Mark's vast experience organisa-
tional considerations right down writing code. In this
book, you're offered an opportunity to build on that experience. Use it."

— *Adam Ralph, speaker, tutor, and software simplifier, Particular Software*

"I've been reading Mark's blogs for years and he always manages to entertain while at the same time offering deep technical insights. *Code That Fits in Your Head* follows in that vein, offering a wealth of information to any software developer looking to take their skills to the next level."

— *Adam Tornhill, founder of CodeScene, author of* Software Design X-Rays *and* Your Code as a Crime Scene

"My favorite thing about this book is how it uses a single code base as a working example. Rather than having to download separate code samples, you get a single Git repository with the entire application. Its history is hand-crafted to show the evolution of the code alongside the concepts being explained in the book. As you read about a particular principle or technique, you'll find a direct reference to the commit that demonstrates it in practice. Of course, you're also free to navigate the history at your own leisure, stopping at any stage to inspect, debug, or even experiment with the code. I've never seen this level of interactivity in a book before, and it brings me special joy because it takes advantage of Git's unique design in a new constructive way."

— *Enrico Campidoglio, independent consultant, speaker and Pluralsight author*

"Mark Seemann not only has decades of experience architecting and building large software systems, but is also one of the foremost thinkers on how to scale and manage the complex relationship between such systems and the teams that build them."

— *Mike Hadlow, freelance software consultant and blogger*

"Mark Seemann is well known for explaining complex concepts clearly and thoroughly. In this book he condenses his wide-ranging software development experience into a set of practical, pragmatic techniques for writing sustainable and human-friendly code. This book will be a must read for every programmer."

—*Scott Wlaschin, author of* Domain Modeling Made Functional

"Mark writes, 'Successful software endures'—this book will help you to write that kind of software."

—*Bryan Hogan, software architect, podcaster, blogger*

"Mark has an extraordinary ability to help others think deeply about the industry and profession of software development. With every interview on *.NET Rocks!* I have come away knowing I would have to go back and listen to my own show to really take in everything we discussed."

—*Richard Campbell, co-host*, .NET Rocks!

Code That Fits in Your Head

Robert C. Martin Series

Visit **informit.com/martinseries** for a complete list of available publications.

The **Robert C. Martin Series** is directed at software developers, team-leaders, business analysts, and managers who want to increase their skills and proficiency to the level of a Master Craftsman. The series contains books that guide software professionals in the principles, patterns, and practices of programming, software project management, requirements gathering, design, analysis, testing, and others.

Make sure to connect with us!
informit.com/socialconnect

Code That Fits in Your Head

HEURISTICS FOR SOFTWARE ENGINEERING

Mark Seemann

✦Addison-Wesley

Boston • Columbus • New York • San Francisco • Amsterdam • Cape Town
Dubai • London • Madrid • Milan • Munich • Paris • Montreal • Toronto • Delhi • Mexico City
São Paulo • Sydney • Hong Kong • Seoul • Singapore • Taipei • Tokyo

Cover: Mark Seeman
Page xxix, author photo: © Linea Vega Seemann Jacobsen
Page 12, Queen Alexandrine's Bridge, Denmark: Ulla Seemann
Page 33, baseball and bat: buriy/123RF
Page 38, illustration of human brain: maglyvi/Shutterstock
Page 38, illustration of laptop computer: grmarc/Shutterstock
Page 157, Figure 8.2: © Microsoft 2021
Page 158, Figure 8.3, scissors: Hurst Photo/Shutterstock
Page 158, Figure 8.3, hand saw: Andrei Kuzmik/Shutterstock
Page 158, Figure 8.3, utility knife: Yogamreet/Shutterstock
Page 158, Figure 8.3, Phillips-head screwdriver: bozmp/Shutterstock
Page 158, Figure 8.3, Swiss military knife: Billion Photos/Shutterstock
Page 159, Figure 8.4: Roman Babakin/Shutterstock
Page 170, Figure 8.5: © Microsoft 2021
Page 239, Figure 12.1: ajt/Shutterstock
Page 259, Figure 13.2, bursting star: Arcady/Shutterstock
Page 269, Figure 13.5: Verdandi/123RF
Page 277, Figure 14.1: Tatyana Pronina/Shutterstock
Page 291, Figure 15.2: kornilov007/Shutterstock
Page 291, hammer: bozmp/Shutterstock
Pages 306, Figure 15.3: Figure based on a screen shot from codescene.io
Pages 307, Figure 15.4: Figure based on a screen shot from codescene.io

For information about buying this title in bulk quantities, or for special sales opportunities (which may include electronic versions; custom cover designs; and content particular to your business, training goals, marketing focus, or branding interests), please contact our corporate sales department at corpsales@pearsoned.com or (800) 382-3419.

For government sales inquiries, please contact governmentsales@pearsoned.com.

For questions about sales outside the U.S., please contact intlcs@pearson.com.

Visit us on the Web: informit.com/aw

Library of Congress Control Number: 2021944424

ISBN-13: 978-0-13-746440-1
ISBN-10: 0-13-746440-1

1 2021

To my parents:
My mother, Ulla Seemann, to whom I owe my attention to detail.
My father, Leif Seemann, from whom I inherited my contrarian streak.

"The future is already here — it's just not very evenly distributed"
—*William Gibson*

Contents

SERIES EDITOR FOREWORD

My grandson is learning to code.

Yes, you read that right. My 18-year-old grandson is learning to program computers. Who's teaching him? His aunt, my youngest daughter, who was born in 1986, and who 16 months ago decided to change careers from chemical engineering to programming. And who do they both work for? My eldest son, who along with my youngest son, is in the process of starting up his second software consultancy.

Yeah, software runs in the family. And, yeah, I've been programming for a long, long time.

Anyway, my daughter asked me to spend an hour with my grandson teaching him about the basics and the beginnings of computer programming. So we started up a Tuple session and I lectured him on what computers were, and how they got started, and what early computers looked like, and . . . well, you know.

By the end of the lecture I was coding up the algorithm for multiplying two binary integers, in PDP-8 assembly language. For those of you who aren't aware, the PDP-8 had no multiply instruction; you had to write an algorithm to multiply numbers. Indeed, the PDP-8 didn't even have a subtract instruction; you had to use two's complement and add a pseudo-negative number (let the reader understand).

As I finished up the coding example, it occurred to me that I was scaring my grandson to death. I mean, when I was 18 this kind of geeky detail thrilled me; but maybe it wasn't so attractive to an 18-year-old whose aunt is trying to teach him how to write simple Clojure programs.

Anyway, it made me think of just how hard programming actually is. And it is hard. It's really hard. It may be the hardest thing that humans have ever attempted.

Oh, I don't mean it's hard to write the code to calculate a bunch of prime numbers, or a Fibonacci sequence, or a simple bubble sort. That's not too hard. But an Air Traffic Control system? A luggage management system? A bill of materials system? *Angry Birds*? Now that's hard. That's really, really hard.

I've known Mark Seemann for quite a few years now. I don't remember ever actually meeting him. It may be that we have never actually been together in the same room. But he and I have interacted quite a bit in professional newsgroups and social networks. He's one of my favourite people to disagree with.

He and I disagree on all kinds of things. We disagree on static versus dynamic typing. We disagree on operating systems and languages. We disagree on, well, lots of intellectually challenging things. But disagreeing with Mark is something you have to do very carefully because the logic of his arguments is impeccable.

So when I saw this book, I thought about how much fun it was going to be to read through and disagree with. And that's exactly what happened. I read through it. I disagreed with some things. And I had fun trying to find a way to make my logic supersede his. I think I may have even succeeded in one or two cases—in my head—maybe.

But that's not the point. The point is that software is hard; and much of the last seven decades have been spent trying to find ways to make it a little bit easier. What Mark has done in this book is to gather all the best ideas from those seven decades and compile them in one place.

More than that, he has organized them into a set of heuristics and techniques, and placed them in the order that you would execute them. Those heuristics and techniques build on each other, helping you move from stage to stage while developing a software project.

In fact, Mark develops a software project throughout the pages of this book, while explaining each stage and the heuristics and techniques that benefit that stage.

Mark uses C# (one of the things I disagree with ;-), but that's not relevant. The code is simple, and the heuristics and techniques are applicable to any other language you might be using.

He covers things such as Checklists, TDD, Command Query Separation, Git, Cyclomatic Complexity, Referential Transparency, Vertical Slicing, Legacy Strangulation, and Outside-In Development, just to mention a few.

Moreover, there are gems scattered literally everywhere throughout these pages. I mean, you'll be reading along, and all of a sudden he'll say something like, "Rotate your test function 90 degrees and see if you can balance it on the Act of the Arrange/Act/Assert triplet" or "The goal is not to write code fast. The goal is sustainable software" or "Commit database schema to git".

Some of these gems are profound, some are just idle mentions, others are speculations, but all of them are examples of the deep insight that Mark has acquired over the years.

So read this book. Read it carefully. Think through Mark's impeccable logic. Internalise these heuristics and techniques. Stop and consider the insightful gems as they pop out at you. And just maybe, when it comes time for you to lecture your grandchildren, you won't scare the devil out of them.

—*Robert C. Martin*

PREFACE

In the second half of the 2000s, I began doing technical reviews for a publisher. After reviewing a handful of books, the editor contacted me about a book on Dependency Injection.

The overture was a little odd. Usually, when they contacted me about a book, it would already have an author and a table of contents. This time, however, there was none of that. The editor just requested a phone call to discuss whether the book's subject matter was viable.

I thought about it for a few days and found the topic inspiring. At the same time, I couldn't see the need for an entire book. After all, the knowledge was out there: blog posts, library documentation, magazine articles, even a few books all touched on related topics.

On reflection, I realised that, while the information was all out there, it was scattered, and used inconsistent and sometimes conflicting terminology. There'd be value in collecting that knowledge and presenting it in a consistent pattern language.

Two years later, I was the proud author of a published book.

After some years had gone by, I began to think about writing another book. Not this one, but a book about some other topic. Then I had a third idea, and a fourth, but not this one.

A decade went by, and I began to realise that when I consulted teams on writing better code, I'd suggest practices that I'd learned from better minds than mine. And again, I realised that most of that knowledge is already available, but it's scattered, and few people have explicitly connected the dots into a coherent description of how to develop software.

Based on my experience with the first book, I know that there's value in collecting disparate information and presenting it in a consistent way. This book is my attempt at creating such a package.

WHO SHOULD READ THIS BOOK

This book is aimed at programmers with at least a few years of professional experience. I expect readers to have suffered through a few bad software development projects; to have experience with unmaintainable code. I also expect readers seeking to improve.

The core audience is 'enterprise developers'—particularly back-end developers. I've spent most of my career in that realm, so this simply reflects my own expertise. But if you're a front-end developer, a games programmer, a development tools engineer, or something else entirely, I expect you will still gain a lot from reading this book.

You should be comfortable reading code in a compiled, object-oriented language in the C family. While I've been a C# programmer for most of my career, I've learned a lot from books with example code in C++ or Java[1]. This book turns the tables: Its example code is in C#, but I hope that Java, TypeScript, or C++ developers find it useful, too.

---

1. If you're curious about which books I mean, take a look at the bibliography.

PREREQUISITES

This isn't a beginner's book. While it deals with how to organise and structure source code, it doesn't cover the most basic details. I expect that you already understand why indentation is helpful, why long methods are problematic, that global variables are bad, and so on. I don't expect you to have read *Code Complete* [65], but I assume that you know of some of the basics covered there.

A NOTE FOR SOFTWARE ARCHITECTS

The term 'architect' means different things to different people, even when the context is constrained to software development. Some architects focus on the big picture; they help an entire organisation succeed with its endeavours. Other architects are deep in the code and mainly concerned with the sustainability of a particular code base.

To the degree that I'm a software architect, I'm the latter kind. My expertise is in how to organise source code so that it addresses long-term business goals. I write about what I know, so to the degree this book is useful to architects, it will be that type of architect.

You'll find no content about Architecture Tradeoff Analysis Method (ATAM), Failure Mode and Effects Analysis (FMEA), service discovery, and so on. That kind of architecture is outside the scope of this book.

ORGANISATION

While this is a book about methodologies, I've structured it around a code example that runs throughout the book. I decided to do it that way in order to make the reading experience more compelling than a typical 'pattern catalogue'. One consequence of this decision is that I introduce practices and heuristics when they fit the 'narrative'. This is also the order in which I typically introduce the techniques when I coach teams.

The narrative is structured around a sample code base that implements a restaurant reservation system. The source code for that sample code base is available at informit.com/title/9780137464401.

If you want to use the book as a handbook, I've included an appendix with a list of all the practices and information about where in the book you can read more.

ABOUT THE CODE STYLE

The example code is written in C#, which is a language that has rapidly evolved in recent years. It's picking up more and more syntax ideas from functional programming; as an example, *immutable record types* were released while I was writing the book. I've decided to ignore some of these new language features.

Once upon a time, Java code looked a lot like C# code. Modern C# code, on the other hand, doesn't look much like Java.

I want the code to be comprehensible to as many readers as possible. Just as I've learned much from books with Java examples, I want readers to be able to use this book without knowing the latest C# syntax. Thus, I'm trying to stick to a conservative subset of C# that ought to be legible to other programmers.

This doesn't change the concepts presented in the book. Yes, in some instances, a more succinct C#-specific alternative is possible, but that would just imply that extra improvements are available.

TO VAR OR NOT TO VAR

The var keyword was introduced to C# in 2007. It enables you to declare a variable without explicitly stating its type. Instead, the compiler infers the type from the context. To be clear, variables declared with var are exactly as statically typed as variables declared with explicit types.

For a long time the use of this keyword was controversial, but most people now use it; I do, too, but I occasionally encounter pockets of resistance.

While I use var professionally, writing code for a book is a slightly different context. Under normal circumstances, an IDE isn't far away. A modern development environment can quickly tell you the type of an implicitly typed variable, but a book can't.

I have, for that reason, occasionally chosen to explicitly type variables. Most of the example code still uses the var keyword because it makes the code shorter, and line width is limited in a printed book. In a few cases, though, I've deliberately chosen to explicitly declare a variable's type, in the hope that it makes the code easier to understand when read in a book.

CODE LISTINGS

The majority of the code listings are taken from the same sample code base. It's a Git repository, and the code examples are taken from various stages of development. Each such code listing includes a relative path to the file in question. Part of that file path is a Git commit ID.

For example, listing 2.1 includes this relative path: *Restaurant/f729ed9/Restaurant.RestApi/Program.cs*. This means that the example is taken from commit ID f729ed9, and the file is Restaurant.RestApi/Program.cs. In other words, to view this particular version of the file, you check out that commit:

```
$ git checkout f729ed9
```

When you've done that, you can now explore the Restaurant.RestApi/Program.cs file in its full, executable context.

A NOTE ON THE BIBLIOGRAPHY

The bibliography contains a mix of resources, including books, blog posts, and video recordings. Many of my sources are online, so I have of course supplied URLs. I've made an effort to mostly include resources that I have reason to believe have a stable presence on the Internet.

Still, things change. If you're reading this book in the future, and a URL has become invalid, try an internet archive service. As I'm writing this, https://archive.org is the best candidate, but that site could also be gone in the future.

QUOTING MYSELF

Apart from other resources, the bibliography also includes a list of my own work. I'm aware that, as far as making a case, quoting myself doesn't constitute a valid argument in itself.

I'm not including my own work as a sleight of hand. Rather, I'm including these resources for the reader who might be interested in more details. When I cite myself, I do it because you may find an expanded argument, or a more detailed code example, in the resource I point to.

ACKNOWLEDGEMENTS

I'd like to thank my wife Cecilie for love and support during all the years we've been together, and my children Linea and Jarl for staying out of trouble.

Apart from family, my first thanks go to my invaluable long-time friend Karsten Strøbæk, who not only has tolerated my existence for 25 years, but who was also the first reviewer on this book. He also helped me with various LATEX tips and tricks, and added more entries to the index than I did.

I'd also like to thank Adam Tornhill for his feedback on the section about his work.

I'm indebted to Dan North for planting the phrase *Code That Fits in Your Head* in my subconscious, which might have happened as early as 2011 [72].

Register your copy of *Code That Fits in Your Head* on the InformIT site for convenient access to updates and/or corrections as they become available. To start the registration process, go to informit.com/register and log in or create an account. Enter the product ISBN (9780137464401) and click Submit. Look on the Registered Products tab for an Access Bonus Content link next to this product, and follow that link to access any available bonus materials. If you would like to be notified of exclusive offers on new editions and updates, please check the box to receive email from us.

ABOUT THE AUTHOR

Mark Seemann is a bad economist who's found a second career as a programmer, and he has worked as a web and enterprise developer since the late 1990s. As a young man Mark wanted to become a rock star, but unfortunately had neither the talent nor the looks – later, however, he became a Certified Rockstar Developer. He has also written a Jolt Award-winning book about Dependency Injection, given more than a 100 international conference talks, and authored video courses for both Pluralsight and Clean Coders. He has regularly published blog posts since 2006. He lives in Copenhagen with his wife and two children.

I

ACCELERATION

The first part of this book is loosely structured around a programming narrative. The code examples all follow an example code base, from creation of the first file, to completion of the first feature.

In the beginning, you'll see detailed explanations of changes to the code. As the chapters progress, I'll skip some details. The purpose of the code examples is to give you a context for the various practices and techniques being introduced.

If I've skipped a detail that you'd like to know more about, you can consult the Git repository that accompanies the book. Each code listing is tagged with the commit ID that identifies the source.

The history of the commits that belong to this part is quite polished. If you read through that part of the Git history, it'll look as though I barely made any mistakes. That's not the case.

To err is human, and I make as many mistakes as you. One of the wonderful features of Git, however, is that you can rewrite history. I've been rebasing that part of the repository multiple times to make it as polished as I wanted it.

I didn't do that to cover my mistakes. I did it because I felt that for those readers who'd like to learn from the repository, it'd be more educational if I removed the noise of my mistakes.

The example code forms a narrative from which to introduce the practices that I describe. In this part of the book, you'll see the code *accelerate* from zero to a deployed feature. But even if you aren't working with greenfield development, you should be able to use the techniques to increase your efficiency.

ART OR SCIENCE?

1

Are you a scientist or an artist? An engineer or a craftsman? Are you a gardener or a chef? A poet or an architect?

Are you a programmer or a software developer? If so, then what are you?

My response to these questions is: *Yes, none of the above.*

While I self-identify as a programmer, I'm a little of all of the above. And yet, none of those.

Questions like these are important. The software development industry is about 70 years old, and we're still figuring it out. One persistent problem is how to *think* about it. Hence these questions. Is software development like building a house? Is it like composing a poem?

Over the decades, we've tried sundry metaphors, but they all fall apart. Developing software is like building a house, except when it isn't. Developing software is like growing a garden, except when it isn't. Ultimately, none of the metaphors fit.

I believe, though, that how we think about software development shapes how we work.

If you think that developing software is like building a house, you'll make mistakes.

1.1   BUILDING A HOUSE

For decades, people have likened developing software to building a house. As Kent Beck puts it:

> *"Unfortunately, design in software has been shackled by metaphors from physical design activities."* [5]

It's one of the most pervasive, beguiling, and obstructive metaphors of software development.

1.1.1   THE PROBLEM WITH PROJECTS

If you think of developing software as being similar to building a house, the first mistake you'll make is to think of it as a *project*. A project has a start and an end. Once you reach the end, the work is done.

Only unsuccessful software ends. Successful software endures. If you're fortunate enough to develop successful software, when you're done with a release you'll move on to develop the next. This can go on for years. Some successful software lasts for decades[1].

Once you've built a house, people can move in. You'll need to maintain it, but the cost of that is only a fraction of what it cost to build it. Granted, software like that exists. Particularly in the enterprise segment, once you've built[2] an internal line-of-business application, it's done and users are fettered to it. Such software enters maintenance mode once the project is done.

---

1. I'm writing this book in LaTeX—a program first released in 1984!
2. This is a verb I aspire to never use about software development, but in this particular context, it makes sense.

But most software isn't like that. Software that competes with other software is never done. If you're caught in the house-building metaphor, you may think of it as a series of projects. You may plan to release the next version of your product in nine months, but to your horror find that your competitor publishes improvements every three months.

So you work hard at making the 'projects' shorter. When you're finally able to deliver every three months, your competitor is on a one-month release cycle. You can see where this ends, can't you?

It ends with Continuous Delivery [49]. That, or you'll eventually go out of business. Based on research, the book *Accelerate* [29] argues convincingly that the key capability distinguishing high-performing from low-performing teams is the ability to release at the drop of a hat.

When you can do that, the notion of a software development *project* no longer makes sense.

1.1.2 THE PROBLEM WITH PHASES

Another misconception often produced by the house-building metaphor is that software development should happen in distinct *phases*. When building a house, an architect first draws the plans. Then you prepare the logistics, move materials on site, and only then can you begin to build.

When this metaphor is applied to software development, you appoint a *software architect* whose responsibility it is to produce a plan. Only when the plan is done should development start. This perspective on software development sees the planning phase as the phase where intellectual work happens. According to the metaphor, the programming phase is like the actual construction phase of a house. Developers are seen as interchangeable workers[3], basically little more than glorified typists.

Nothing could be farther from the truth. As Jack Reeves pointed out in 1992 [87], the *construction* phase of software development is when you

---

3. I've nothing against construction workers; my beloved father was a mason.

compile source code. It's virtually free, quite unlike construction of a house. All work happens in the *design* phase, or as Kevlin Henney so eloquently put it:

> *"The act of describing a program in unambiguous detail and the act of programming are one and the same."* [42]

In software development, there's no construction phase to speak of. This doesn't imply that planning isn't useful, but it does indicate that the house-building metaphor is at best unhelpful.

1.1.3 DEPENDENCIES

When you build a house, physical reality imposes constraints. You must first lay the foundations, then raise the walls, and only then can you put on the roof. In other words, the roof depends on the walls, which depend on the foundation.

This metaphor tricks people into thinking that they need to manage dependencies. I've had project managers who produced elaborate Gantt charts to plan a project.

I've worked with numerous teams, and most of them start any new development project by designing a relational database schema. The database is the foundation of most online services, and teams seem incapable of shaking the notion that you could develop a user interface before you have a database.

Some teams never manage to produce a working piece of software. After they've designed the database, they figure that they need a *framework* to go with it. So they proceed to reinvent an object-relational mapper, that Vietnam of computer science [70].

The house-building metaphor is harmful because it deceives you into thinking about software development in a particular way. You'll miss opportunities that you don't see because your perspective doesn't align with reality. The reality of software development is that, metaphorically speaking, you *can* start with the roof. You'll see an example of this later in this book.

1.2 GROWING A GARDEN

The house-building metaphor is wrong, but perhaps other metaphors work better. The gardening metaphor has been gaining traction in the 2010s. It's not accidental that Nat Pryce and Steve Freeman named their excellent book *Growing Object-Oriented Software, Guided by Tests* [36].

This view on software development sees software as a living organism that must be tended, coaxed, and pruned. It's another compelling metaphor. Have you ever felt that a code base has a life of its own?

It can be illuminating to view software development in this light. At least it forces a change in perspective that might shake your belief that software development is like building a house.

By viewing software as a living organism, the gardening metaphor emphasises pruning. Left to itself, a garden will grow wild. In order to extract value from a garden, a gardener must tend to it by killing weeds while aiding and supporting the desired plants. Translated into software development, it helps focusing on activities that *prevent* code rot, such as refactoring and deletion of dead code.

I don't find this metaphor nearly as problematic as the house-building metaphor, but I still don't think that it paints the whole picture.

1.2.1 WHAT MAKES A GARDEN GROW?

I like the gardening metaphor's emphasis on activities that combat disorder. Just as you must prune and weed a garden, you must refactor and pay off technical debt in your code bases.

The gardening metaphor, on the other hand, says little about where code comes from. In a garden, plants grow automatically. All they need are nutrients, water, and light. Software, on the other hand, doesn't grow automatically. You can't just throw a computer, crisps, and soft drinks into a dark room and expect software to grow from that. You'd be lacking an important ingredient: programmers.

Code is written by someone. This is an active process, and the gardening metaphor doesn't have much to say about it. How do you decide what to write, and what not to write? How do you decide *how* to structure a piece of code?

If we wish to improve the software development industry, we have to address these questions, too.

1.3   TOWARDS ENGINEERING

Other metaphors for software development exist. For example, I already mentioned the term *technical debt*, which implies an accountant's view. I've also touched on the process of *writing* code, which suggests a similarity to other kinds of authoring. Few metaphors are entirely wrong, but none are perfectly right either.

There are reasons I've targeted the house-building metaphor in particular. One is that it's so pervasive. Another is that it seems so wrong as to be unsalvageable.

1.3.1   SOFTWARE AS A CRAFT

I came to the conclusion that the house-building metaphor is harmful many years ago. Once you dispose of a viewpoint, you typically go looking for a new one. I found it in *software craftsmanship*.

It seems compelling to view software development as a craft, as essentially *skilled work*. While you *can* take an education in computer science, you don't have to. I didn't[4].

The skills you need to work as a professional software developer tend to be situational. Learn how this specific code base is structured. Learn how to use that particular framework. Suffer through the ordeal of wasting three days troubleshooting a bug in production. Things like that.

---

4. In case you're wondering, I do have a university degree. It's in economics, but apart from a stint in the Danish Ministry of Economic Affairs, I never used it.

The more you do that, the more skilled you become. If you stay in the same company, and work in the same code base for years, you may become a specialised authority, but will that help you if you decide to work somewhere else?

You can learn faster by moving from code base to code base. Try some back-end development. Do some front-end development. Perhaps try some game programming, or some machine learning. This will expose you to a wide range of problems that will accumulate as experience.

This is strikingly similar to the old European tradition of *journeyman years*. A craftsman like a carpenter or roofer would travel around Europe, working for a while in a place before moving on to the next. Doing so exposed them to alternative solutions to problems. It made them better at their craft.

It's compelling to think of software developers like that. The book *The Pragmatic Programmer* is even subtitled *From Journeyman to Master* [50].

If this is true, it follows that we should structure our industry accordingly. We should have apprentices who work alongside masters. We could even organise guilds.

If it's true, that is.

Software craftsmanship is another metaphor. I find it illuminating, but when you shine a bright light on a subject, you also produce shadows. The brighter the light, the darker the shadow, as illustrated in figure 1.1.

Figure 1.1 The brighter the light you shine on an object, the darker the shadows seem.

There's still something missing from the picture.

1.3.2 HEURISTICS

My software craftsmanship years were, in some sense, a period of utter disillusionment. I saw skill as nothing but accumulated experience. It seemed to me that there was no methodology to software development. That everything depended on circumstances. That there was no right or wrong way to do things.

That programming was basically an art.

That suited me well. I've always liked art. When I was young, I wanted to be an artist[5].

The problem with that viewpoint is that it doesn't seem to scale. In order to 'create' new programmers, you'd have to take them on as apprentices until they have learned enough to become journeymen. From there, mastery is several more years away.

Another issue with viewing programming as an art or a craft is that it, too, doesn't fit reality. Around 2010, it began to occur to me [106] that I was following heuristics when I programmed—rules of thumb and guidelines that can be taught.

At first, I didn't make much of it. Over the years, however, I regularly found myself in positions where I was coaching other developers. When I did that, I'd often formulate reasons for writing code in particular ways.

I began to realise that I'd probably been wrong in my nihilism. That perhaps, guidelines might be the key to turning programming into an engineering discipline.

---

5. My oldest aspiration was to become a comic book artist in the European tradition. Later, in my teenage years, I picked up the guitar and dreamt of becoming a rock star. It turned out that while I enjoyed both drawing and playing, I wasn't particularly talented.

1.3.3 EARLIER NOTIONS OF SOFTWARE ENGINEERING

The notion of software engineering dates back to the late 1960s[6]. It was related to the contemporary *software crisis*, the dawning realisation that programming is *hard*.

Programmers back then actually had a good grasp of what they were doing. Many of the illustrious figures of our industry were active in those days: Edsger Dijkstra, Tony Hoare, Donald Knuth, Alan Kay. If you'd asked people back then if they thought that programming would be an engineering discipline in the 2020s, they'd probably say yes.

You may have noticed that I discuss the notion of software engineering as an aspirational goal, rather than a fact of everyday software development. It's possible that there are pockets of actual software engineering in the world[7], but in my experience, most software development is conducted in a different style.

I'm not alone in feeling that software engineering is still a future goal. Adam Barr puts it beautifully:

"If you're like me, you dream of a day when software engineering is studied in a thoughtful, methodical way, and the guidance given to programmers sits atop a foundation of experimental results rather than the shifting sands of individual experience." [4]

He explains how software engineering was well on its way, but then something happened that derailed it. What happened, according to Barr, was personal computers. They created a generation of programmers who'd taught themselves to program at home. Since they could tinker with computers in solitude, they remained largely ignorant of the body of knowledge that already existed.

---

6. The term may be older than that. It's not entirely clear to me, and I wasn't alive back then, so I don't recall. It seems uncontroversial, though, that two NATO conferences held in 1968 and 1969 popularised the term software engineering [4].

7. NASA seems like a good bet on being one of those pockets.

This state of affairs seems to persist to this day. Alan Kay calls computing *Pop Culture*:

> *"But pop culture holds a disdain for history. Pop culture is all about identity and feeling like you're participating. It has nothing to do with cooperation, the past or the future—it's living in the present. I think the same is true of most people who write code for money. They have no idea where [their culture came from]"* [52]

We may have squandered fifty years by making little progress on software engineering, but I think that we may have made progress in other ways.

1.3.4 MOVING FORWARD WITH SOFTWARE ENGINEERING

What does an engineer do? Engineers design and oversee the construction of things, from big structures such as bridges, tunnels, skyscrapers, and power plants, to tiny objects like microprocessors[8]. They help produce physical objects.

Dronning Alexandrine's bridge, popularly called *Mønbroen*. Completed in 1943, it connects Sealand with the smaller island of Møn, Denmark.

---

8. I once had a friend who was a chemical engineer by education. After university, he became a brewer with Carlsberg. Engineers also brew beer.

Programmers don't do that. Software is intangible. As Jack Reeves pointed out [87], since there's no physical object to produce, construction is virtually free. Software development is principally a design activity. When we type code into an editor it corresponds to engineers drawing plans, rather than workers constructing things.

'Real' engineers follow methodologies that usually lead to successful outcomes. That's what we programmers want to do as well, but we have to be careful to copy only those activities that make sense in our context. When you design a physical object, real construction is expensive. You can't just try to build a bridge, experiment with it for a while, only to decide that it's no good, tear it down, and start over. Because real-world construction is expensive, engineers engage in calculations and simulations. It takes less time and fewer materials to calculate the strength of a bridge than it does to build it.

There's an entire engineering discipline that relates to logistics. People engage in meticulous planning because that's the safest and least expensive way to build physical things.

That's the part of engineering we *don't* need to copy.

But there's plenty of other engineering methodologies that can inspire us. Engineers also do creative, human work, but it's often structured in a framework. Specific activities should be followed by other activities. They review and sign off on each other's work. They follow checklists [40].

You can do that as well.

That's what this book is about. It's a guided tour of heuristics I've found useful. I'm afraid it's closer to what Adam Barr calls *the shifting sands of individual experience* than to a scientifically founded set of laws.

I believe that this reflects the current state of our industry. Anyone who believes that we have firm scientific evidence for anything should read *The Leprechauns of Software Engineering* [13].

1.4 CONCLUSION

If you think about the history of software development, you probably think of advances at orders of magnitudes. Yet, many of those advances are advances in hardware, not software. Still, in the last fifty years, we've witnessed tremendous progress in software development.

Today, we have much more advanced programming languages than fifty years ago, access to the Internet (including de facto online help in the form of Stack Overflow), object-oriented and functional programming, automated testing frameworks, Git, integrated development environments, and so on.

On the other hand, we're still struggling with the *software crisis*, although it's debatable whether anything can be called a crisis if it's been going on for half a century.

Despite serious efforts, the software development industry still doesn't resemble an engineering discipline. There are some fundamental differences between engineering and programming. Until we understand that, we can't make progress.

The good news is that you can do many of the things that engineers do. There's a mindset, and a collection of processes you can follow.

As the science-fiction author William Gibson said:

> *"The future is already here—it's just not very evenly distributed"*[9]

As the book *Accelerate* charts, some organisations use advanced techniques today, while other lag behind [29]. The future is, indeed, unevenly distributed. The good news is that the advanced ideas are free for the taking. It's up to you to start using them.

In chapter 2, you'll get your first taste of concrete activities you can perform.

---

9. This is one of those quotes that have a nebulous origin. It seems uncontroversial that the idea and overall phrasing is Gibson's, but exactly when he first stated it is unclear [76].

2 CHECKLISTS

How do you transition from programmer to software engineer? I don't want to claim that this book has the definitive answer to that question, but I hope it can set you on the path.

I believe that it's so early in the history of software development that there are lots of things we still don't understand. On the other hand, we can't wait until we've figured it all out. We learn by experimentation. The activities and methodologies presented in this book are inspired by many great people who came before me[1]. These practices have worked for me and the many people I've taught. I hope that they'll work for you as well, or that they'll inspire you to identify even better ways to work.

2.1 AN AID TO MEMORY

A fundamental problem with software development is that there's a lot going on. Our brains aren't good at keeping track of many things at the same time.

---

1. There are too many to be listed here, but take a look at the bibliography. I've done my best to credit everyone for their contributions, but I've certainly forgotten some, for which I apologise.

We also have a tendency to skip doing things that don't seem important right now.

The problem isn't that you don't know how to do a thing; it's that you forget to do it, even though you know that you ought to.

This problem isn't isolated to programming. Pilots suffer from it, and they invented a simple solution to the problem: *checklists*.

I realise that this sounds incredibly dull and constraining, but consider the origins of the checklist. According to Atul Gawande [40] it started in 1935 with the B-17 bomber. Compared to previous airplanes, the B-17 was much more complex. In fact, it was so complex that it crashed on a demonstration flight for potential army buyers, killing two crew members, including the pilot.

An investigation into the crash concluded that it was due to 'pilot error'. Given that the pilot was one of the army air corps' most experienced test pilots, this could hardly be written off as lack of training. As one newspaper put it, the plane was just "too much airplane for one man to fly." [40]

A group of test pilots came up with a solution: a checklist of *simple* actions to perform during take-off, and another to follow during landing.

Simple checklists empower skilled professionals such as airplane pilots. When a task is complex, it's almost inevitable that you forget to consider a thing or two. A checklist helps you focus on the hard parts of your task by taking your mind off the trivial things. You don't have to make an effort to remember to do all the trivial things; you just have to remember to refer to the checklist at various *pause points*.

It's important to understand that checklists are supposed to enable, support, and liberate practitioners. They're not there to monitor or audit. The power of checklists is that you *use* them in the situation—not that they leave any trail of evidence. Perhaps the most powerful lists are those that specifically *don't* leave any audit trail. These could simply be lists on a wall poster, a clipboard, in a ring binder, or similar.

Checklists are not intended to constrain you, but rather to improve results. As one of Atul Gawande's informants put it:

> *"When surgeons make sure to wash their hands or to talk to everyone on the team"* – he'd seen the surgery checklist – *"they improve their outcomes with no increase in skill. That's what we are doing when we use the checklist."* [40]

If pilots and surgeons can follow checklists, then so can you. The key is to *improve the outcome with no increase in skill*.

At various points in the coming chapters, I'm going to present you with checklists. This isn't the only 'engineering method' that you'll learn, but it's the simplest. It's a good place to start.

A checklist is just an aid to memory. It doesn't exist to restrict you; it exists to help you remember to perform trivial, but important actions, such as washing your hands before surgery.

2.2 CHECKLIST FOR A NEW CODE BASE

The checklists I'll present in this book are *suggestions*. They're based on how I approach programming, but your circumstances differ from mine, so they may not fit perfectly. Just like the take-off checklist for an Airbus A380 is different from the take-off checklist for the B-17.

Use my checklist suggestions verbatim, or as inspiration.

Here's a checklist for starting a new code base:

- ☑ Use Git
- ☑ Automate the build
- ☐ Turn on all error messages

That doesn't look like much, and that's deliberate. A checklist isn't a complex flowchart with detailed instructions. It's a simple list of items that you can cover in a few minutes.

Checklists come in two forms: *read-do* and *do-confirm* [40]. With a *read-do* checklist, you read each item on the list and immediately perform the action before you move on to the next item. With a *do-confirm* checklist, you do all the things, and then you run through the checklist and confirm that you've done all the activities.

I've deliberately left the above list vague and conceptual, but since it's worded in the imperative form, it suggests a *read-do* checklist. You could easily turn it into a *do-confirm* checklist, but if you do, you should make sure to go through it with at least one other person. That's what pilots do. One reads the checklist and the other confirms. It's too easy to skip a step if you're by yourself, but a copilot can keep you honest.

Exactly how to *use Git*, *automate the build*, and *turn on all error messages* is up to you, but in order to make the above checklist concrete, I'll show you a detailed, running example.

2.2.1   USE GIT

Git has become the de-facto standard source control system. Use it[2]. Compared to centralised source control systems such as CVS or Subversion, a distributed source control system offers a tremendous advantage. If you know how to use it, that is.

Git isn't the most user-friendly piece of technology on the planet, but you're a programmer. You've managed to learn at least one programming language. Compared to that, learning the basics of Git is easy. Do yourself a favour and invest one or two days learning the basics of it. Not a graphical user interface on top of it, but how it actually works.

Git gives you the ability to boldly *experiment* with your code. Try something out, and if it doesn't work, just undo your changes. It's the ability to work as a

---

2. Despite being superior to most alternatives, Git has plenty of issues. The biggest problem is its complicated and inconsistent command-line interface. If a better distributed source control system comes along in the future, feel free to migrate. At the time when I'm writing this, however, there's no better alternative.

source control system *on your hard drive* that makes Git stand above centralised version control systems.

There are several graphical user interfaces (GUIs) on top of Git, but in this book, I'll stick to the command line. Not only is it the foundation of Git, it's also the way I normally prefer to work with it. Although I'm on Windows, I work in Git Bash.

The first thing you should do in a new code base is to initialise a local Git repository[3]. Open your command-line window in the directory where you'd like to put the code. At this time you don't have to worry about online Git services like GitHub; you can always connect the repository later. Then write[4]:

```
$ git init
```

That's it. You may also consider following the advice from my friend Enrico Campidoglio [17] and add an empty commit:

```
$ git commit --allow-empty -m "Initial commit"
```

I usually do this because it enables me to rewrite the history of my repository before I publish it to an online Git service. You don't have to do this, though.

2.2.2 AUTOMATE THE BUILD

When you have hardly any code, it's easy to automate compilation, testing, and deployment. Trying to retrofit Continuous Delivery [49] onto an existing code base can seem a formidable undertaking. That's the reason I think you should do this right away.

Currently there's no code, only a Git repository. You'll need a minimal application in order to have something to compile. Create the minimal amount

---

3. I'd stick to this rule for any code base that I expect will live for more than a week. I sometimes don't bother initialising a Git repository for truly ephemeral code, but my threshold for creating a Git repository is quite low. You can always undo it again by deleting the .git directory.

4. Don't write the $—it's just there to indicate the command-line prompt. I'll include it throughout the book when showing what happens on the command line.

of code that you're able to deploy, and then deploy it. This is an idea similar to a Walking Skeleton [36], but one step earlier in the development process, as suggested by figure 2.1.

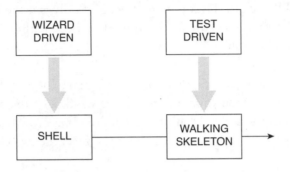

Figure 2.1 Use a wizard or scaffolding program to create a shell of the application, commit it, and deploy it. Then use an automated test to create a Walking Skeleton [36] that you commit and deploy.

A Walking Skeleton is an implementation of the thinnest possible slice of real functionality that you can automatically build, deploy, and test end-to-end [36]. You can do that next, but I think that there's value in first establishing a deployment pipeline [49].

Common Issues Related to Establishing a Deployment Pipeline

What if you can't set up a deployment pipeline yet? Perhaps you don't have a Continuous Integration server. If so, make it a priority to get one. You don't have to get an actual server. These days, there's plenty of cloud-based Continuous Delivery services.

Perhaps you don't have a production environment yet. Try to work around this issue by configuring your deployment pipeline so that you can release to some preproduction environment. Preferably one that looks as much like the production environment as possible. Even if you can't get your hands on hardware that resembles the production environment, at least try to simulate the production system's network topology. You can use smaller machines, virtual machines, or containers.

Most of the policies that I suggest in this book are free. This one tends to cost money, for servers, software, or cloud-based services. The amounts are typically only fractions of a programmer's salary, so compared to the total cost of developing software, it's money well spent.

Before you set up a deployment pipeline, however, you should make sure that you can easily compile the code and run developer tests. You'll need some code.

This book is composed around an example that acts as its backbone. You'll see how to develop a simple online restaurant reservation system in C#. Right now, we need a web service that'll handle HTTP requests.

In order to move in that direction, the simplest way to get started is to create an ASP.NET Core web project. I'll be using Visual Studio to do this[5]. While I like to use command-line interfaces for interactions I frequently perform, I like the guidance an IDE can give me for actions I only do now and then. You can, if you'd like, use a command-line tool instead, but the result should be the same: a few files and a working web site. Listings 2.1 and 2.2 show[6] the files that Visual Studio created.

When you run the web site, it serves a single text file with the contents:

```
Hello World!
```

That's good enough for now, so commit the code to Git.

---

5. I'll not show any screen shots or otherwise get into details about this process. Before the book is published, these would be out of date. It is, however, a simple process involving only one or two steps.

6. C# is a relatively verbose language, so I generally only show the highlights of a file. I've left out using directives and namespace declarations.

Listing 2.1 Default ASP.NET Core web service entry point, generated by Visual Studio.
(Restaurant/f729ed9/Restaurant.RestApi/Program.cs)

```
public class Program
{
    public static void Main(string[] args)
    {
        CreateHostBuilder(args).Build().Run();
    }

    public static IHostBuilder CreateHostBuilder(string[] args) =>
        Host.CreateDefaultBuilder(args)
            .ConfigureWebHostDefaults(webBuilder =>
            {
                webBuilder.UseStartup<Startup>();
            });
}
```

The goal in this step is to automate the build. While you can open your IDE and use it to compile the code, that's not automatable. Create a script file that performs the build, and commit that to Git as well. Initially, it's as simple as listing 2.3 shows.

I spend all of my command-line time in Bash, despite working in Windows, so I've defined a shell script. You can create a `.bat` file, or a PowerShell script instead, if that's more to your liking[7]. The important part is that right now, it calls `dotnet build`. Notice that I'm configuring a Release build. The automated build should reflect what will eventually go into production.

As you add more build steps, you should add them to the build script as well. The point of the script is that it should serve as a low-friction tool that developers can run on their own machine. If the build script passes on a developer's machine, it's OK to push the changes to the Continuous Integration server.

---

7. If you need to do something more complex, such as assemble documentation, compile reusable packages for package managers, and so on, you may consider a full-blown build tool. But start simple, and only add complexity if you need it. Often, you don't.

Listing 2.2 Default `Startup` file, generated by Visual Studio. I've edited the comment line breaks to make them fit on the page. *(Restaurant/f729ed9/Restaurant.RestApi/Startup.cs)*

```
public class Startup
{
    // This method gets called by the runtime. Use this method to add
    // services to the container.
    // For more information on how to configure your application,
    // visit https://go.microsoft.com/fwlink/?LinkID=398940
    public void ConfigureServices(IServiceCollection services)
    {
    }

    // This method gets called by the runtime. Use this method to configure
    // the HTTP request pipeline.
    public void Configure(IApplicationBuilder app, IWebHostEnvironment env)
    {
        if (env.IsDevelopment())
        {
            app.UseDeveloperExceptionPage();
        }

        app.UseRouting();

        app.UseEndpoints(endpoints =>
        {
            endpoints.MapGet("/", async context =>
            {
                await context.Response.WriteAsync("Hello World!");
            });
        });
    }
}
```

Listing 2.3 Build script. *(Restaurant/f729ed9/build.sh)*

```
#!/usr/bin/env bash
dotnet build --configuration Release
```

The next step should be to establish your deployment pipeline. When you've added new commits to *master* this should trigger a process that (if successful) deploys the changes to your production environment, or at least makes everything ready so that deployment is but a manual sign-off away.

The details involved in doing this are beyond the scope of this book. They depend on which Continuous Integration server or service you use, as well as its version. This changes all the time. I could show you how to enable this on Azure DevOps Services, Jenkins, TeamCity, and so on, but then this would become a book about that particular technology.

2.2.3 TURN ON ALL ERROR MESSAGES

I once sat with another programmer to teach him how to add unit tests to an existing code base. Soon we ran into trouble. The code compiled, but didn't do what it was supposed to do. He started to frantically navigate around the code base, chaotically changing a thing here, a line of code there. I asked him:

"Could we see if there are any compiler warnings?"

I had a fairly good idea about what the problem was, but I try to help people by letting them discover things for themselves. You learn better that way.

"That's no use," he replied. "There are hundreds of compiler warnings in this code base."

That turned out to be true, but I insisted that we looked through the list, and I quickly found the warning I knew would be there. It correctly identified the problem.

Compiler warnings and other automated tools can detect problems with code. Use them.

In addition to using Git, this is one of the lowest-hanging fruits you can pick. I'm bemused that so few people use the tools that are readily available to them.

Most programming languages and environments come with various tools that'll check your code, such as compilers, linters, code analysis tools, and style and formatting guards. Use as many as you can; they're rarely wrong.

In this book I'll be using C# for examples. It's a compiled language, and compilers typically emit warnings whenever they detect code that compiles, but is most likely wrong. These warnings are usually correct, so it pays to take heed of them.

As the anecdote illustrates, it can be difficult to discover a new compiler warning if you already have 124 other warnings. For that reason, you should have zero tolerance for warnings. You should have zero warnings.

In fact, you should treat warnings as errors.

All compiled languages I've worked with come with an option to turn compiler warnings into compiler errors. That's an effective way to prevent warnings from accumulating.

It can seem like a formidable task to address hundreds of existing warnings. It's much easier to address a single warning the moment it appears. For that reason, turn the warnings-as-errors option on as one of the first things you do in a new code base. That effectively prevents any compiler warnings from accumulating.

When I do that in the code base introduced in section 2.2.2, the code still compiles. What little code Visual Studio had generated for me fortunately doesn't emit any warnings[8].

Many languages and programming environments come with additional automated tools you can use. A *linter*, for example, is a tool that warns you if a piece of code seems to be exhibiting a code smell. Some even check spelling errors. There are linters for such diverse languages as JavaScript and Haskell.

C# comes with a similar set of tools called *analysers*. While turning warnings into errors is only a checkbox somewhere, adding analysers is a little more involved. Still, with the latest version of Visual Studio, it's straightforward[9].

---

8. In Visual Studio, the warnings-as-errors settings is associated with a build configuration. You should definitely treat warnings as errors in Release mode, but I also do it in Debug mode. If you want to change this setting for both configurations, you have to remember to do it twice. Perhaps you should make that part of your checklist.

9. Again, I'm not describing the actual steps required to do this, because a detailed description is likely to be outdated before the book is published.

These analysers represent decades of knowledge about how to write .NET code. They began as an internal tool called *UrtCop*. It was used during early development of the .NET framework itself, so it predates .NET 1.0. It was later renamed to *FxCop* [23]. It has lived an uneasy existence in the .NET ecosystem, but has recently been re-implemented on top of the Roslyn compiler tool chain.

It's an extensible framework that contains an abundance of guidelines and rules. It looks for violations of naming conventions, potential security problems, incorrect use of known library APIs, performance issues, and much more.

When activated in the sample code shown in listings 2.1 and 2.2, the default rule set emits no fewer than seven warnings! Since the compiler now treats warnings as errors, the code no longer compiles. At first blush, this may seem to get in the way of getting work done, but the only thing this should upset is the illusion that code is maintainable without careful contemplation.

Seven warnings today are easier to address than hundreds of warnings in the future. Once you get over the shock, you realise that most of the fixes involve deleting code. You only have to make one change to the `Program` class. You can see the result in listing 2.4. Can you spot the change?

Listing 2.4 ASP.NET Core web service entry point, after analyser warnings have been addressed. *(Restaurant/caafdf1/Restaurant.RestApi/Program.cs)*

```
public static class Program
{
    public static void Main(string[] args)
    {
        CreateHostBuilder(args).Build().Run();
    }

    public static IHostBuilder CreateHostBuilder(string[] args) =>
        Host.CreateDefaultBuilder(args)
            .ConfigureWebHostDefaults(webBuilder =>
            {
                webBuilder.UseStartup<Startup>();
            });
}
```

The change to the `Program` class is that it's now marked with the `static` keyword. There's no reason for a class to support instantiation when it has only shared members. That's an example of a code analysis rule. It's hardly of much import here, but on the other hand, the fix is as simple as adding a single keyword to the class declaration, so why not follow the advice? In other cases, that rule can help you make the code base easier to understand.

Most of the changes that I had to make affect the `Startup` class. Since they involve deletion of code, I think the result is an improvement. Listing 2.5 shows the result.

Listing 2.5 Startup file after analyser warnings have been addressed. Compare with listing 2.2. *(Restaurant/caafdf1/Restaurant.RestApi/Startup.cs)*

```
public sealed class Startup
{
    // This method gets called by the runtime. Use this method to configure
    // the HTTP request pipeline.
    public static void Configure(
        IApplicationBuilder app,
        IWebHostEnvironment env)
    {
        if (env.IsDevelopment())
        {
            app.UseDeveloperExceptionPage();
        }

        app.UseRouting();

        app.UseEndpoints(endpoints =>
        {
            endpoints.MapGet("/", async context =>
            {
                await context.Response.WriteAsync("Hello World!")
                    .ConfigureAwait(false);
            });
        });
    }
}
```

What changed? Most noticeably, I deleted the `ConfigureServices` method, since it didn't do anything. I also `sealed` the class and added a call to `ConfigureAwait`.

Each code analysis rule comes with online documentation. You can read about the motivation for the rule, and how to address warnings.

Nullable Reference Types

C# 8 introduces an optional feature known as *Nullable reference types[a]*. It enables you to use the static type system to declare whether or not an object can be null. When the feature is enabled, objects are assumed to be non-nullable, that is, that they *can't* be null.

If you want to declare that an object *can* be null, you adorn the type declaration with a ? (question mark), as in `IApplicationBuilder? app`.

Being able to distinguish between objects that aren't supposed to be null from objects that may be null helps reduce the amount of defensive coding you need to add. The feature has the potential to reduce the number of run-time defects in your system, so turn it on. Turn it on when the code base is new, so that you don't have to deal with too many compiler errors.

When I turn on this feature for the sample code base shown in this chapter, the code still compiles.

---

[a]The way Microsoft names concepts and features can be confusing. Like all other mainstream C-based languages, reference types have always been *nullable* in the sense that objects can be null. The feature should really be called *non-nullable reference types*.

Static code analysis is like an automated code review. In fact, when a development organisation contacts me because they'd like me to do a C# code review, I first tell them to run the analysers. That'll save them hours off my fee.

I typically don't hear from that potential customer again[10]. When you run such analysers over an existing code base, you can easily get thousands of warnings and feel overwhelmed. To prevent that, start using those tools right away.

---

10. I'm a terrible businessman... or am I?

Contrary to compiler warnings, static code analysis tools like linters or the .NET Roslyn analysers tend to produce some false positives[11]. The automated tools typically give you various options to suppress false positives, so that's hardly a reason to spurn them.

Treat compiler warnings as errors. Treat linter and static code analysis warnings as errors. At first it'll be frustrating, but it'll improve the code. It might make you a better programmer as well.

Is that *engineering?* Is that it? It's not all you can do, but it's a good first step. Engineering, broadly speaking, is to use all the heuristics and deterministic machinery you can to improve the chance of ultimate success. Those tools are like automated checklists. Every time you run them, they control for thousands of potential issues.

Some of them have been around for a long time, but in my experience few people use them. The future is unevenly distributed. Turn the controls on. *Improve the outcome with no increase in skill.*

Treating warnings as errors is easiest to do at the beginning. When a code base is brand-new, there's no code to warn about. This lets you deal with errors one at a time.

2.3 ADDING CHECKS TO EXISTING CODE BASES

In the real world, you rarely get the opportunity to begin a new code base. Most professional software development involves working with existing code. While it's less demanding to treat warnings as errors in a new code base, it's not impossible in an existing code base.

---

11. I realise that this is confusing, but here it is: a *positive* means a warning, that is that the code looks wrong. That doesn't sound positive, but in the terminology of binary classification, *positive* indicates the presence of a signal, whereas *negative* indicates absence. It's also used in software testing and medicine. Just consider what it means to be *Covid-19-positive!*

2.3.1 GRADUAL IMPROVEMENT

The key is to gradually turn on the extra guards. Most existing code bases contain several libraries[12], as exemplified in figure 2.2. Turn on the extra checks one library at a time.

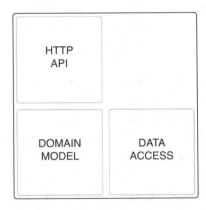

Figure 2.2 A code base made from packages. In this example, the packages are *HTTP API*, *Domain Model*, and *Data Access*.

You can often turn on one type of warning at a time. In an existing code base, you may already have hundreds of compiler warnings. Extract the list and group it by type. Then pick a particular type of warning that has perhaps a dozen instances, and fix all of those warnings. Fix them while they're still compiler warnings, so that you can keep working with the code. Check your changes into Git every time you've made an improvement. Merge those gradual improvements into *master*.

Once you've eliminated the last warning of a given type (in that part of the code base), turn those warnings into errors. Then move on to another type of warning, or address the same type in another part of the code base.

You can do the same with linters and analysers. With .NET analysers, for example, you can configure which rules to enable. Address one rule at a time,

---

12. Libraries are also known as *packages*. Visual Studio developers will often refer to libraries as *projects* within a *solution*.

and once you've eliminated all warnings produced by a given rule, turn that rule on so that it prevents all future instances.

Likewise, C#'s *nullable reference types* feature can be gradually enabled.

The key, in all cases, is to follow the Boy Scout Rule [61]: leave the code in a better state than you found it.

2.3.2 Hack Your Organisation

When I talk at conferences and in user groups, people often approach me. Usually they are inspired, but feel that their manager will not let them focus on *internal quality*.

The benefit of treating warnings as errors is that you add an *institutional* quality gate. If you treat warnings as errors and turn on static code analysis, you relinquish some control. Loss of control doesn't sound good, but it can sometimes be an advantage.

When you're facing pressure to 'just deliver' because 'we don't have time to do it by the book', imagine replying,

"Sorry, but if I do that, the code doesn't compile."

Such a reply has the potential to curb stakeholders' insistence on ignoring engineering discipline. It's not strictly the case that you can't possibly circumvent any of those automatic checks, but you don't have to tell everyone that. The stratagem is that you turn what used to be a human decision into a machine-enforced rule.

Is this morally appropriate? Use your judgment. As a professional software developer, you're the technical expert. It's literally your job to make technical decisions. You can report all details to your superiors, but a lot of the information will be meaningless to nontechnical managers. Providing technical expertise includes *not* confusing stakeholders with details they can't make sense of or use.

In a healthy organisation, the best strategy is to be open and honest about what you do. In an unhealthy organisation, for example an organisation with a substantial 'hustle culture', adopting a counter-strategy might be more appropriate. You can use automated quality gates to hack the culture of your organisation. Even if this involves mild subterfuge, you could still argue that the ultimate goal is to support good software engineering. This should also be advantageous to the entire organisation.

Use your moral judgment. Do this for the good of the organisation, not just to further your own personal agenda.

2.4   CONCLUSION

Checklists will improve outcomes with no increase in skill [40]. Use them. Checklists help you remember to make the right decisions. They support you; they don't control you.

In this chapter, you've seen an example of a simple checklist to use when you start a new code base. You then read about the consequences of instituting that checklist. A checklist can be simple, and yet have a big effect.

You saw how to enable Git right away. That's the simplest of the three items on the checklist. When you consider how easy it is to take that step, though, that small effort pays manifold.

You also saw how to automate the build. This, too, is easy to do when you do it right away. Have a build script. Use it.

Finally, you saw how to turn compiler warnings into errors. You can also use additional automated checks such as linters or static code analysis. Given how easy it is to turn these features on, there's little reason to pass them by.

In the rest of the book, you'll see the impact these early decisions have on the code base as I add features.

Engineering is more than following a checklist, or automating what can be automated, but those measures represent a step in the right direction. They're small improvements you can make today.

TACKLING COMPLEXITY

Try to solve the following simple puzzle by listening to your intuition; don't try to solve it with mathematics or calculation.

A baseball bat and ball costs $1.10. The bat costs a dollar more than the ball. How much does the ball cost?

Take note of your immediate response.

This seems like an easy question. Since this is supposed to be a book about *engineering*, an intellectually demanding discipline, you probably suspect a trap.

We'll return to the bat and ball shortly.

This chapter takes a step back and attempts to answer a fundamental question: *Why is software development so difficult?*

The answer that it proposes is equally fundamental. It has to do with how the human brain works. This is the central thesis of the entire book. Before discussing how to write code that fits in your head, we must discuss what *does* fit in your head.

Subsequent chapters then put this knowledge into practice.

3.1 PURPOSE

After reading the first two chapters, you may be underwhelmed. Perhaps you thought that software engineering was going to be a cerebral, sophisticated, arcane, and esoteric discipline. We can easily make it more sophisticated than what you've seen so far, but we have to start somewhere. Why not start with the easy parts? As figure 3.1 alludes, climbing a hill starts at ground level.

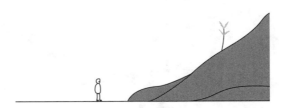

Figure 3.1 Climbing a hill starts at ground level.

Before we continue I think that we should pause and discuss the problem that we're trying to address. Which problem is that?

The problem that this book is trying to solve is one of sustainability. Not in the usual, environmental, sense of the word, but suggesting that code can sustain the organisation that owns it.

3.1.1 SUSTAINABILITY

An organisation creates software for various reasons. Often, it's to make money. Sometimes, it's to *save* money. Once in a while, governments institute software projects to supply digital infrastructure for its citizens; there are no direct profits or savings to be gained from the software, but there's a mission to fulfil.

It often takes a long time to develop a complex piece of software—months, if not years.

Much software lives for years or decades. During its lifetime, it undergoes changes, gets new features, bugs are fixed, and so on. This requires regular work on the code base.

The software exists to support the organisation in some way or other. When you add new features, or address defects, you support the organisation. It's best served if you can support it as well today as you could half a year ago. And when you can support it as well in another half year.

This is a continual effort. It must be *sustainable*.

As Martin Fowler explains: without an eye to internal quality, you soon lose the ability to make improvements in reasonable time.

> *"This is what happens with poor internal quality. Progress is rapid initially, but as time goes on it gets harder to add new features. Even small changes require programmers to understand large areas of code, code that's difficult to understand. When they make changes, unexpected breakages occur, leading to long test times and defects that need to be fixed."* [32]

This is the situation I believe that software engineering should address. It should make the software development process more regular. It should sustain its organisation. For months and years and decades.

Software engineering should make the software development process more *regular*. It should *sustain* its organisation.

3.1.2 VALUE

Software exists to serve a purpose. It should provide *value*. I often run into software professionals who seem blinded by that word. If the code you wrote doesn't provide value, then why did you write it?

A certain focus on value seems warranted. I've also met more than one programmer who, if left to him- or herself, will while away hours dilly-dallying with some clever framework of their own devising.

This happens to commercial companies as well. Richard P. Gabriel tells the story of the rise and fall of a company called Lucid [38]. While they were tinkering with the perfect commercial implementation of Common Lisp, C++ came along and took over the market for cross-platform software development languages.

The Lucid people considered C++ inferior to Common Lisp, but Gabriel ultimately came to understand why customers chose it. C++ may be less consistent and more complicated, but it worked and was available to customers. Lucid's product wasn't. This lead Gabriel to formulate the aphorism that *worse is better*. Lucid went out of business.

People who tinker with technology without regard for its purpose occupy the right-hand side of figure 3.2.

Figure 3.2 Some programmers never consider the value of the code they write, while others have difficulty seeing past immediately quantifiable results. Sustainability lies somewhere in-between.

The focus on value seems to be a reaction to this mindset. It makes sense to ask whether code serves a purpose. The term *value* is often used as a proxy for *purpose*, despite the fact that you can't measure it. There's a school of project management based on the idea [88] that you should:

1. form a hypothesis about the impact of the change you're about to make
2. make the change
3. measure the impact and compare it to your prediction

This isn't a book about project management, but that seems a reasonable approach. It fits the observations of *Accelerate* [29].

The notion that code should produce value unfortunately leads to the logical fallacy that code not producing value is prohibited. The notion that *worse is better* isn't far off.

This is a fallacy because some code produces no *immediately measurable* value. You might, on the other hand, be able to measure the absence of it. A straightforward example is security. You may not be able to measure the value of adding authentication to an online system, but you can probably measure the absence of it.

The same goes for Fowler's argument about internal quality [32]. A lack of architecture is going to be measurable, but only when it's too late. I've seen more than one company go out of business because of poor internal quality.

Sustainability occupies the middle ground in figure 3.2. It discourages technology for technology's sake, but it also advises against a myopic focus on value.

Software engineering ought to encourage sustainability. By following checklists, by treating warnings as errors, et cetera, you prevent some cruft [32] from forming. None of the methodologies and heuristics presented in this book guarantee a perfect result, but they pull in the right direction. You'll still have to use your experience and judgment. This is, after all, the *art* of software engineering.

3.2   WHY PROGRAMMING IS DIFFICULT

What makes software development so hard? There's more than one reason. One is, as discussed in section 1.1, that we're using the wrong metaphors. That clouds our thinking, but that's not the only reason.

Another problem is that a computer is quantitatively different from a brain. Yes, that's another problematic metaphor.

3.2.1   THE BRAIN METAPHOR

It seems obvious to liken a computer to a brain, and vice versa. Surely, there are superficial similarities. Both can perform calculations. Both can recall events that happened in the past. Both can store and retrieve information.

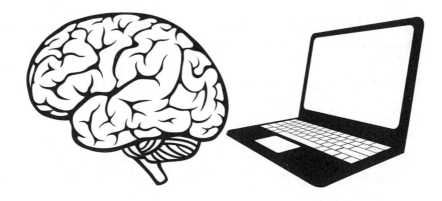

Is the brain like a computer? Don't be misled by the obvious similarities.

Is a computer like a brain? I think that there are more differences than similarities. A computer can't make intuitive inferences. It doesn't interpret sight and sound well[1]. It doesn't have intrinsic motivation.

Is a brain like a computer? Compared to a computer, our ability to calculate is glacially slow, and our memory is so unreliable as to be disreputable. We forget

---

1. So-called *AI* has made advances in recent years, but the problems researchers are struggling with are still at a level that a toddler can easily solve. Show a computer a children's book with drawings of farm animals and ask it what's in each picture.

important things. Memories can be fabricated or manipulated [109], and you're not even aware that this happens. You're certain that you were at a particular party twenty years ago with your best friend, but she's sure she never went. Either your memory is wrong, or hers is.

What about *working memory?* A computer can keep track of millions of things in RAM. Human short-term memory can hold from four to seven[2] pieces of information [80][109].

This has profound implications for programming. Even a modest subroutine can easily create dozens of variables and branching instructions. When you try to understand what source code does, you're essentially running an emulator of the programming language in your mind. If too many things are going on, you can't keep track of it all.

How much is too much?

This book uses the number *seven* as a token for the limit of the brain's short-term memory. You may be able to keep track of nine things from time to time, but seven represents the concept well.

3.2.2 CODE IS READ MORE THAN IT'S WRITTEN

This brings us to a fundamental problem of programming.

> You spend more time reading code than writing it.

You write a line of code once and read it multiple times [61]. You rarely get to work with a pristine code base. When you work with an existing code base, you must understand it before you can successfully edit it. When you add a

---

2. You may also have encountered *the magical number seven, plus or minus two*. I don't consider the exact number important. What I do find crucial is that it's orders of magnitude less than a computer's working memory.

new feature, you read the existing code to figure out how to best reuse what's already there and to learn what new code you'll have to add. When you struggle to fix a bug, you must first understand what causes it. You'll typically spend the majority of your programming time reading existing code.

> Optimise code for readability.

You constantly hear about new programming languages, new libraries, new frameworks, or new IDE features that enable you to produce more code faster. As the Lucid story shows, it sells well, but is hardly a good strategy for sustainable software development. More code faster means more code that you'll have to read. The more you produce, the more you have to read. Automated code generation only makes matters worse.

As Martin Fowler writes about low code quality:

> *"Even small changes require programmers to understand large areas of code, code that's difficult to understand."* [32]

Code that's difficult to understand slows you down. On the other hand, every minute you invest in making the code easier to understand pays itself back tenfold.

3.2.3 READABILITY

It's easy to say that you should favour readable code over code that's easy to write, but what, exactly, is readable code?

Have you ever looked at some code and asked yourself: *Who wrote this crap?!* Then, once you investigate[3] it turns out that it was you?

This happens to everyone. When you're writing code, you're in a situation where you're aware of all the context that gives rise to the code. When you're reading code, all that contextual information is gone.

---

3. git blame is a great tool for such forensics.

Ultimately, the code is the only artefact that matters. Documentation may be out of date, or absent. The person who wrote the code may be on vacation, or may have left the organisation.

To add insult to injury, the brain performs poorly when reading and evaluating formal statements. How did you respond to the baseball-bat-and-ball question at the beginning of this chapter?

The number that immediately jumped into your head was *10*. That's the answer that most people give [51].

It's the wrong answer. If the ball costs 10 cents then the bat must cost $1.10, and the total price would be $1.20. The correct answer is 5 cents.

The point is that we make mistakes all the time. When we solve trivial maths problems, and when we read code.

How do you write readable code? You can't trust your intuition. You'll need something more actionable. Heuristics, checklists... software engineering. We'll return to this topic throughout the book.

3.2.4 INTELLECTUAL WORK

Have you ever driven your car somewhere, and after ten minutes of driving, you suddenly 'wake up' and horrified ask yourself: *How did I get here?*

I have. Not that I've literally fallen asleep behind the wheel, but I've been so lost in thought that I've been oblivious that I was driving. I've also accomplished the feat of bicycling past my own home, as well as trying to unlock the door to my downstairs neighbour instead of my own.

Based on these confessions I realise that you probably don't want to get into a car with me, but my point isn't that I'm easily distracted. The point is that the brain works even when you aren't aware of it.

You know that your brain controls your breathing, even when you aren't thinking of it. It takes care of a lot of motor functions without your explicit control. It seems that it does much more than that.

After one of the incidents where I'd found myself behind the wheel of my car, wondering how I got where I was, I was as astounded as I was appalled. I'd been driving in my home city of Copenhagen, and I *must* have performed a series of complex manoeuvres to get where I was. Stopping for red, turning left, turning right without hitting any of the city's omnipresent bicyclists, correctly navigating to my destination. Yet I had no recollection of doing any of that.

Your conscious awareness isn't a required ingredient for complex intellectual work.

Have you ever been *in the zone* while programming? Looking up from the screen and realising that it's suddenly dark outside and that you've been at it for hours? In psychology, this mental state is called *flow* [51]. In it, you're so fully engrossed in your activity that you lose awareness of the self.

You can program without deliberate thinking. Of course, you can also write code while being aware that you're doing it. The point is that a lot goes on in your brain that you're not explicitly aware of. Your brain performs the work; your consciousness may be nothing but a passive spectator.

You'd think that intellectual work would be one hundred percent deliberate thinking, but the truth is probably that a lot of involuntary activity also takes place. Psychologist and Nobel laureate Daniel Kahneman suggests a model of thought comprising two systems: *System 1* and *System 2*.

> *"System 1 operates automatically and quickly, with little or no effort and no sense of voluntary control.*
>
> *System 2 allocates attention to the effortful mental activities that demand it, including complex computations. The operations of System 2 are often associated with the subjective experience of agency, choice, and concentration."* [51]

You probably think of programming as belonging exclusively to the realm of System 2, but that doesn't have to be the case. It seems that System 1 is always running in the background, trying to make sense of the code it's looking at. The problems is that System 1 is fast, but not particularly accurate. It can easily make incorrect inferences. That's what's happening when *10* is the first number that comes to your mind when confronted with the baseball-bat-and-ball puzzle.

In order to organise source code such that our brains can make sense of it, you have to keep System 1 from going off the rails. Kahneman also writes:

> *"An essential design feature [of System 1] is that it represents only activated ideas. Information not retrieved (even unconsciously) from memory might as well not exist. System 1 excels at constructing the best possible story that incorporates ideas currently activated, but it does not (cannot) allow for information it does not have.*
>
> *The measure of success for System 1 is the coherence of the story it manages to create. The amount and quality of the data on which the story is based are largely irrelevant. When information is scarce, which is a common occurrence, System 1 operates as a machine for jumping to conclusions."* [51]

There's a *machine for jumping to conclusions* in your brain[4], and it's looking at your code. You'd better organise code so that the relevant information is *activated*. As Kahneman puts it, *what you see is all there is* (WYSIATI) [51].

This already goes a long way explaining why global variables and hidden side effects make code obscure. A global variable is typically not visible when you look at a piece of code. Even if your System 2 knows about it, that knowledge is not activated, so System 1 doesn't take it into account.

Place related code close together. All the dependencies, variables, and decisions required should be visible at the same time. This is a theme that runs throughout the book, so you'll see plenty of examples, particularly in chapter 7.

---

4. Why is System 1 running all the time, while System 2 may not be? One reason could be that effortful thinking burns more glucose [51]. That would imply that System 1 is an energy-saving mechanism.

3.3 TOWARDS SOFTWARE ENGINEERING

The purpose of software engineering should be to support the organisation that owns the software. You should be able to make changes at a sustainable pace.

But writing code is difficult because it's so intangible. You spend more time reading code than writing it, and the brain is easily misled—even by unremarkable matters like the bat-and-ball problem.

Software engineering must address this problem.

3.3.1 RELATIONSHIP TO COMPUTER SCIENCE

Can computer science help? I don't see why not, but computer science isn't (software) engineering, just like physics isn't the same as mechanical engineering.

Such disciplines can interact, but they aren't the same. Successful practices can provide inspiration and insight for scientists, and results from science can be applied to engineering, as suggested by figure 3.3.

Figure 3.3 Science and engineering interact, but aren't the same.

For example, results from computer science can be encapsulated in reusable packages.

I had a couple of years of professional experience with software development before I learned about sorting algorithms. I don't have a formal education in computer science; I taught myself to code. If I needed to sort an array in C++, Visual Basic, or VBScript, I'd call a method.

You don't have to be able to implement quicksort or merge sort to sort collections. You don't have to know about hash indexes, SSTables, LSM-trees, and B-trees to query a database[5].

Computer science helps the software development industry to progress, but the knowledge gained there can often be packaged into reusable software. It doesn't hurt to know about computer science, but you don't have to. You can still do software engineering.

3.3.2 HUMANE CODE

Sorting algorithms can be encapsulated and distributed as reusable libraries. Sophisticated storage and retrieval data structures can be packaged as general-purpose database software, or offered as cloud-based infrastructure.

You still have to write code.

You have to organise it in a sustainable manner. You must structure it in such a way that it fits in your brain.

As Martin Fowler put it:

> *"Any fool can write code that a computer can understand. Good programmers write code that humans can understand."* [34]

The brain comes with cognitive constraints that are completely different from a computer's limits. A computer can keep track of millions of things in RAM. Your brain can keep track of seven.

A computer will only make decisions based on the information it's instructed to consult. Your brain tends to jump to conclusions. What you see is all there is.

---

5. These are some of the data structures that power databases [55].

Obviously, you must write code such that the resulting software works as desired. That's no longer the main problem of software engineering. The challenge is to organise it so that it fits in your brain. Code must be humane.

This implies writing small, self-contained functions. Throughout this book, I'll use the number seven as a proxy for the limits of human short-term memory. Humane code, then, implies fewer than seven dependencies, that cyclomatic complexity is at most seven, and so on.

The devil's in the details, though, so I'll show you plenty of examples.

3.4 CONCLUSION

The core problem that software engineering should solve is that it's so complex that it doesn't fit the human brain. Fred Brooks offered this analysis in 1986:

> *"Many of the classical problems of developing software products derive from this essential complexity and its nonlinear increases with size [...] From the complexity comes the difficulty of enumerating, much less understanding, all the possible states of the program"* [14]

I use the term *complexity* in the same way that Rich Hickey uses it [45]: as an antonym to simplicity. *Complex* means 'assembled from parts', as opposed to *simple*, which implies unity.

The human brain can deal with limited complexity. Our short-term memory can only keep track of seven objects. If we don't pay attention, we can easily write code that handles more than seven things at once. The computer doesn't care, so it's not going to stop us.

Software engineering should be the deliberate process of preventing complexity from growing.

Perhaps you recoil from all of this. You may think that it's going to slow you down.

Yes, that's the point. To paraphrase J.B. Rainsberger [86], you probably need slowing down. The faster you type, the more code you make that everyone has to maintain. Code isn't an asset; it's a liability [77].

As Martin Fowler argues, it's by applying good architecture that you can keep a sustainable pace [32]. Software engineering is a means to that end. It's an attempt to shift software development from being a pure art towards being *a methodology*.

VERTICAL 4 SLICE

Some years ago, a regular client of mine asked me to come help with a project. When I arrived, I learned that a team had been working on a task for about half a year without getting anywhere.

Their task was indeed daunting, but they were stuck in Analysis Paralysis [15]. There were so many requirements that the team couldn't figure out how to address them all. I've seen this happen more than once, with different teams.

Sometimes, the best strategy is to just get started. You should still think and plan ahead. There's no reason to be wilfully nonchalant or blasé about thinking ahead, but just as too little planning can be bad for you, so can too much. If you've already established your deployment pipeline [49], the sooner you can deploy a piece of working software, no matter how trivial, the sooner you can start to collect feedback from stakeholders [29].

Start by creating and deploying a vertical slice of the application.

4.1 START WITH WORKING SOFTWARE

How do you know that software works? Ultimately, you don't know until you've shipped it. Once it's deployed or installed, and being used by real users, you may be able to verify whether or not it works. That's not even the final assessment. The software that you've developed may work as you intended it to work, while not solving users' actual problems. How to address that problem is beyond the scope of the book, so I'll leave it at that[1]. I interpret *software engineering* as a methodology to make sure that the software works as intended, and that it stays that way.

The idea behind vertical slicing is to get to working software as soon as possible. You do that by implementing the simplest feature you can think of—*all the way* from user interface to data store.

4.1.1 FROM DATA INGRESS TO DATA PERSISTENCE

Most software comes with two types of boundaries to the wider world. You've probably seen diagrams similar to figure 4.1 before. Data arrives at the top. The application may subject the input to various transformations, and may ultimately decide to save it.

Even a *read* operation can be considered input, although it doesn't result in data being saved. A query typically comes with query parameters that identify the data being requested. The software still transforms those input values to an interaction with its data store.

Sometimes, the data store is a dedicated database. At other times, it's just another system. It could be an HTTP-based service somewhere on the internet, a message queue, the file system, or even just the local computer's standard output stream.

Such downstream targets can be write-only systems (e.g. the standard output stream), read-only systems (e.g. a third-party HTTP API), or read-write systems (e.g. the file system or databases).

---

1. *The Lean Startup* [88] and *Accelerate* [29] are good starting points if you need to explore that topic.

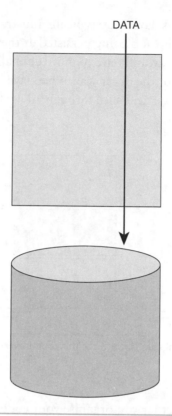

Figure 4.1 Typical architecture diagram. Data arrives at the top, flows through the application (the box), and is persisted at the bottom (in the can).

Thus, at a sufficiently high level of abstraction, the diagram in figure 4.1 describes most software, from web sites to command-line utilities.

4.1.2 MINIMAL VERTICAL SLICE

You can organise code in various ways. A conventional architecture is to organise constituent elements into layers [33][26][50][60]. You don't have to do it like that, but the context of layered application architecture helps explain why it's called a *vertical* slice.

> You don't have to organise your code in layers. This section only discusses layered architecture to explain why it's called a *vertical* slice.

As figure 4.2 shows, layers are typically illustrated as horizontal strata, with data arriving on top and being persisted at the bottom. In order to implement a complete feature, you'll have to move data all the way from entry point to persistence layer, or the other way. When layers are horizontal shapes, then a single feature is a vertical slice through all of them.

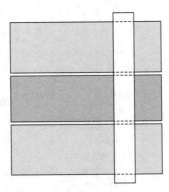

Figure 4.2 A vertical slice through the horizontal layers of a stereotypical application architecture.

Regardless of whether you organise your code in layers or in another way, implementing an end-to-end feature has at least two benefits:

1. It gives you early feedback about the entire life cycle of your software development process.
2. It's working software. It might already be useful to someone.

I've met programmers who spent months perfecting a home-grown data-access framework before even trying to use it to implement a feature. They often learn that they've made assumptions about usage patterns that don't fit reality. You should avoid Speculative Generality [34], the tendency to add features to code because you 'might need it later'. Instead, implement features with the simplest possible code, but look out for duplication as you add more.

Implementing a vertical slice is an effective way to learn what sort of code you need, and what you can do without.

4.2 WALKING SKELETON

Find a motivation for making changes to the code. Such motivation acts as a *driver* of the change, so to speak.

You've already seen examples of such drivers. When you treat warnings as errors, when you turn on linters and other static code analysers, you introduce extrinsic motivations for changing the code. This can be beneficial because it removes a degree of subjective judgement.

Using drivers of change gives rise to a whole family of *x-driven* software development methodologies:

1. Test-driven development [9] (TDD)
2. Behaviour-driven development (BDD)
3. Domain-driven design [26] (DDD)
4. Type-driven development
5. Property-driven development[2]

Recall the bat-and-ball-problem from chapter 3. It demonstrates how easy it is to make mistakes. Using an extrinsic driver works a bit like double-entry bookkeeping [63]. You somehow interact with the driver, and it induces you to modify the code.

While the driver can be a linter, it can also be code, in the form of automated tests. I often follow an outside-in style of test-driven development. This is a technique where the first tests you write exercise the high-level boundary of the system under test. From there, you can work your way from the outside in by adding tests of more fine-grained implementation details, as needed. You'll find a more detailed explanation, including an example, in section 4.3.

You're going to need a test suite.

---

2. See subsection 15.3.1 for an example of property-based testing.

4.2.1   CHARACTERISATION TEST

In the rest of this chapter, I'm going to show you how to add a vertical slice to the restaurant reservation HTTP API I began developing in subsection 2.2.2. Right now, it only serves the plain text Hello World!

If you add a simple automated test of the system, you're on track to enabling test-driven development. You'll have a thin slice of functionality that you can automatically test and deploy: a Walking Skeleton [36].

Follow the *new-code-base checklist* introduced in section 2.2 when adding a unit test project to the Visual Studio solution: add the new test project to Git, treat warnings as errors, and make sure that the automated build runs the test.

Once you've done that, add your first test case, like listing 4.1.

Listing 4.1 Integration test of the HTTP home resource.
(Restaurant/3ee0733/Restaurant.RestApi.Tests/HomeTests.cs)

```
[Fact]
public async Task HomeIsOk()
{
    using var factory = new WebApplicationFactory<Startup>();
    var client = factory.CreateClient();

    var response = await client
        .GetAsync(new Uri("", UriKind.Relative))
        .ConfigureAwait(false);

    Assert.True(
        response.IsSuccessStatusCode,
        $"Actual status code: {response.StatusCode}.");
}
```

To be clear, I wrote this test after the fact, so I didn't follow test-driven development. Rather, this type of test is called a Characterisation Test [27] because it characterises (i.e. *describes*) the behaviour of existing software.

I did this because the software already exists. You may recall from chapter 2 that I used a wizard to generate the initial code. Right now it works as intended, but how do we know that it'll keep working?

I find it prudent to add automated tests to protect against regressions.

The test shown in listing 4.1 uses the *xUnit.net* unit testing framework. This is the framework I'll use throughout the book. Even if you're not familiar with it, it should be easy to follow the examples, as it follows well-known patterns for unit testing [66].

It uses the test-specific `WebApplicationFactory<T>` class to create a self-hosted instance of the HTTP application. The `Startup` class (shown in listing 2.5) defines and bootstraps the application itself.

Notice that the assertion only considers the most superficial property of the system: does it respond with an HTTP status code in the `200` range (e.g. `200 OK` or `201 Created`)? I decided to refrain from verifying anything stronger than that, because the current behaviour (it returns `Hello World!`) only acts as a placeholder. It should change in the future.

When only asserting that a Boolean expression is true, the only message you'll get from the assertion library is that `true` was expected, but the actual value was `false`. That's hardly illuminating, so it may prove helpful to provide a bit of extra context. I did that here by using the overload to `Assert.True` that takes an additional message as its second argument.

I find the test too verbose as presented, but it compiles and the test passes. We'll improve the test code in a moment, but first, keep the *new-code-base checklist* in mind. Did I do anything that the build script should automate? Yes, indeed, I added a test suite. Change the build script to run the tests. Listing 4.2 shows how I did that.

Listing 4.2 Build script with tests. *(Restaurant/3ee0733/build.sh)*

```
#!/usr/bin/env bash
dotnet test --configuration Release
```

Compared to listing 2.3, the only change is that it calls `dotnet test` instead of `dotnet build`.

Remember to follow the checklist. Commit the changes to Git.

4.2.2   ARRANGE ACT ASSERT

There's structure to the test in listing 4.1. It starts with two lines followed by a blank line, then a single statement spanning three lines followed by a blank line, and finally another single statement spanning three lines.

Most of that structure is the result of deliberate methodology. For now, I'll skip the reason that some statements span multiple lines. You can read about that in subsection 7.1.3.

The blank lines, on the other hand, are there because the code follows the Arrange Act Assert pattern [9], also known as the AAA pattern. The idea is to organise a unit test into three phases.

1. In the *arrange* phase you prepare everything required for the test.
2. In the *act* phase you invoke the operation you'd like to test.
3. In the *assert* phase you verify that the actual outcome matches the expected outcome.

You can turn that pattern into a heuristic. I usually indicate the three phases by separating them with a blank line. That's what I've done in listing 4.1.

This only works if you can avoid additional blank lines in the test. A common problem is when the *arrange* section grows so big that you get the urge to apply some formatting by adding blank lines. If you do that, you'll have more than two blank lines in your test, and it's unclear which of them delineate the three phases.

In general, consider it a code smell [34] when test code grows too big. I like it best when the three phases balance. The *act* section is typically the smallest, but if you imagine that you rotate the code 90° as shown in figure 4.3, you should be able to balance the code approximately on the *act* section.

If the test code is so big that you must add additional blank lines, you'll have to resort to code comments to identify the three phases [92], but try to avoid this.

At the other extreme, you may occasionally write a miniscule test. If you only have three lines of code, and if each line belongs to each of the different AAA phases, you can dispense with the blank lines; similarly if you have only one or two lines of code. The purpose of the AAA pattern is to make a test more readable by the addition of a well-known structure. If you only have two or three lines of code, odds are that the test is so small that it's already readable as is.

4.2.3 Moderation of Static Analysis

While listing 4.1 is only a few lines of code, I still consider it too verbose. Particularly the *act* section could be more readable. There are two problems:

1. The call to `ConfigureAwait` adds what seems like redundant noise.
2. That's quite a convoluted way to pass an empty string as an argument.

Let's address each in turn.

Figure 4.3 Imagine that you rotate your test code 90°. (Code shown here is illustrative and represents *any* unit test code block.) If you can position it approximately on its *act* phase, then it's in balance.

If `ConfigureAwait` is redundant, then why is it there? It's there because otherwise the code doesn't compile. I've configured the test project according to the *new-code-base checklist*, which includes adding static code analysis and turning all warnings into errors.

One of these rules[3] recommends calling `ConfigureAwait` on awaited tasks. The rule comes with documentation that explains the motivation. In short, by default a task resumes on the thread that originally created it. By calling `ConfigureAwait(false)` you indicate that the task can instead resume on any thread. This can avoid deadlocks and certain performance issues. The rule strongly suggests to call this method in code that implements a reusable library.

A test library, however, isn't a generally reusable library. The clients are known in advance: two or three standard test runners, including the built-in Visual Studio test runner, and the one used by your Continuous Integration server.

The documentation for the rule also contains a section on when it's safe to deactivate the rule. A unit testing library fits the description, so you can turn it off to remove the noise from your tests.

Be aware that while it's fine to turn off this particular rule for unit tests, it should remain in effect for production code. Listing 4.3 shows the Characterisation Test after clean-up.

Another issue with listing 4.1 is that the `GetAsync` method includes an overload that takes a `string` instead of a `Uri` object. The test would be more readable with `""` instead of `new Uri("", UriKind.Relative)`. Alas, another static code analysis rule[4] discourages use of that overload.

You should avoid 'stringly typed' [3] code[5]. Instead of passing strings around, you should favour objects with good encapsulation. I salute that design principle, so I have no intention to deactivate the rule, like I did with the rule about `ConfigureAwait`.

I do believe, however, that we can make a principled exception from the rule. As you may have noticed, you have to populate a `Uri` object with a `string`.

---

3. CA2007: Do not directly await a Task.
4. CA2234: Pass System.Uri objects instead of strings.
5. Also known as Primitive Obsession [34].

The advantage of a `Uri` object over a `string` is that, at the *receiving* side, you know that an encapsulated object carries stronger guarantees than a `string` does[6]. At the site where you create the object, there's little difference. Therefore, I think it's fair to suppress the warning since the code contains a `string` *literal* – not a variable.

Listing 4.3 Test with relaxed code analysis rules.
(Restaurant/d8167c3/Restaurant.RestApi.Tests/HomeTests.cs)

```
[Fact]
[SuppressMessage(
    "Usage", "CA2234:Pass system uri objects instead of strings",
    Justification = "URL isn't passed as variable, but as literal.")]
public async Task HomeIsOk()
{
    using var factory = new WebApplicationFactory<Startup>();
    var client = factory.CreateClient();

    var response = await client.GetAsync("");

    Assert.True(
        response.IsSuccessStatusCode,
        $"Actual status code: {response.StatusCode}.");
}
```

Listing 4.3 shows the result of suppressing the `ConfigureAwait` rule for all tests, and the `Uri` rule for the specific test. Notice that the *act* section shrank from three to one line of code. Most importantly, the code is easier to read. The code I removed was (in this context) noise. Now it's gone.

You can see that I suppressed the `Uri` recommendation by using an attribute on the test method. Notice that I supplied a written `Justification` of my decision. As I argued in chapter 3, the code is the only artefact that really matters. Future readers may need to understand why the code is organised as it is[7].

> Documentation should prioritise explaining *why* a decision was made, rather than *what* was decided.

---

6. Read more about guarantees and encapsulation in chapter 5.
7. You can typically reconstruct *what* changed from your Git history. It's much harder to reconstruct *why* things changed.

As useful as static code analysis is, false positives come with the territory. It's okay to disable rules or suppress specific warnings, but don't do this lightly. At least, document why you decide to do it, and if possible, get feedback on the decision.

4.3   OUTSIDE-IN

Now we're up to speed. There's a system that responds to HTTP requests (although it doesn't do much) and there's an automated test. That's our Walking Skeleton [36].

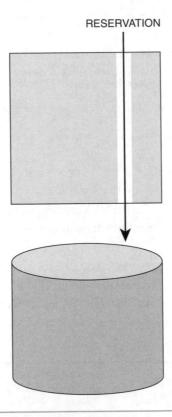

Figure 4.4 The plan is to create a vertical slice through the system that receives a valid reservation and saves it in a database.

The system ought to do something useful. In this chapter, the goal is to implement a vertical slice through the system from HTTP boundary to data store. Recall from subsection 2.2.2 that the system should be a simple online restaurant reservation system. I think a good candidate for a slice is the ability to receive a valid reservation and save it in a database. Figure 4.4 illustrates the plan.

The system should be an HTTP API that receives and replies with JSON documents. This is how the rest of the world interacts with the system. That's the contract with external clients, so it's important that once you've established it, you keep it.

How do you prevent regressions in the contract? One way is to write a set of automated tests against the HTTP boundary. If you write the tests before the implementation, then you have a *driver* for it.

Such a test can serve double duty as an automated acceptance test [49], so you might call the process *acceptance-test-driven development*. I prefer to call it *outside-in test-driven development*[8], because while you *begin* at the boundary, you can (and should) work your way in. You'll see an example of this soon.

4.3.1 RECEIVE JSON

When you're beginning a new code base, there's so much that has to be done. It can be hard to move in small steps, but try, nonetheless. The smallest change I can think of in the restaurant reservation example is to verify that the response from the API is a JSON document.

We know that right now, it isn't. At the moment, the web application just returns the hard-coded string `Hello World!` as a plain-text document.

In good test-driven style, you could write a new test that asserts that the response should be in JSON, but most of it would repeat the existing test shown in listing 4.3. Instead of duplicating the test code, you can elaborate on the existing test. Listing 4.4 shows the expanded test.

---

8. I didn't invent this term, but I don't recall where I first heard it. The *idea*, however, I first encountered in *Growing Object-Oriented Software, Guided by Tests* [36].

Listing 4.4 Test that asserts that the home resource returns JSON.
(Restaurant/316beab/Restaurant.RestApi.Tests/HomeTests.cs)

```
[Fact]
[SuppressMessage(
    "Usage", "CA2234:Pass system uri objects instead of strings",
    Justification = "URL isn't passed as variable, but as literal.")]
public async Task HomeReturnsJson()
{
    using var factory = new WebApplicationFactory<Startup>();
    var client = factory.CreateClient();

    using var request = new HttpRequestMessage(HttpMethod.Get, "");
    request.Headers.Accept.ParseAdd("application/json");
    var response = await client.SendAsync(request);

    Assert.True(
        response.IsSuccessStatusCode,
        $"Actual status code: {response.StatusCode}.");
    Assert.Equal(
        "application/json",
        response.Content.Headers.ContentType?.MediaType);
}
```

Three things have changed:

1. I changed the name of the test to be more specific.
2. The test now explicitly sets the `request`'s `Accept` header to `application/json`.
3. I added a second assertion.

By setting the `Accept` header, the client engages HTTP's content negotiation [2] protocol. If the server can serve a JSON response, it ought to do so.

To verify that, I added a second assertion that examines the `response`'s `Content-Type`[9].

---

9. You may have heard that a test should have only one assertion. You may also have heard that having multiple assertions is called Assertion Roulette, and that it's a code smell. Assertion Roulette is, indeed, a code smell, but multiple assertions per test isn't necessarily an example of it. Assertion Roulette is either when you repeatedly interleave *assert* sections with additional *arrange* and *act* code, or when an assertion lacks an informative assertion message [66].

The test now fails at the second assertion. It expects the Content-Type header to be application/json, but it's actually null. This is more like test-driven development: write a failing test, then make it pass.

When working with ASP.NET you're expected to follow the Model View Controller [33] (MVC) pattern. Listing 4.5 shows the simplest Controller implementation I could pull off.

Listing 4.5 First incarnation of HomeController. *(Restaurant/316beab/Restaurant.RestApi/HomeController.cs)*

```
[Route("")]
public class HomeController : ControllerBase
{
    public IActionResult Get()
    {
        return Ok(new { message = "Hello, World!" });
    }
}
```

This, in itself, however, isn't enough. You also have to tell ASP.NET to use its MVC framework. You can do this in the Startup class, as shown in listing 4.6.

Listing 4.6 Setting up ASP.NET for MVC. *(Restaurant/316beab/Restaurant.RestApi/Startup.cs)*

```
public sealed class Startup
{
    public static void ConfigureServices(IServiceCollection services)
    {
        services.AddControllers();
    }

    public static void Configure(
        IApplicationBuilder app,
        IWebHostEnvironment env)
    {
        if (env.IsDevelopment())
            app.UseDeveloperExceptionPage();

        app.UseRouting();
        app.UseEndpoints(endpoints => { endpoints.MapControllers(); });
    }
}
```

Compared to listing 2.5 this looks simpler. I consider that an improvement.

With these changes, the test in listing 4.4 passes. Commit the changes to Git, and consider pushing them through your deployment pipeline [49].

4.3.2 POST A RESERVATION

Recall that the purpose of a vertical slice is to demonstrate that the system works. We've spent some time getting into position. That's normal with a new code base, but now it's ready.

When picking a feature for the first vertical slice, I look for a few things. You could call this a heuristic as well.

1. The feature should be simple to implement.
2. Prefer data input if possible.

When developing systems with persisted data, you quickly find that you need some data in the system in order to test other things. Starting with a feature that adds data to the system neatly addresses that concern.

In that light, it seems useful to enable the web application to receive and save a restaurant reservation. Using outside-in test-driven development, you could write a test like listing 4.7.

When pursuing a vertical slice, aim for the happy path [66]. For now, ignore all the things that could go wrong[10]. The goal is to demonstrate that the system has a specific capability. In this example, the desired capability is to receive and save a reservation.

Thus, listing 4.7 posts a *valid* reservation to the service. The reservation should include a valid date, email, name, and quantity. The test uses an anonymous type to emulate a JSON object. When serialised, the resulting JSON has the same structure, and the same field names.

---

10. But if you think of any, write them down so you don't forget about them [9].

Listing 4.7 Testing that a valid reservation can be posted to the HTTP API. The PostReservation method is in listing 4.8.
(Restaurant/90e4869/Restaurant.RestApi.Tests/ReservationsTests.cs)

```
[Fact]
public async Task PostValidReservation()
{
    var response = await PostReservation(new {
        date = "2023-03-10 19:00",
        email = "katinka@example.com",
        name = "Katinka Ingabogovinanana",
        quantity = 2 });

    Assert.True(
        response.IsSuccessStatusCode,
        $"Actual status code: {response.StatusCode}.");
}
```

High-level tests should go easy on the assertions. During development, many details will change. If you make the assertions too specific, you'll have to correct them often. Better to keep a light touch. The test in listing 4.7 only verifies that the HTTP status code represents success, as discussed in section 4.2.1. As you add more test code, you'll be describing the expected behaviour of the system in increasing detail. Do this iteratively.

You may have noticed that the test delegates all the action to a method called PostReservation. This is the Test Utility Method [66] shown in listing 4.8.

Much of the code is similar to listing 4.4. I could have written it in the test itself. Why didn't I? There's a couple of reasons, but this is where software engineering is more art than science.

One reason is that I think it makes the test itself more readable. Only the essentials are visible. You post some values to the service, the response indicates success. This is a great example of an *abstraction*, according to Robert C. Martin:

> *"Abstraction is the elimination of the irrelevant and the amplification of the essential"* [60]

Listing 4.8 PostReservation helper method. This method is defined in the test code base. *(Restaurant/90e4869/Restaurant.RestApi.Tests/ReservationsTests.cs)*

```
[SuppressMessage(
    "Usage",
    "CA2234:Pass system uri objects instead of strings",
    Justification = "URL isn't passed as variable, but as literal.")]
private async Task<HttpResponseMessage> PostReservation(
    object reservation)
{
    using var factory = new WebApplicationFactory<Startup>();
    var client = factory.CreateClient();

    string json = JsonSerializer.Serialize(reservation);
    using var content = new StringContent(json);
    content.Headers.ContentType.MediaType = "application/json";
    return await client.PostAsync("reservations", content);
}
```

Another reason I wanted to define a helper method is that I'd like to reserve the right to change how this is done. Notice that the last line of code calls PostAsync with the hard-coded relative path "reservations". This implies that the *reservations* resource exists at a URL like https://api.example.com /reservations. This might be the case, but you may not want this to be part of your contract.

You can write an HTTP API with published URL templates, but it wouldn't be REST because it's hard to change the API without breaking the contract [2]. APIs that expect clients to use documented URL templates use HTTP verbs, but not hypermedia controls[11].

It's too big a detour to insist on hypermedia controls (i.e. *links*) right now, so in order to reserve the right to change things later, you can abstract the service interaction in a SUT[12] Encapsulation Method [66].

The only other remark I'll make about listing 4.8 is that I chose to suppress the code analysis rule that suggests Uri objects, for the same reason as explained in section 4.2.3.

---

11. The Richardson Maturity Model for REST distinguishes between three levels: 1. Resources. 2. HTTP verbs. 3. Hypermedia controls [114].

12. SUT: System Under Test.

When you run the test it fails as expected. The Assertion Message [66] is *Actual status code: NotFound*. This means that the `/reservations` resource doesn't exist on the server. Hardly surprising, since we've yet to implement it.

That's straightforward to do, as listing 4.9 shows. It's the minimal implementation that passes all existing tests.

Listing 4.9 Minimal `ReservationsController`.
(Restaurant/90e4869/Restaurant.RestApi/ReservationsController.cs)

```
    [Route("[controller]")]
    public class ReservationsController
    {
#pragma warning disable CA1822 // Mark members as static
        public void Post() { }
#pragma warning restore CA1822 // Mark members as static
    }
```

The first detail that you see is the ugly `#pragma` instructions. As their comments suggest, they suppress a static code analysis rule that insists on making the `Post` method `static`. You can't do that, though: if you make the method `static` then the test fails. The ASP.NET MVC framework matches HTTP requests with controller methods by convention, and methods must be instance methods (i.e. not `static`).

There are multiple ways to suppress warnings from the .NET analysers and I deliberately chose the ghastliest alternative. I did that instead of leaving a `//TODO` comment. I hope those `#pragma` instructions have the same effect.

The `Post` method is currently a no-op, but it obviously shouldn't stay like that. You have to temporarily suppress the warning, though, because otherwise the code doesn't compile. Treating warnings as errors isn't a free ride, but I find the slowdown worthwhile. Remember: The goal isn't to write as many lines of code as fast as you can. The goal is sustainable software.

> The goal it not to write code fast. The goal is sustainable software.

All tests now pass. Commit the changes in Git, and consider pushing them through your deployment pipeline [49].

4.3.3   UNIT TEST

As listing 4.9 shows, the web service doesn't handle the posted reservation. You can use another test to drive the behaviour closer to the goal, like the test in listing 4.10.

Listing 4.10 Unit test of posting a valid reservation.
(Restaurant/bc1079a/Restaurant.RestApi.Tests/ReservationsTests.cs)

```
[Fact]
public async Task PostValidReservationWhenDatabaseIsEmpty()
{
    var db = new FakeDatabase();
    var sut = new ReservationsController(db);

    var dto = new ReservationDto
    {
        At = "2023-11-24 19:00",
        Email = "juliad@example.net",
        Name = "Julia Domna",
        Quantity = 5
    };
    await sut.Post(dto);

    var expected = new Reservation(
        new DateTime(2023, 11, 24, 19, 0, 0),
        dto.Email,
        dto.Name,
        dto.Quantity);
    Assert.Contains(expected, db);
}
```

Unlike the previous tests you've seen, this isn't a test against the system's HTTP API. It's a unit test[13]. This illustrates the key idea behind *outside-in test-driven development*. While you start at the boundary of the system, you should work your way in.

---

13. The term *unit test* is ill-defined. There's little consensus about its definition. I lean towards defining it as *an automated test that tests a unit in isolation of its dependencies*. Note that this definition is still vague, since it doesn't define *unit*. I normally think of a unit as a small piece of behaviour, but exactly how small is, again, ill-defined.

"But the boundary of the system is where the system interacts with the outside world," you object. "Shouldn't we be testing its *behaviour?*"

That sounds appropriate, but is, unfortunately, impractical. Trying to cover all behaviour and edge cases via boundary tests leads to a combinatorial explosion. You'd have to write tens of thousands of tests to do this [85]. Going from testing the outside to testing units in isolation addresses that problem.

While the unit test in listing 4.10 looks simple on the surface, much is going on behind the scenes. It's another example of an abstraction: amplify the essentials and eliminate the irrelevant. Clearly, no code is irrelevant. The point is that in order to understand the overall purpose of the test, you don't (yet) need to understand all the details of `ReservationDto`, `Reservation`, or `FakeDatabase`.

The test is structured according to the Arrange Act Assert [9] heuristic [92]. A blank line separates each phase. The *arrange* phase creates a `FakeDatabase` as well as the System Under Test (SUT) [66].

The *act* phase creates a Data Transfer Object (DTO) [33] and passes it to the `Post` method. You could also have created the `dto` as part of the *arrange* phase. I think you can argue for both alternatives, so I tend to go with what balances best, as I described in section 4.2.2. In this case there are two statements in each phase. I think that this *2-2-2* structure balances better than the *3-1-2* shape that would result if you move initialisation of the `dto` to the *arrange* phase.

Finally, the *assert* phase verifies that the database contains the `expected` reservation.

This describes the overall flow of the test, as well as the reason that it's structured the way it is. Hopefully, the abstractions introduced here enabled you to follow along even though you have yet to see the new classes. Before consulting listing 4.11, imagine what `ReservationDto` looks like.

4.3.4 DTO AND DOMAIN MODEL

When you looked, were you surprised? It's a completely normal C# DTO. Its only responsibility is to mirror the structure of the incoming JSON document and capture its constituent values.

Listing 4.11 Reservation DTO. This is part of the production code.
(Restaurant/bc1079a/Restaurant.RestApi/ReservationDto.cs)

```
public class ReservationDto
{
    public string? At { get; set; }
    public string? Email { get; set; }
    public string? Name { get; set; }
    public int Quantity { get; set; }
}
```

How do you think `Reservation` looks? Why does the code even contain two classes with similar names? The reason is that while they both represent *a reservation*, they play different *roles*.

The role of a DTO is to capture incoming data in a data structure, or to help transform a data structure to output. You should use it for nothing else, as it offers no encapsulation. Martin Fowler puts it this way:

> "A Data Transfer Object *is one of those objects our mothers told us never to write.*" [33]

The purpose of the `Reservation` class, on the other hand, is to encapsulate the business rules that apply to a reservation. It's part of the code's Domain Model [33][26]. Listing 4.12 shows the initial version of it. While it looks more complex[14] than listing 4.11, it actually isn't. It's made from exactly the same number of constituent parts.

---

14. Keep in mind that I use the word *complex* to mean *assembled from parts* [45]. It's not a synonym for *complicated.*

Listing 4.12 Reservation class. This is part of the Domain Model.
(Restaurant/bc1079a/Restaurant.RestApi/Reservation.cs)

```
public sealed class Reservation
{
    public Reservation(
        DateTime at,
        string email,
        string name,
        int quantity)
    {
        At = at;
        Email = email;
        Name = name;
        Quantity = quantity;
    }

    public DateTime At { get; }
    public string Email { get; }
    public string Name { get; }
    public int Quantity { get; }

    public override bool Equals(object? obj)
    {
        return obj is Reservation reservation &&
            At == reservation.At &&
            Email == reservation.Email &&
            Name == reservation.Name &&
            Quantity == reservation.Quantity;
    }

    public override int GetHashCode()
    {
        return HashCode.Combine(At, Email, Name, Quantity);
    }
}
```

"But there's so much more code there! Didn't you cheat? Where are the tests that drove you to this implementation?" you ask.

I wrote no tests of the Reservation class (apart from listing 4.10). I never claimed that I'd stick strictly to test-driven development.

Earlier in this chapter I discussed how I don't trust myself to write correct code. Again, recall the bat-and-ball problem if you need a reminder of how easily fooled the brain is. I do, however, trust *a tool* to write code for me. While I'm not a big fan of auto-generated code, Visual Studio wrote most of listing 4.12 for me.

I wrote the four read-only properties and then used Visual Studio's *generate constructor* tool to add the constructor, and the *generate Equals and GetHashCode* tool for the rest. I trust that Microsoft tests the features they include in their products.

How does `Reservation` better encapsulate the business rules about reservations? For now, it barely does. The major difference is that, as opposed to the DTO, the domain object requires all four constituent values to be present[15]. In addition, the `Date` is declared as a `DateTime`, which guarantees that the value is a proper date, and not just any arbitrary `string`. If you aren't yet convinced, section 5.3 and subsection 7.2.5 returns to the `Reservation` class to make it more compelling.

Why does `Reservation` look like a Value Object[16]? Because this offers a number of advantages. You should prefer Value Objects for your Domain Model [26]. It also makes testing easier [104].

Consider the assertion in listing 4.10. It looks for `expected` in `db`. How did `expected` get into `db`? It didn't, but an object that *looks just like it* did. Assertions use objects' own definitions of equality to compare expected and actual values, and `Reservation` overrides `Equals`. You can only safely implement such *structural equality* when the class is immutable. Otherwise, you might compare two mutable objects and think they're the same, only to later see them diverge.

Structural equality makes elegant assertions possible [104]. In the test, just create an object that represents the expected outcome, and compare it to the actual result.

---

15. Recall that the *nullable reference types* feature is enabled. The absence of question marks in the property declarations indicate that none of them may be null. Contrast with listing 4.11, which has question marks on all string properties, indicating that all may be null.

16. A *Value Object* [33] is an immutable object that composes other values and makes them look like a single, albeit complex, value. The archetypical example would be a `Money` class consisting of a currency and an amount [33].

4.3.5 FAKE OBJECT

The final new class implied by listing 4.10 is `FakeDatabase`, shown in listing 4.13. As its name implies, this is a Fake Object [66], a kind of Test Double [66][17]. It pretends that it's a database.

Listing 4.13 Fake database. This is part of the test code.
(Restaurant/bc1079a/Restaurant.RestApi.Tests/FakeDatabase.cs)

```
[SuppressMessage(
    "Naming",
    "CA1710:Identifiers should have correct suffix",
    Justification = "The role of the class is a Test Double.")]
public class FakeDatabase :
    Collection<Reservation>, IReservationsRepository
{
    public Task Create(Reservation reservation)
    {
        Add(reservation);
        return Task.CompletedTask;
    }
}
```

It's just an ordinary in-memory collection that implements an interface called `IReservationsRepository`. Since it derives from `Collection<Reservation>` it comes with various collection methods, including `Add`. That's also the reason that it works with `Assert.Contains` in listing 4.10.

A Fake Object [66] is a test-specific object that nonetheless has proper behaviour. When you use it as a stand-in for a real database, you can think of it as a kind of in-memory database. It works well with state-based testing [100]. That's the kind of test shown in listing 4.10. In the *assert* phase, you verify that the actual state fits the expected state. That particular test considers the state of `db`.

---

17. You may know Test Doubles as *mocks* and *stubs*. Like the word *unit test*, there's no consensus about what these words actually mean. I try to avoid them for that reason. For what it's worth, the excellent book *xUnit Test Patterns* [66] offers clear definitions of those terms, but alas, no one uses them.

4.3.6 REPOSITORY INTERFACE

The FakeDatabase class implements the IReservationsRepository interface shown in listing 4.14. This early in the lifetime of the code base, the interface only defines a single method.

For now, I chose to name the interface after the Repository pattern [33], although it only has a passing similarity to the original pattern description. I did that because most people are familiar with the name and understand that it models data access in some way. I may decide to rename it later.

Listing 4.14 Repository interface. This is part of the Domain Model. (*Restaurant/bc1079a/Restaurant.RestApi/IReservationsRepository.cs*)

```
public interface IReservationsRepository
{
    Task Create(Reservation reservation);
}
```

4.3.7 CREATE IN REPOSITORY

As you can see by the distance between this page and listing 4.10, that single test sparked the creation of several new types. This is normal early in the life of a code base. There's almost no existing code, so even a simple test is likely to set off a small avalanche of new code.

Based on the test, you also have to modify ReservationsController's constructor and Post method to support the interaction driven by the test. The constructor must take an IReservationsRepository parameter, and the Post method a ReservationDto parameter. Once you've made these changes, the test finally compiles so that you can run it.

When you execute it, it fails, as it's supposed to do.

To make it pass, you must add a Reservation object to the repository in the Post method. Listing 4.15 shows how.

The `ReservationsController` uses Constructor Injection [25] to receive the injected `repository` and save it as a read-only property for later use. This means that in any properly initialised instance of the class, the `Post` method can use it. Here, it calls `Create` with a *hard-coded* `Reservation`. While this is obviously wrong, it passes the test. It's the simplest[18] thing that could possibly work [22].

Listing 4.15 Saving a reservation in the injected repository.
(Restaurant/bc1079a/Restaurant.RestApi/ReservationsController.cs)

```
[ApiController, Route("[controller]")]
public class ReservationsController
{
    public ReservationsController(IReservationsRepository repository)
    {
        Repository = repository;
    }

    public IReservationsRepository Repository { get; }

    public async Task Post(ReservationDto dto)
    {
        if (dto is null)
            throw new ArgumentNullException(nameof(dto));

        await Repository
            .Create(
                new Reservation(
                    new DateTime(2023, 11, 24, 19, 0, 0),
                    "juliad@example.net",
                    "Julia Domna",
                    5))
            .ConfigureAwait(false);
    }
}
```

If you're wondering what drove the Guard Clause [7] against null into existence, that was prompted by a static code analysis rule. Again, keep in

---

18. You might argue that it'd be just as simple to copy the values from dto. It's true that this would have the same cyclomatic complexity and the same number of lines of code, but in the spirit of *The Transformation Priority Premise* [64] (TPP), I consider a constant to be simpler than a variable. See subsection 5.1.1 for more details on the TPP.

mind that you can use more than one *driver* at the same time: test-driven development *and* analysers or linters. There's lots of tooling that can drive creation of code. In fact, I used Visual Studio's *add null check* tool to add the guard.

The code in listing 4.15 passes the test in listing 4.10, but now another test fails!

4.3.8 CONFIGURE DEPENDENCIES

While the new test succeeds, the boundary test in listing 4.7 now fails because `ReservationsController` no longer has a parameterless constructor. The ASP.NET framework needs help creating instances of the class, particularly because no classes in the production code implement the required `IReservationsRepository` interface.

The simplest way to make all tests pass is to add a Null Object [118] implementation of the interface. Listing 4.16 shows a temporary class nested within the `Startup` class. It's an implementation of `IReservationsRepository` that doesn't do anything.

Listing 4.16 Null Object implementation. This is a temporary, nested private class. (*Restaurant/bc1079a/Restaurant.RestApi/Startup.cs*)

```
private class NullRepository : IReservationsRepository
{
    public Task Create(Reservation reservation)
    {
        return Task.CompletedTask;
    }
}
```

If you register it with ASP.NET's built-in Dependency Injection Container [25] it'll solve the problem. Listing 4.17 shows how to do that. Since `NullRepository` is stateless, you can register a single object with the Singleton lifetime [25], which means that the same object will be shared between all threads during the process lifetime of the web service.

Listing 4.17 Register `NullRepository` with ASP.NET's built-in DI Container.
(Restaurant/bc1079a/Restaurant.RestApi/Startup.cs)

```
public static void ConfigureServices(IServiceCollection services)
{
    services.AddControllers();

    services.AddSingleton<IReservationsRepository>(
        new NullRepository());
}
```

All tests now pass. Commit the changes in Git, and consider pushing them through your deployment pipeline.

4.4 COMPLETE THE SLICE

Pursuing the vertical slice, figure 4.5 implies that something is missing. You need a proper implementation of `IReservationsRepository` to save the reservation to persistent storage. Once you have that, you've completed the slice.

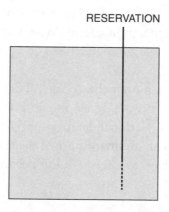

RESERVATION

Figure 4.5 Progress so far. Compare to the plan shown in figure 4.4.

"Wait a minute," you say, "it doesn't work at all! It'd just save a hard-coded reservation! And what about input validation, logging, or security?"

We'll get to all of this in time. Right now, I'll be satisfied if a stimulus can produce a persistent state change, even if that's a hard-coded reservation. It'll still demonstrate that an external event (an HTTP POST) can modify the state of the application.

4.4.1 SCHEMA

How should we save the reservation? In a relational database? A graph database [89]? A document database?

If you were to follow the spirit of *Growing Object-Oriented Software, Guided by Tests* [36] (GOOS) you should pick the technology that best supports test-driven development. Preferably something that you can host within your automated tests. That suggests a document database.

Despite of this, I'll pick a relational database—specifically, SQL Server. I do this for educational reasons. First, GOOS [36] is already an excellent resource if you want to learn principled outside-in test-driven development. Second, in reality, relational databases are ubiquitous. Having a relational database is often non-negotiable. Your organisation may have a support agreement with a particular vendor. Your operations team may prefer a specific system because they know how to maintain it, and do backups. Your colleagues may be most comfortable with a certain database.

Despite the *NoSQL* movement, relational databases remain an unavoidable part of enterprise software development. I hope that this book is more useful because I include a relational database as part of the example. I'll use SQL Server because it's an idiomatic part of the standard Microsoft stack, but the techniques you'd have to apply wouldn't change much if you chose another database.

Listing 4.18 shows the initial schema for the Reservations table.

I prefer defining a database schema in SQL, since that's the native language of the database. If you instead prefer to use an object-relational mapper or a domain-specific language then that's fine too. The important part is that you

Listing 4.18 Database schema for the `Reservations` table.
(Restaurant/c82d82c/Restaurant.RestApi/RestaurantDbSchema.sql)

```
CREATE TABLE [dbo].[Reservations] (
    [Id]        INT            NOT NULL IDENTITY,
    [At]        DATETIME2      NOT NULL,
    [Name]      NVARCHAR (50)  NOT NULL,
    [Email]     NVARCHAR (50)  NOT NULL,
    [Quantity]  INT            NOT NULL
    PRIMARY KEY CLUSTERED ([Id] ASC)
)
```

commit the database schema to the same Git repository that holds all the other source code.

> Commit database schema to the Git repository.

4.4.2 SQL REPOSITORY

Now that you know what the database schema looks like, you can implement the `IReservationsRepository` interface against the database. Listing 4.19 shows my implementation. As you can tell, I'm not a fan of object-relational mappers (ORMs).

You may argue that using the fundamental ADO.NET API is verbose compared to, say, Entity Framework, but keep in mind that you shouldn't be optimising for writing speed. When optimising for readability, you can still argue that using an object-relational mapper would be more readable. I think that there's a degree of subjective judgement involved.

If you want to use an object-relational mapper instead, then do so. That's not the important point. The important point is that you keep your Domain Model [33] unpolluted by implementation details[19].

---

19. This is the Dependency Inversion Principle applied. *Abstractions should not depend upon details. Details should depend upon abstractions* [60]. The abstraction in this context is the Domain Model, that is, `Reservation`.

What I like about the implementation in listing 4.19 is that it has simple invariants. It's a stateless, thread-safe object. You can create a single instance of it and reuse it during the lifetime of your application.

"But Mark," you protest, "now you're cheating again! You didn't test-drive that class."

Listing 4.19 SQL Server implementation of the Repository interface.
(Restaurant/c82d82c/Restaurant.RestApi/SqlReservationsRepository.cs)

```
public class SqlReservationsRepository : IReservationsRepository
{
    public SqlReservationsRepository(string connectionString)
    {
        ConnectionString = connectionString;
    }

    public string ConnectionString { get; }

    public async Task Create(Reservation reservation)
    {
        if (reservation is null)
            throw new ArgumentNullException(nameof(reservation));

        using var conn = new SqlConnection(ConnectionString);
        using var cmd = new SqlCommand(createReservationSql, conn);
        cmd.Parameters.Add(new SqlParameter("@At", reservation.At));
        cmd.Parameters.Add(new SqlParameter("@Name", reservation.Name));
        cmd.Parameters.Add(new SqlParameter("@Email", reservation.Email));
        cmd.Parameters.Add(
            new SqlParameter("@Quantity", reservation.Quantity));

        await conn.OpenAsync().ConfigureAwait(false);
        await cmd.ExecuteNonQueryAsync().ConfigureAwait(false);
    }

    private const string createReservationSql = @"
        INSERT INTO
            [dbo].[Reservations] ([At], [Name], [Email], [Quantity])
        VALUES (@At, @Name, @Email, @Quantity)";
}
```

True, I didn't do that because I consider `SqlReservationsRepository` a Humble Object [66]. This is an implementation that's hard to unit test because it depends on a subsystem that you can't easily automate. Instead, you drain the object of branching logic and other kinds of behaviour that tend to cause defects.

The only branching in `SqlReservationsRepository` is the null guard that was driven by static code analysis and created by Visual Studio.

All that said, in section 12.2 you'll see how to add automated tests that involve the database.

4.4.3 CONFIGURATION WITH DATABASE

Now that you have a proper implementation of `IReservationsRepository` you have to tell ASP.NET about it. Listing 4.20 shows the changes you need to make to the `Startup` class.

Listing 4.20 The parts of the `Startup` file that configure the application to run against SQL Server. *(Restaurant/c82d82c/Restaurant.RestApi/Startup.cs)*

```
public IConfiguration Configuration { get; }

public Startup(IConfiguration configuration)
{
    Configuration = configuration;
}

public void ConfigureServices(IServiceCollection services)
{
    services.AddControllers();

    var connStr = Configuration.GetConnectionString("Restaurant");
    services.AddSingleton<IReservationsRepository>(
        new SqlReservationsRepository(connStr));
}
```

You call `AddSingleton` with the new `SqlReservationsRepository` class instead of the `NullRepository` class from listing 4.16. You can now delete that class.

You can't create a `SqlReservationsRepository` instance unless you supply a connection string, so you must get that from the ASP.NET's configuration.

When you add a constructor to `Startup`, as shown in listing 4.20, the framework automatically supplies an instance of `IConfiguration`.

You'll have to configure the application with a proper connection string. Among the many options available, you can use a configuration file. Listing 4.21 shows what I commit to Git at this point. While it's helpful to your colleagues to commit the structure of required configuration, don't include actual connection strings. They're going to vary according to environments and may contain secrets that shouldn't be in your version control system.

Listing 4.21 Structure of connection string configuration. This is what you should commit to Git. Be sure to avoid committing secrets.
(Restaurant/c82d82c/Restaurant.RestApi/appsettings.json)

```
{
  "ConnectionStrings": {
    "Restaurant": ""
  }
}
```

If you put a real connection string in the configuration file, the application ought to work.

4.4.4 PERFORM A SMOKE TEST

How do you know that the software works? After all, we didn't add an automated systems test.

While you should favour automated tests, you shouldn't forget manual testing. Once in a while, turn the system on and see if it catches fire. This is called a Smoke Test.

If you put a proper connection string in the configuration file and start the system on your development machine, you can try to `POST` a reservation to it. There's a wide selection of tools available to interact with an HTTP API. .NET developers tend to prefer GUI-based tools like Postman or Fiddler, but do yourself a favour and learn to use something that's easier to automate. I often use *cURL*. Here's an example (broken into multiple lines to fit the page):

```
$ curl -v http://localhost:53568/reservations
  -H "Content-Type: application/json"
  -d "{ \"at\": \"2022-10-21 19:00\",
        \"email\": \"caravan@example.com\",
        \"name\": \"Cara van Palace\",
        \"quantity\": 3 }"
```

This posts a JSON reservation to the appropriate URL. If you look in the database you configured the application to use, you should now see a row with a reservation... for *Julia Domna!*

Recall that the system still saves a hard-coded reservation, but at least you now know that if you supply a stimulus, something happens.

4.4.5 BOUNDARY TEST WITH FAKE DATABASE

The only remaining problem is that the boundary test in listing 4.7 now fails. The `Startup` class configures the `SqlReservationsRepository` service with a connection string, but there's no connection string in the test context. There's also no database.

It's possible to automate setting up and tearing down a database for automated test purposes, but it's cumbersome and slows down the tests. Maybe later[20], but not now.

Instead, you can run the boundary test against the `FakeDatabase` shown in listing 4.13. In order to do that, you must change how the test's `WebApplicationFactory` behaves. Listing 4.22 shows how to override its `ConfigureWebHost` method.

The code in the `ConfigureServices` block runs after the `Startup` class' `ConfigureServices` method has executed. It finds all the services that implement the `IReservationsRepository` interface (there's only one) and removes them. It then adds a `FakeDatabase` instance as a replacement.

---

20. In section 12.2, in fact.

Listing 4.22 How to replace a real dependency with a Fake for testing purposes.
(Restaurant/c82d82c/Restaurant.RestApi.Tests/RestaurantApiFactory.cs)

```
public class RestaurantApiFactory : WebApplicationFactory<Startup>
{
    protected override void ConfigureWebHost(IWebHostBuilder builder)
    {
        if (builder is null)
            throw new ArgumentNullException(nameof(builder));

        builder.ConfigureServices(services =>
        {
            services.RemoveAll<IReservationsRepository>();
            services.AddSingleton<IReservationsRepository>(
                new FakeDatabase());
        });
    }
}
```

You have to use the new `RestaurantApiFactory` class in your unit test, but that's just a change to a single line in the `PostReservation` helper method. Compare listing 4.23 with listing 4.8.

Listing 4.23 Test helper method with updated web application factory. Only the highlighted line that initialises the `factory` has changed compared to listing 4.8.
(Restaurant/c82d82c/Restaurant.RestApi.Tests/ReservationsTests.cs)

```
[SuppressMessage(
    "Usage",
    "CA2234:Pass system uri objects instead of strings",
    Justification = "URL isn't passed as variable, but as literal.")]
private async Task<HttpResponseMessage> PostReservation(
    object reservation)
{
    using var factory = new RestaurantApiFactory();
    var client = factory.CreateClient();

    string json = JsonSerializer.Serialize(reservation);
    using var content = new StringContent(json);
    content.Headers.ContentType.MediaType = "application/json";
    return await client.PostAsync("reservations", content);
}
```

Once more, all tests pass. Commit the changes in Git, and push them through your deployment pipeline. Once the changes are in production, perform another manual Smoke Test against the production system.

4.5 CONCLUSION

A thin vertical slice is an effective way to demonstrate that the software may actually work. Combined with Continuous Delivery [49] you're able to quickly put working software in production.

You may think that the first vertical slice is so 'thin' that it's pointless. The example in this chapter showed how to save a reservation in a database, but the values being saved aren't the values supplied to the system. How does that add any value?

Granted, it hardly does, but it establishes a running system, as well as a deployment pipeline [49]. Now you can improve on it. Small improvements, continuously delivered, inch closer towards a useful system. Other stakeholders are better equipped to evaluate when the system becomes useful. Your task is to enable them to perform that evaluation. Deploy as often as you can, and let other stakeholders tell you when you're done.

ENCAPSULATION 5

Have you ever bought something significant, like a house, a plot of land, a company, or a car?

If so, you probably signed a contract. A *contract* stipulates a set of rights and obligations on both sides. The seller promises to hand over the property. The buyer commits to pay the specified amount at a prescribed time. The seller may give some guarantees as to the state of the property. The buyer may promise not to hold the seller liable for damages after the transaction completes. And so on.

A contract introduces and formalises a level of trust that would otherwise not be present. Why should you trust a stranger? It's too risky to do that, but the institution of a contract fills the gap.

That's what *encapsulation* is about. How can you trust an object to behave reasonably? By making objects engage in contracts.

5.1 SAVE THE DATA

Chapter 4 closed without resolving an unbearable tension. Listing 4.15 shows how the Post method saves a hard-coded reservation while it ignores the data it received.

This is a defect. To fix it, you have to add some code, and that puts us in a good position to start discussing encapsulation. Since this kills two birds with one stone, let's do that first.

5.1.1   THE TRANSFORMATION PRIORITY PREMISE

Don't forget to use a *driver* if you can. The hard-coded values in listing 4.15 were driven by a single test case. How can you improve the situation?

It's tempting to just fix the code. After all, what has to happen is hardly rocket science. When I coach teams, I constantly have to remind developers to slow down. Write production code as answers to drivers like tests or analysers. Moving forward in small steps reduces the risk of mistakes.

When you edit code, you *transform* it from one working state to another. This doesn't happen atomically. During modification, the code may not compile. Keep the time when the code is invalid as short as possible, as implied by figure 5.1. This reduces the number of things your brain has to keep track of.

Figure 5.1 Editing code is the process of going from one working state to another. Keep the time when the code is in transition (i.e. doesn't work) as short as possible.

In 2013 Robert C. Martin published a prioritised list of code transformations [64]. While he only intended it as a preliminary suggestion, I find it useful as a guideline. It goes like this:

- ({}→nil) no code at all → code that employs nil
- (nil→constant)
- (constant→constant+) a simple constant to a more complex constant
- (constant→scalar) replacing a constant with a variable or an argument
- (statement→statements) adding more unconditional statements
- (unconditional→if) splitting the execution path

- (scalar→array)
- (array→container)
- (statement→recursion)
- (if→while)
- (expression→function) replacing an expression with a function or algorithm
- (variable→assignment) replacing the value of a variable

The list is ordered roughly so that the simpler transformations are at the top, and the more complex changes are at the bottom.

Don't worry if some of the words seem cryptic or obscure. As with so many other guidelines in this book, they're food for thought rather than rigid rules. The point is to move in small increments, for example by using a hard-coded constant instead of null[1], or by turning a singular value into an array.

At the moment, the Post method saves a *constant*, but it ought to save data from dto; a set of *scalar* values. This is the *constant→scalar* transformation (or a set of them).

The point with the *Transformation Priority Premise* is that we should aim to make changes to our code using the small transformations from the list.

Since we've identified the change we're aiming for as one of the warranted changes, let's go ahead and make it.

5.1.2 PARAMETRISED TEST

The idea behind the Transformation Priority Premise is that once you've identified which transformation to aim for, you should write a test driving that change.

You could write a new test method, but it'd be a duplicate of listing 4.10, just with some different property values for the dto. Instead, turn the existing test into a Parametrised Test [66].

---

1. In the article [64] Robert C. Martin calls an undefined value *nil*, but from the context, it seems that he means *null*. Some languages (e.g. Ruby) call null *nil*.

Listing 5.1 Parametrised Test of posting a valid reservation. Compared to listing 4.10, only the highlighted test case is new.
(Restaurant/4617450/Restaurant.RestApi.Tests/ReservationsTests.cs)

```
[Theory]
[InlineData(
    "2023-11-24 19:00", "juliad@example.net", "Julia Domna", 5)]
[InlineData("2024-02-13 18:15", "x@example.com", "Xenia Ng", 9)]
public async Task PostValidReservationWhenDatabaseIsEmpty(
    string at,
    string email,
    string name,
    int quantity)
{
    var db = new FakeDatabase();
    var sut = new ReservationsController(db);

    var dto = new ReservationDto
    {
        At = at,
        Email = email,
        Name = name,
        Quantity = quantity
    };
    await sut.Post(dto);

    var expected = new Reservation(
        DateTime.Parse(dto.At, CultureInfo.InvariantCulture),
        dto.Email,
        dto.Name,
        dto.Quantity);
    Assert.Contains(expected, db);
}
```

Listing 5.1 shows the change. Instead of the [Fact] attribute, it uses the [Theory][2] attribute to indicate a Parametrised Test, as well as two [InlineData] attributes that supply the data. Notice that the top [InlineData] attribute supplies the same test values as listing 4.10, while the second attribute contains a new test case.

---

2. This is *xUnit.net's* API for Parametrised Tests. Other frameworks provide that feature in similar or not-so-similar ways. A few unit testing frameworks don't support this at all. In my opinion, that's reason enough to find another framework. The ability to write Parametrised Tests is one of the most important features of a unit testing framework.

One thing that should bother you is that the assertion phase of the test now seems to duplicate what would essentially be the implementation code. That's clearly not perfect. You shouldn't trust your brain to write production code without some sort of double-entry bookkeeping, but that only works if the two views are different. That's not the case here.

Perfect, however, is the enemy of the good. While this change introduces a problem in the test code, its purpose is to demonstrate that the Post method doesn't work. And indeed, when you run the test suite, the new test case fails.

5.1.3 COPY DTO TO DOMAIN MODEL

Listing 5.2 shows the simplest transformation you can make to the Post method to make all tests pass.

Listing 5.2 The Post method now saves the dto data.
(Restaurant/4617450/Restaurant.RestApi/ReservationsController.cs)

```
public async Task Post(ReservationDto dto)
{
    if (dto is null)
        throw new ArgumentNullException(nameof(dto));

    var r = new Reservation(
        DateTime.Parse(dto.At!, CultureInfo.InvariantCulture),
        dto.Email!,
        dto.Name!,
        dto.Quantity);
    await Repository.Create(r).ConfigureAwait(false);
}
```

This seems like an improvement compared to listing 4.15, but there are still issues that you ought to address. Fight the urge to make further improvements right now. By adding the test case shown in listing 5.1, you've driven a small transformation. While the code isn't perfect, it's *improved*. All tests pass. Commit the changes to Git and push them through your deployment pipeline.

If you're wondering about the exclamation marks after dto.At, dto.Email, and dto.Name, those are some of the remaining imperfections.

This code base uses C#'s *nullable reference types* feature, and most of the dto properties are declared as nullable. Without the exclamation mark, the compiler complains that the code accesses a nullable value without checking for null. The ! operator suppresses the compiler's complaints. With the exclamation marks, the code compiles.

This is a terrible hack. While the code compiles, it could easily cause a NullReferenceException at run time. Trading a compile-time error for a run-time exception is a poor trade-off. We should do something about that.

Another potential run-time exception lurking in listing 5.2 is that there's no guarantee that the DateTime.Parse method call succeeds. We should do something about that as well.

5.2 VALIDATION

With the code in listing 5.2, what happens if a client posts a JSON document without an at property?

You might think that Post would throw a NullReferenceException, but in reality, DateTime.Parse throws an ArgumentNullException instead. At least that method performs input validation. You should do the same.

How Is ArgumentNullException Better Than NullReferenceException?

Does it matter which exception is thrown by a method? After all, if you don't handle it, your program will crash.

Exception types seem to matter most if you can handle them. If you know that you can handle a particular type of exception, you can write a try/catch block. The problem is all the exceptions that you can't handle.

Typically, `NullReferenceException` happens when a required object is missing (null). If the object is required, but not available, there's not much that you can do about it. This is as true for `NullReferenceException` as it is for `ArgumentNullException`, so why bother to check for null only to throw an exception?

The difference is that a `NullReferenceException` carries no helpful information in its exception message. You're only told that some object was null, but not which one.

An `ArgumentNullException`, on the other hand, carries information about which argument was null.

If you encounter an exception message in a log or error report, which would you rather like to see? A `NullReferenceException` with no information, or an `ArgumentNullException` with the name of the argument that was null?

I'll take the `ArgumentNullException` any time, thank you.

The ASP.NET framework translates an unhandled exception to a `500 Internal Server Error` response. That's not what we want in this case.

5.2.1 BAD DATES

When input is invalid, an HTTP API should return `400 Bad Request` [2]. That's not what happens. Add a test that reproduces the problem.

Listing 5.3 shows how to test what happens when the reservation date and time is missing. You may wonder why I wrote it as a `[Theory]` with only a single test case. Why not a `[Fact]`?

I admit that I cheated a bit. Once again, the *art* of software engineering manifests itself. This is based on *the shifting sands of individual experience* [4] – I know that I'm going to add more test cases soon, so I find it easier to start with a `[Theory]`.

Listing 5.3 Test what happens when you post a reservation DTO with a missing at value. *(Restaurant/9e49134/Restaurant.RestApi.Tests/ReservationsTests.cs)*

```
[Theory]
[InlineData(null, "j@example.net", "Jay Xerxes", 1)]
public async Task PostInvalidReservation(
    string at,
    string email,
    string name,
    int quantity)
{
    var response =
        await PostReservation(new { at, email, name, quantity });
    Assert.Equal(HttpStatusCode.BadRequest, response.StatusCode);
}
```

The test fails because the response's status code is `500 Internal Server Error`.

You can easily pass the test with the code in listing 5.4. The major difference from listing 5.2 is the addition of the Null Guard.

Listing 5.4 Guard against null At property. *(Restaurant/9e49134/Restaurant.RestApi/ReservationsController.cs)*

```
public async Task<ActionResult> Post(ReservationDto dto)
{
    if (dto is null)
        throw new ArgumentNullException(nameof(dto));
    if (dto.At is null)
        return new BadRequestResult();

    var r = new Reservation(
        DateTime.Parse(dto.At, CultureInfo.InvariantCulture),
        dto.Email!,
        dto.Name!,
        dto.Quantity);
    await Repository.Create(r).ConfigureAwait(false);

    return new NoContentResult();
}
```

The C# compiler is clever enough to detect the Guard Clause, which means that you can remove the exclamation mark after `dto.At`.

You can add another test case where the `email` property is missing, but let's fast-forward one more step. Listing 5.5 contains two new test cases.

Listing 5.5 More test cases with invalid reservations.
(Restaurant/3fac4a3/Restaurant.RestApi.Tests/ReservationsTests.cs)

```
[Theory]
[InlineData(null, "j@example.net", "Jay Xerxes", 1)]
[InlineData("not a date", "w@example.edu", "Wk Hd", 8)]
[InlineData("2023-11-30 20:01", null, "Thora", 19)]
public async Task PostInvalidReservation(
    string at,
    string email,
    string name,
    int quantity)
{
    var response =
        await PostReservation(new { at, email, name, quantity });
    Assert.Equal(HttpStatusCode.BadRequest, response.StatusCode);
}
```

The bottom `[InlineData]` attribute contains a test case with a missing `email` property, while the middle test case supplies an `at` value that's not a date and time.

Listing 5.6 Guard against various invalid input values.
(Restaurant/3fac4a3/Restaurant.RestApi/ReservationsController.cs)

```
public async Task<ActionResult> Post(ReservationDto dto)
{
    if (dto is null)
        throw new ArgumentNullException(nameof(dto));
    if (dto.At is null)
        return new BadRequestResult();
    if (!DateTime.TryParse(dto.At, out var d))
        return new BadRequestResult();
    if (dto.Email is null)
        return new BadRequestResult();

    var r = new Reservation(d, dto.Email, dto.Name!, dto.Quantity);
    await Repository.Create(r).ConfigureAwait(false);

    return new NoContentResult();
}
```

Listing 5.6 passes all tests. Notice that I could remove another exclamation mark by guarding against a null email.

5.2.2 RED GREEN REFACTOR

Consider listing 5.6. It's grown in complexity since listing 4.15. Can you make it simpler?

This is an important question to regularly ask. In fact, you should ask it after each test iteration. It's part of the *Red Green Refactor* [9] cycle.

- **Red.** Write a failing test. Most test runners render a failing test in *red*.
- **Green.** Make as minimal change as possible to pass all tests. Test runners often render passing tests in *green*.
- **Refactor.** Improve the code without changing its behaviour.

Once you've moved through all three phases, you start over with a new failing test. Figure 5.2 illustrates the process.

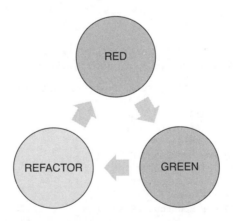

Figure 5.2 The Red Green Refactor cycle.

So far in the book's running example, you've only seen oscillations of red-green, red-green, and red-green. It's time to add the third phase.

The Science of Test-Driven Development

The Red Green Refactor process is one of the most scientific methodologies of software engineering that I can think of.

In the scientific method, you first form a hypothesis in the form of a prediction of a falsifiable outcome. Then you perform an experiment and measure the result. Finally, you compare the actual to the predicted outcome.

Does that sound familiar?

That sounds like the Arrange Act Assert [9] pattern, although we should be careful not to overextend the metaphor. The *act* phase is the experiment, and the *assert* phase is where you compare expected and actual outcomes.

The red and green phases in the Red Green Refactor cycle are small, ready-made science experiments in their own right.

In the red phase, the ready-made hypothesis is that when you run the test you just wrote, it should fail. This is a measurable experiment that you can perform. It has a quantitative outcome: it'll either pass or fail.

If you adopt Red Green Refactor as a consistent process, you may be surprised how often you get a passing test in this phase. Remember how easily the brain jumps to conclusions [51]. You'll inadvertently write tautological assertions [105]. Such false negatives happen, but you wouldn't discover them if you didn't perform the experiment.

Likewise, the green phase is a ready-made hypothesis. The prediction is that when you run the test, it'll succeed. Again, the experiment is to run the test, which has a quantifiable result.

(continues)

> If you want to move towards software engineering, and if you believe
> that there's a relationship between science and engineering, I can't think
> of anything more appropriate than test-driven development.

In the *refactor* phase, you consider the code you wrote in the green phase. Can
you improve it? If so, that would be refactoring.

> *"Refactoring is the process of changing a software system in such a way that it does
> not alter the external behavior of the code yet improves its internal structure."* [34]

How do you know that you don't change the external behaviour? It's difficult
to prove a universal conjecture, but it'd be easy to disprove. If just one
automated test were to fail after a change, you'd know that you broke
something. Thus, a minimum bar is that if you change the structure of the
code, all tests should still pass.

Can listing 4.15 be improved while still passing all tests? Yes, it turns out that
the null guard of `dto.At` is redundant. Listing 5.7 shows the simplified `Post`
method.

Listing 5.7 It's not necessary to guard against a null `At` property – `DateTime.TryParse` already
does that. *(Restaurant/b789ef1/Restaurant.RestApi/ReservationsController.cs)*

```
public async Task<ActionResult> Post(ReservationDto dto)
{
    if (dto is null)
        throw new ArgumentNullException(nameof(dto));
    if (!DateTime.TryParse(dto.At, out var d))
        return new BadRequestResult();
    if (dto.Email is null)
        return new BadRequestResult();

    var r = new Reservation(d, dto.Email, dto.Name!, dto.Quantity);
    await Repository.Create(r).ConfigureAwait(false);

    return new NoContentResult();
}
```

Why does this still work? It works because `DateTime.TryParse` already checks for null, and if the input is null, the return value is `false`.

How could you have known that? I'm not sure that I can give an answer that leads to reproducible results. I thought of this refactoring because I knew the behaviour of `DateTime.TryParse`. This is another example of programming based on *the shifting sands of individual experience* [4] – the *art* in software engineering.

5.2.3 NATURAL NUMBERS

Encapsulation is more than just checking for null. It's a contract that describes valid interactions between objects and callers. One way to specify validity is to state what's considered *invalid*. By implication all else is valid.

When you prohibit null references, you're implicitly allowing all non-null objects. Unless you add more constraints, that is. Listing 5.7 already does that for `dto.At`. Not only is null prohibited, but the string must also represent a proper date and time.

Design by Contract

Encapsulation is the idea that you should be able to interact with an object without intimate knowledge of its implementation details. This serves at least two purposes:

- It enables you to change the implementation; that is to *refactor*.
- It allows you to think of an object in an abstract way.

The second point is important when it comes to software engineering. Recall from chapter 3 that a fundamental problem is the brain's cognitive constraints. You can only keep track of seven things in your short-term memory. Encapsulation enables you to 'replace' the many details of an object's implementation with a simpler contract.

(continues)

Recall Robert C. Martin's definition of abstraction:

"Abstraction is the elimination of the irrelevant and the amplification of the essential" [60]

The *essential* quality of an object is its contract. It's usually simpler than the underlying implementation, so it fits better in your brain.

The idea of making contracts an explicit part of object-oriented programming is closely associated with Bertrand Meyer and the Eiffel language. In Eiffel, contracts are an explicit part of the language [67].

While no modern languages have made contracts explicit to the degree that Eiffel did, you can still design with contracts in mind. A Guard Clause [7], for example, can enforce a contract by rejecting invalid input.

Design explicitly with an eye to what does and does not constitute valid input, and what guarantees you can give about output.

What about the other constituent elements of a reservation? Using C#'s static type system, the `ReservationDto` class shown in listing 4.11 already (by its lack of the `?` symbol) declares that `Quantity` can't be null. But would *any* integer be an appropriate reservation quantity? *2? 0? -3?*

2 seems like a reasonable number of people, but clearly not *-3*. What about *0?* Why would you want to make a reservation for no people?

It seems to make most sense that a reservation quantity is a natural number. In my experience, this frequently happens when you evolve a Domain Model [33][26]. A model is an attempt to describe the real world[3], and in the real world, natural numbers abound.

Listing 5.8 shows the same test method as listing 5.5, but with two new test cases with invalid quantities.

---

3. Even when the 'real world' is only a business process.

Listing 5.8 More test cases with invalid quantities. The highlighted test cases are new, compared to listing 5.5. *(Restaurant/a6c4ead/Restaurant.RestApi.Tests/ReservationsTests.cs)*

```
[Theory]
[InlineData(null, "j@example.net", "Jay Xerxes", 1)]
[InlineData("not a date", "w@example.edu", "Wk Hd", 8)]
[InlineData("2023-11-30 20:01", null, "Thora", 19)]
[InlineData("2022-01-02 12:10", "3@example.org", "3 Beard", 0)]
[InlineData("2045-12-31 11:45", "git@example.com", "Gil Tan", -1)]
public async Task PostInvalidReservation(
    string at,
    string email,
    string name,
    int quantity)
{
    var response =
        await PostReservation(new { at, email, name, quantity });
    Assert.Equal(HttpStatusCode.BadRequest, response.StatusCode);
}
```

These new test cases in turn drove the revision of the Post method you can see in listing 5.9. The new Guard Clause [7] only accepts natural numbers.

Listing 5.9 Post now also guards against invalid quantities. *(Restaurant/a6c4ead/Restaurant.RestApi/ReservationsController.cs)*

```
public async Task<ActionResult> Post(ReservationDto dto)
{
    if (dto is null)
        throw new ArgumentNullException(nameof(dto));
    if (!DateTime.TryParse(dto.At, out var d))
        return new BadRequestResult();
    if (dto.Email is null)
        return new BadRequestResult();
    if (dto.Quantity < 1)
        return new BadRequestResult();

    var r = new Reservation(d, dto.Email, dto.Name!, dto.Quantity);
    await Repository.Create(r).ConfigureAwait(false);

    return new NoContentResult();
}
```

Most programming languages come with built-in data types. There are typically several integer data types: 8-bit integers, 16-bit integers, and so on.

Normal integers, however, are signed. They describe negative numbers as well as positive numbers. That's frequently not what you want.

You can sometimes get around the issue by using unsigned integers, but it wouldn't work in this case, because an unsigned integer would still allow zero. To reject a reservation for no people, you'd still need a Guard Clause.

The code in listing 5.9 compiles and all tests pass. Commit the changes in Git, and consider pushing them through your deployment pipeline.

5.2.4 POSTEL'S LAW

Let's recapitulate the process so far. What constitutes a valid reservation? The date must be a proper date, and the quantity must be a natural number. It's also a requirement that Email isn't null, but is that it?

Shouldn't we require a *valid* email address? And what about the name?

Email addresses are notoriously difficult to validate [41], and even if you had a full implementation of the SMTP specification, what good would it do you?

Users can easily give you a bogus email address that fits the spec. The only way to really validate an email address is to send a message to it and see if that provokes a response (such as the user clicking on a validation link). That would be a long-running asynchronous process, so even if you'd want to do that, you can't do it as a blocking method call.

The bottom line is that it makes little sense to validate the email address, apart from checking that it isn't null. For that reason, I'm not going to validate it more than I've already done.

What about the name? It's mostly a convenience. When you show up at the restaurant, the maître d' will ask for your name rather than your email address or a reservation ID. If you never gave your name when you made the reservation, the restaurant can probably find you by email address instead.

Instead of rejecting a null name, you can convert it to an empty string. That design decision follows Postel's law, because you're being liberal with the input name.

Postel's Law

Designing object interactions according to contract means thinking explicitly about pre- and postconditions. Which conditions must the client fulfil before interacting with the object? Which guarantees does the object give about the conditions after the interaction? These questions are closely related to declarations about input and output.

You can use *Postel's law* to deliberately contemplate pre- and postconditions. I'll paraphrase it as:

Be conservative in what you send, be liberal in what you accept.

Jon Postel originally formulated the guideline as part of the TCP specification, but I find it a useful guideline in the wider context of API design.

When you issue a contract, the stronger guarantees you give, and the less you demand of the other part, the more attractive you make the contract.

When it comes to API design, I usually interpret Postel's law as allowing input as long as I can meaningfully work with it, but no longer. A corollary is that while you should be liberal in what you accept, there's still going to be input you can't accept. As soon as you detect that that's the case, fail fast and reject the input.

You should still have a *driver* for that change, so add another test case like listing 5.10. The biggest change compared to listing 5.1 is the new test case, which is given by the third [InlineData] attribute. That test case initially fails, as it's supposed to do according to the Red Green Refactor process.

Listing 5.10 Another test case with a null name. The highlighted test case is new compared to listing 5.1. *(Restaurant/c31e671/Restaurant.RestApi.Tests/ReservationsTests.cs)*

```
[Theory]
[InlineData(
    "2023-11-24 19:00", "juliad@example.net", "Julia Domna", 5)]
[InlineData("2024-02-13 18:15", "x@example.com", "Xenia Ng", 9)]
[InlineData("2023-08-23 16:55", "kite@example.edu", null, 2)]
public async Task PostValidReservationWhenDatabaseIsEmpty(
    string at,
    string email,
    string name,
    int quantity)
{
    var db = new FakeDatabase();
    var sut = new ReservationsController(db);

    var dto = new ReservationDto
    {
        At = at,
        Email = email,
        Name = name,
        Quantity = quantity
    };
    await sut.Post(dto);

    var expected = new Reservation(
        DateTime.Parse(dto.At, CultureInfo.InvariantCulture),
        dto.Email,
        dto.Name ?? "",
        dto.Quantity);
    Assert.Contains(expected, db);
}
```

In the green phase, make the test pass. Listing 5.11 shows one way to do that. You could have used a standard ternary operator, but C#'s null coalescing operator (??) is a more compact alternative. In a way, it replaces the ! operator, but it's a good trade-off, because ?? doesn't suppress the compiler's null-check engine.

In the *refactor* phase, you ought to consider if you can make any improvements to the code. I think that you can, but that's going to be a longer discussion. There's no rule that prohibits a check-in between the *green* and the *refactor* phases. For now, commit the current changes to Git and push them through your deployment pipeline.

Listing 5.11 The Post method converts null names to the empty string. *(Restaurant/c31e671/Restaurant.RestApi/ReservationsController.cs)*

```
public async Task<ActionResult> Post(ReservationDto dto)
{
    if (dto is null)
        throw new ArgumentNullException(nameof(dto));
    if (!DateTime.TryParse(dto.At, out var d))
        return new BadRequestResult();
    if (dto.Email is null)
        return new BadRequestResult();
    if (dto.Quantity < 1)
        return new BadRequestResult();

    var r =
        new Reservation(d, dto.Email, dto.Name ?? "", dto.Quantity);
    await Repository.Create(r).ConfigureAwait(false);

    return new NoContentResult();
}
```

5.3 Protection of Invariants

Do you see anything wrong with listing 5.11? How does it look?

If we're concerned with complexity, it doesn't look too bad. Visual Studio comes with a built-in calculator of simple code metrics, such as cyclomatic complexity, depth of inheritance, lines of code, and so on. The metric I mostly pay attention to is cyclomatic complexity. If it exceeds seven[4] I think you should do something to reduce the number, but currently it's at six.

On the other hand, if you consider the entire system, there's more going on. While the Post method checks the preconditions of what constitutes a valid reservation, that knowledge is immediately lost. It calls the Create method on its Repository. Recall that this method is implemented by the SqlReservationsRepository class in listing 4.19.

If you're a maintenance programmer, and the first glimpse you get of the code base is listing 4.19, you may have questions about the reservation parameter.

---

4. Recall from section 3.2.1 that I use the number seven as a token for the brain's short-term memory limit.

Is At a proper date? Is Email guaranteed to not be null? Is Quantity a natural number?

You can look at the Reservation class in listing 4.12 and see that, indeed, Email is guaranteed to not be null, because you've used the type system to declare it non-nullable. The same is true for the date, but what about the quantity? Can you be sure that it isn't negative, or zero?

At the moment, the only way you can answer that question is by some detective work. What other code calls the Create method? Currently, there's only one call site, but this could change in the future. What if there were multiple callers? That's a lot to keep track of in your head.

Wouldn't it be easier if there were some way that would guarantee that the object has already been validated?

5.3.1 ALWAYS VALID

Reduced to its essence, *encapsulation* should guarantee that an object can never be in an invalid state. There are two dimensions to that definition: validity and state.

You've already encountered heuristics such as Postel's law that help you think about what's valid and invalid. What about state?

The state of an object is the combination of its constituent values. That combination should always be valid. If an object supports mutation then each operation that changes its state must guarantee that the operation doesn't result in an invalid state.

One of the many attractive qualities of immutable objects is that you only have to consider validity in one place: the constructor. If initialisation succeeded, the object should be in a valid state. That's currently not true for the Reservation class shown in listing 4.12.

That's an imperfection. You should make sure that you can't create a Reservation object with a negative quantity. Use a Parametrised Test [66] like listing 5.12 to drive this change.

Listing 5.12 A parametrised test that verifies that you can't create `Reservation` objects with invalid quantities. *(Restaurant/b3ca85e/Restaurant.RestApi.Tests/ReservationTests.cs)*

```
[Theory]
[InlineData( 0)]
[InlineData(-1)]
public void QuantityMustBePositive(int invalidQantity)
{
    Assert.Throws<ArgumentOutOfRangeException>(
        () => new Reservation(
            new DateTime(2024, 8, 19, 11, 30, 0),
            "mail@example.com",
            "Marie Ilsøe",
            invalidQantity));
}
```

I chose to parametrise this test method because I consider the value *zero* fundamentally different from negative numbers. Perhaps you think that zero is a natural number. Perhaps you don't. As with so many other things[5] there's no consensus. Despite this, the test makes it clear that zero is an invalid quantity. It also uses `-1` as an example of a negative number.

The test asserts that when you try to initialise a `Reservation` object with an invalid quantity, it should throw an exception. Notice that it doesn't assert on the exception message. The text of an exception message isn't part of the object's *behaviour*. That's not to say that the message isn't important, but there's no reason to couple tests to implementation details more than necessary. It would only mean that if you later want to change the exception message, you'd have to edit both the System Under Test and the test. Don't repeat yourself [50].

In the red phase of Red Green Refactor this test fails. Move to the green phase by making it pass. Listing 5.13 shows the resulting constructor.

Since the `Reservation` class is immutable, this effectively guarantees that it'll never be in an invalid state[6]. This means that all code that handles

---

5. What's a *unit*? What's a *mock*?

6. I'm pretending that `FormatterServices.GetUninitializedObject` doesn't exist. Don't use that method.

Listing 5.13 Reservation constructor with guard against non-positive quantity.
(Restaurant/b3ca85e/Restaurant.RestApi/Reservation.cs)

```
public Reservation(
    DateTime at,
    string email,
    string name,
    int quantity)
{
    if (quantity < 1)
        throw new ArgumentOutOfRangeException(
            nameof(quantity),
            "The value must be a positive (non-zero) number.");

    At = at;
    Email = email;
    Name = name;
    Quantity = quantity;
}
```

Reservation objects can dispense with defensive coding. The At, Email, Name, and Quantity properties are guaranteed to be populated, and the Quantity will be a positive number. Subsection 7.2.5 returns to the Reservation class to take advantage of these guarantees.

5.4 CONCLUSION

Encapsulation is one of the most misunderstood concepts of object-oriented programming. Many programmers believe that it's a prohibition against exposing class fields directly – that class fields should be 'encapsulated' behind getters and setters. That has little to do with encapsulation.

The most important notion is that an object should guarantee that it'll never be in an invalid state. That's not the callers' responsibility. The object knows best what 'valid' means, and how to make that guarantee.

The interaction between an object and a caller should obey a contract. This is a set of pre- and postconditions.

The preconditions describe the responsibilities of the caller. If the calling code fulfils those obligations, however, the postconditions describe the guarantees given by the object.

Pre- and postconditions together form *invariants*. You can use Postel's law to design a useful contract. The less you ask of the caller, the easier it is for the caller to interact with the object. The better guarantees you can give, the less defensive code the caller has to write.

6 TRIANGULATION

Some years ago I visited a client who wanted my help with their legacy code base. I had the opportunity to interview a few of the developers, and I asked the newest team member how long it took before he felt that he could contribute on his own.

"Three months," he replied.

It took him that long to memorise the code base to a degree where he felt confident editing it. I saw some of it, and it was truly complex. There were more than seven things going on. In fact, there were easily more than *seventy* things going on in some methods.

It takes time to learn to navigate such a code base, but it isn't impossible. You may think that this disproves the thesis that the human brain can only keep track of seven things. I think, however, that the thesis still holds, as I'll now explain.

6.1 SHORT-TERM VERSUS LONG-TERM MEMORY

Recall from subsection 3.2.1 that the number *seven* relates to *short-term* memory. Besides working memory, the brain also has long-term memory with capacity on an entirely different scale [80].

As covered in subsection 3.2.1, we should be careful with the brain-as-a-computer metaphor. Still, it seems obvious that we have a sort of memory store with vast capacity and tremendous span, although fickle. It's a different system than short-term memory, although there's some connection between the two, as implied by figure 6.1.

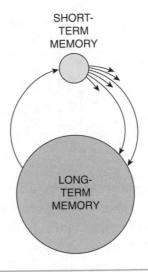

SHORT-
TERM
MEMORY

LONG-
TERM
MEMORY

Figure 6.1 Short-term memory is much smaller than long-term memory (figure not to scale). Most chunks of short-term memory 'disappear' when they 'go out of scope', but some occasionally make it to long-term memory, where they may stay for a long time. Information from long-term memory can also be retrieved and 'loaded' into short-term memory. It's tempting to think of RAM and hard drive, but we should be careful that we don't push the metaphor too far.

When you wake up from a strange dream, you can remember parts of it, but the memory quickly fades.

In the old days, you sometimes had to memorise a phone number for a few seconds in order to dial it. These days, you may have to remember a two-factor authentication one-time code a few seconds to type it in. The next minute, you've forgotten that number.

Some pieces of information, however, may first appear in short-term memory, but then you decide that it's important enough to commit to long-term memory. When I met my future wife in 1995, I quickly decided to memorise her phone number.

Conversely, you can recall information from long-term memory and work with it in short-term memory. For example, you may have memorised various APIs. When you write code, you retrieve the relevant methods into your short-term memory and combine them.

6.1.1 LEGACY CODE AND MEMORY

I believe that when you work with legacy code, you slowly, painstakingly commit the structure of the code base to long-term memory. You *can* work with legacy code, but there's (at least) two problems:

- It takes time to learn the code base
- Change is hard

The first point alone should give pause to hiring managers. If it takes three months before a new employee can be productive, programmers become irreplaceable. From an employee's perspective, if you want to be cynical, there's a degree of job security in being a legacy code programmer. Even so, it can be disenchanting, and it may also make it harder for you to find a new job. Legacy skills transfer poorly.

What's even worse is the second point. Information committed to long-term memory is harder to change. What would happen if you try to improve the code?

The book *Working Effectively with Legacy Code* [27] contains lots of techniques to ameliorate complicated code. It involves changing the structure of it.

What happens when you change the structure of code, as illustrated in figure 6.2? The information in your long-term memory becomes outdated. It gets *harder* to work with the code base, because your painstakingly acquired knowledge no longer applies.

Not only is legacy code difficult to work with. It's also hard to escape from.

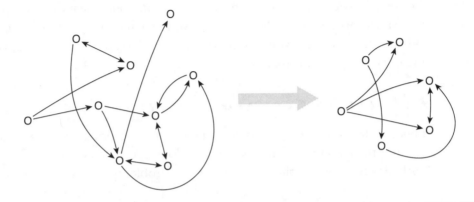

Figure 6.2 Refactoring legacy code comes with its own set of problems. Imagine that the diagram on the left is a complex system. You may be able to refactor it to a less complex system. What happens if the system to the right, while simpler, is still too complex to fit in your head? You may have had the system on the left memorised, but the system on the right is new. Your painstakingly acquired knowledge is now void, and something unknown has taken its place. It'd be better to avoid writing legacy code in the first place.

6.2   CAPACITY

Software engineering should sustain the organisation that owns the software. You develop sustainable code bases by making sure that the code fits in your brain. The capacity of your working memory is seven, so only a few things should be going on at the same time.

Any non-trivial piece of software is going to have much more going on, so you need to decompose and compartmentalise the code structure into small chunks that each fit in your brain.

As Kent Beck puts it:

"The goal of software design is to create chunks or slices that fit into a human mind. The software keeps growing but the human mind maxes out, so we have to keep chunking and slicing differently if we want to keep making changes." [10]

How to do that is the most important discipline of software engineering. Fortunately, there's a set of heuristics you can use to guide you.

I think that you learn best from examples. At the moment, the book's running example is still so simple that it all fits in your brain. We need a more complex code base to warrant decomposition.

6.2.1 OVERBOOKING

Apart from minimal input validation, the current restaurant system tolerates any reservation, in the future or in the past, for any positive quantity. The restaurant that it supports, however, has a physical capacity. Additionally, it may already be fully booked on a given date. The system should check a reservation against existing reservations and the capacity of the restaurant.

As is the dominant technique in this book, use a test as a driver for the new functionality. Which test should you write?

Listing 5.11 is the most up-to-date version of the Post method. If you follow the Transformation Priority Premise [64], the transformation you'd like to make is *unconditional→if*. You want to split the execution path by returning 204 No Content if all goes well, but return some error status code if the request is beyond the capacity of the restaurant. You should write a test that drives that behaviour. Listing 6.1 shows such a test.

The test first makes a reservation and then attempts to make another. Notice that the code is structured according to the Arrange Act Assert layout heuristic. The blank lines clearly delineate the three phases of the test.

The first reservation for six persons is part of the *arrange* phase, whereas the second reservation is the *act*.

Listing 6.1 Test that overbooking shouldn't be possible. Note that the restaurant capacity is implicit in this test. You should consider making it more explicit. *(Restaurant/b3694bd/Restaurant.RestApi.Tests/ReservationsTests.cs)*

```
[Fact]
public async Task OverbookAttempt()
{
    using var service = new RestaurantApiFactory();
    await service.PostReservation(new
    {
        at = "2022-03-18 17:30",
        email = "mars@example.edu",
        name = "Marina Seminova",
        quantity = 6
    });

    var response = await service.PostReservation(new
    {
        at = "2022-03-18 17:30",
        email = "shli@example.org",
        name = "Shanghai Li",
        quantity = 5
    });

    Assert.Equal(
        HttpStatusCode.InternalServerError,
        response.StatusCode);
}
```

Finally, the assertion verifies that the response is `500 Internal Server Error`[1].

You should wonder why the expected outcome is an error. From looking at the test, it isn't clear. You should make a note to revisit this test later to improve it. This is a technique that Kent Beck describes in *Test-Driven Development By Example* [9]. While you write tests, you think of other things you should improve. Don't get derailed; write down your ideas and move on.

---

1. This design decision is contentious. Whenever I return that status code, people argue that `500 Internal Server Error` is reserved for truly unexpected error conditions. While I sympathise with that opinion, the question then becomes: Which HTTP status code to use instead? I've found neither the HTTP 1.1 specification nor the *RESTful Web Services Cookbook* [2] helpful in this regard. In any case, nothing hinges on this particular status code. If you favour another status code, just mentally replace `500 Internal Server Error` with your preference.

The implicit problem that listing 6.1 reproduces is that both reservations are for the same date. The first reservation is for six people, and while there's no explicit assertion, the test assumes that this reservation succeeds. In other words, the restaurant's capacity must be at least six.

The next reservation for five people fails. As the name of the test implies, the test case is an overbooking attempt. The restaurant doesn't have capacity for eleven people. Implicitly, what the test tells us is that the restaurant capacity is somewhere between six and ten.

Code ought to be more explicit than this. As the Zen of Python goes:

> *"Explicit is better than implicit."* [79]

This rule applies to test code as well as production code. The test in listing 6.1 ought to make the restaurant's capacity more explicit. I could have done this before showing you the code, but I want you to see how to write code in small increments. That includes leaving room for improvement. Take a note of any imperfections, but don't let them slow you down. Perfect is the enemy of the good. Let's keep moving.

I once dined at a hipster restaurant in Brooklyn. The only seating in the entire place was at a counter with a view to the kitchen, as illustrated by figure 6.3. It would seat twelve people, and your party would be seated next to other parties unless you reserved all twelve seats. Serving started at exactly 18:30, regardless of whether you were present or not. Such restaurants exist. I point it out because they represent the simplest reservation rules you can imagine. There's one shared table, and only one seating per day. That's the arrangement we'll aim for—for now.

What's the simplest thing that could possibly work [22]? Listing 6.2 shows a simple solution.

While this implementation is clearly wrong, it passes the new test, so commit the change to Git.

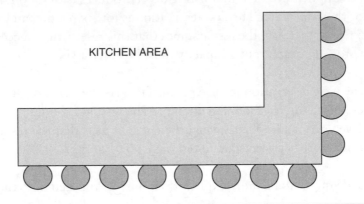

Figure 6.3 Sample table layout. This restaurant only has bar-style seating with a view to the kitchen area.

Listing 6.2 Despite test coverage, the branching performed in this version of the `Post` method doesn't implement the desired business rules.
(Restaurant/b3694bd/Restaurant.RestApi/ReservationsController.cs)

```csharp
public async Task<ActionResult> Post(ReservationDto dto)
{
    if (dto is null)
        throw new ArgumentNullException(nameof(dto));
    if (!DateTime.TryParse(dto.At, out var d))
        return new BadRequestResult();
    if (dto.Email is null)
        return new BadRequestResult();
    if (dto.Quantity < 1)
        return new BadRequestResult();

    if (dto.Email == "shli@example.org")
        return new StatusCodeResult(
            StatusCodes.Status500InternalServerError);

    var r =
        new Reservation(d, dto.Email, dto.Name ?? "", dto.Quantity);
    await Repository.Create(r).ConfigureAwait(false);

    return new NoContentResult();
}
```

6.2.2 THE DEVIL'S ADVOCATE

You've already seen a similar example of what looks like deliberate sabotage: Listing 4.15 hard-coded the data that it saved in the database. I call such intentional obstruction the *Devil's Advocate* technique [98]. You don't have to always apply it, but it can be useful.

I frequently teach test-driven development, and I've observed that beginners often struggle to produce good test cases. How do you know that you've written enough test cases?

The Devil's Advocate is a technique that helps you answer that question. The idea, in all its simplicity, is to deliberately try to pass all tests with an obviously incomplete implementation. That's what the code in listing 6.2 does.

This is useful because it works as a critique of your tests. If you can write a simple but clearly insufficient implementation, it tells you that you need more test cases to drive the desired behaviour. You can think of this process as a sort of triangulation [9], or, as Robert C. Martin puts it:

"As the tests get more specific, the code gets more generic." [64]

You need to add at least one more test case to prompt the correct implementation. Fortunately, a new test case is often just a new line of test data in a Parametrised Test [66], as you can see in listing 6.3.

That may not have been the test method you'd expected. Perhaps you thought the new test case should have been added to the OverbookAttempt method that we are 'currently' working with (listing 6.1). Instead, this is a fourth test case for an 'older' test (PostValidReservationWhenDatabaseIsEmpty). Why is that?

Consider the Transformation Priority Premise [64]. What's wrong with listing 6.2? It branches on a *constant* (the string "shli@example.org"). Which code transformation should you aim for to improve the code? The *constant→scalar* transformation sounds like the best option. You don't want execution to branch on a constant, you want it to branch on a variable.

Listing 6.3 Test of successfully making a reservation. The only change from listing 5.10 is the addition of the highlighted fourth test case.
(Restaurant/5b82c77/Restaurant.RestApi.Tests/ReservationsTests.cs)

```
[Theory]
[InlineData(
    "2023-11-24 19:00", "juliad@example.net", "Julia Domna", 5)]
[InlineData("2024-02-13 18:15", "x@example.com", "Xenia Ng", 9)]
[InlineData("2023-08-23 16:55", "kite@example.edu", null, 2)]
[InlineData("2022-03-18 17:30", "shli@example.org", "Shanghai Li", 5)]
public async Task PostValidReservationWhenDatabaseIsEmpty(
    string at,
    string email,
    string name,
    int quantity)
{
    var db = new FakeDatabase();
    var sut = new ReservationsController(db);

    var dto = new ReservationDto
    {
        At = at,
        Email = email,
        Name = name,
        Quantity = quantity
    };
    await sut.Post(dto);

    var expected = new Reservation(
        DateTime.Parse(dto.At, CultureInfo.InvariantCulture),
        dto.Email,
        dto.Name ?? "",
        dto.Quantity);
    Assert.Contains(expected, db);
}
```

The code in listing 6.2 implies that the email address `shli@example.org` is somehow illegal. That's wide of the mark. Which test case can you add that dispels that implied notion? One where `shli@example.org` is included in a successful reservation. That's what listing 6.3 does. It adds exactly the same reservation, but the circumstances differ. In the `PostValidReservationWhenDatabaseIsEmpty` test method, there's no prior reservation.

Unfortunately, the Devil can counter with the implementation in listing 6.4.

Listing 6.4 Tests force the `Post` method to consider existing reservations to decide whether or not to reject a reservation, but the implementation is still incorrect.
(Restaurant/5b82c77/Restaurant.RestApi/ReservationsController.cs)

```
public async Task<ActionResult> Post(ReservationDto dto)
{
    if (dto is null)
        throw new ArgumentNullException(nameof(dto));
    if (!DateTime.TryParse(dto.At, out var d))
        return new BadRequestResult();
    if (dto.Email is null)
        return new BadRequestResult();
    if (dto.Quantity < 1)
        return new BadRequestResult();

    var reservations =
        await Repository.ReadReservations(d).ConfigureAwait(false);
    if (reservations.Any())
        return new StatusCodeResult(
            StatusCodes.Status500InternalServerError);

    var r =
        new Reservation(d, dto.Email, dto.Name ?? "", dto.Quantity);
    await Repository.Create(r).ConfigureAwait(false);

    return new NoContentResult();
}
```

The new test case in listing 6.3 effectively prevents the Devil from rejecting the reservation based exclusively on the the `dto`. Instead, the method must consider the wider state of the application to pass all tests.

It correctly does this by calling `ReadReservations` on the injected `Repository`, but it incorrectly decides to reject the reservations if there are *any* existing reservations for that date. Still deficient, but closer to proper behaviour.

6.2.3 EXISTING RESERVATIONS

The `ReadReservations` method is a new member of the `IReservationsRepository` interface shown in listing 6.5. Implementations ought to return all reservations on the supplied date.

Listing 6.5 The highlighted ReadReservations method is new, compared to listing 4.14. *(Restaurant/5b82c77/Restaurant.RestApi/IReservationsRepository.cs)*

```
public interface IReservationsRepository
{
    Task Create(Reservation reservation);

    Task<IReadOnlyCollection<Reservation>> ReadReservations(
        DateTime dateTime);
}
```

When you add a new member to an interface, you break existing implementations. In this code base, two of those exist: SqlReservationsRepository and the test-specific FakeDatabase. The Fake [66] implementation is straightforward, as shown in listing 6.6. It uses LINQ to search within itself for all reservations that fall between midnight and the tick[2] before midnight the next day.

Listing 6.6 FakeDatabase implementation of the ReadReservations method. Recall from listing 4.13 that FakeDatabase inherits from a collection base class. That's the reason it can use LINQ to filter itself. *(Restaurant/5b82c77/Restaurant.RestApi.Tests/FakeDatabase.cs)*

```
public Task<IReadOnlyCollection<Reservation>> ReadReservations(
    DateTime dateTime)
{
    var min = dateTime.Date;
    var max = min.AddDays(1).AddTicks(-1);

    return Task.FromResult<IReadOnlyCollection<Reservation>>(
        this.Where(r => min <= r.At && r.At <= max).ToList());
}
```

Write Numeric Expressions in Number-Line Order

Notice that the filter expression in listing 6.6 is written in *number-line order*. Variables are arranged in ascending order from left to right. min is supposed to be the smallest value, so put it farthest to the left, like you'd do on a number line.

---

2. In .NET a *tick* is one hundred nanoseconds. It represents the smallest resolution of the built-in date and time API.

$$min <= r.At <= max$$

On the other hand, max is supposed to be the greatest value, so put it to the extreme right. The variable that the filter expression is concerned with is r.At, so put it between the two extremes.

Organising comparisons like this gives the reader a visual aid [65]. It lays out the values on an implicit contiguous number line.

In practice it means that you'll exclusively be using the *less-than* and *less-than-or-equal* operators, instead of the *greater-than* and *greater-than-or-equal* operators.

The other implementation of the IReservationsRepository interface is SqlReservationsRepository. It, too, must have a proper implementation. Like previously, you can treat that class as a Humble Object [66], so dispense with the automated tests. It's a straightforward SQL SELECT query, so I'm not going to use space to show it here. Consult the book's accompanying source code repository if you're curious about the details.

6.2.4 DEVIL'S ADVOCATE VERSUS RED GREEN REFACTOR

The code in listing 6.4 is still imperfect. While it does query the database for existing reservations, it rejects new reservations if just a single reservation already exists. It passes all tests, though.

Using the triangulation process implied by Robert C. Martin [64], add more test cases until you've defeated the Devil. Which test case should you add next?

The system should accept reservations as long as it has enough remaining capacity, even if it already has one or more reservations for a given day. This suggests a test similar to listing 6.7.

Listing 6.7 Test that it's possible to book a table even when there's already an existing reservation for the same date.
(Restaurant/bf48e45/Restaurant.RestApi.Tests/ReservationsTests.cs)

```
[Fact]
public async Task BookTableWhenFreeSeatingIsAvailable()
{
    using var service = new RestaurantApiFactory();
    await service.PostReservation(new
    {
        at = "2023-01-02 18:15",
        email = "net@example.net",
        name = "Ned Tucker",
        quantity = 2
    });

    var response = await service.PostReservation(new
    {
        at = "2023-01-02 18:30",
        email = "kant@example.edu",
        name = "Katrine Nøhr Troelsen",
        quantity = 4
    });

    Assert.True(
        response.IsSuccessStatusCode,
        $"Actual status code: {response.StatusCode}.");
}
```

Like the test in listing 6.1 it adds one reservation in the *arrange* phase, and another in the *act* phase, but unlike the `OverbookAttempt` test, this one expects a successful outcome. This is because the sum of the quantities is six, and we know that the restaurant can accommodate at least six guests.

Can the Devil's Advocate defeat this test? In other words, is it possible to change the `Post` method so that it passes all tests, yet still doesn't implement the correct business rule?

Yes, that's possible, but it's getting harder. Listing 6.8 shows the relevant snippet from the `Post` method (i.e. not the entire `Post` method). It uses LINQ to first convert the `reservations` to a collection of quantities, and then picks only the first of those.

The `SingleOrDefault` method returns a value if the collection contains a single element, or a default value if the collection is empty. The default `int`

Listing 6.8 The part of the `Post` method that decides whether or not to reject the reservation. The Devil's Advocate still attempts to circumvent the requirements specified by the test suite. The restaurant's capacity is hard-coded at `10`.
(Restaurant/bf48e45/Restaurant.RestApi/ReservationsController.cs)

```
var reservations =
    await Repository.ReadReservations(d).ConfigureAwait(false);
int reservedSeats =
    reservations.Select(r => r.Quantity).SingleOrDefault();
if (10 < reservedSeats + dto.Quantity)
    return new StatusCodeResult(
        StatusCodes.Status500InternalServerError);
```

value is `0`, so as long as there's no reservations, or a single existing reservation, this works.

If the collection contains more than one element, the `SingleOrDefault` method will throw an exception, but since no test cases exercise that situation, all tests pass.

It seems that once again, the Devil's Advocate has thwarted our plans for a proper implementation. Should we write another test case?

We could do that, but on the other hand, don't forget the Red Green Refactor process. Listing 6.7 represents the *red* phase, while listing 6.8 represents the *green* phase. Now it's time to refactor. Can you improve the code in listing 6.8?

It's already using LINQ, so how about using `Sum` instead of `SingleOrDefault`? Listing 6.9 shows the entire `Post` method after this refactoring. Compare the decision logic in the middle of the method to listing 6.8. It's actually simpler!

The code in listing 6.9 still passes all tests, but is also more general. That's an improvement, so check the changes into Git.

How do you detect such an opportunity for refactoring? How do you know that the `Sum` method exists? Such knowledge is still based on experience. I never promised that the *art of software engineering* would be an altogether deterministic process. It's just as well; if it was, machines could do our job.

Listing 6.9 The Post method now correctly decides to accept or reject a reservation based on the total sum of reservation quantities. The restaurant's capacity is hard-coded at 10. That's another imperfection we should address.
(Restaurant/9963056/Restaurant.RestApi/ReservationsController.cs)

```
public async Task<ActionResult> Post(ReservationDto dto)
{
    if (dto is null)
        throw new ArgumentNullException(nameof(dto));
    if (!DateTime.TryParse(dto.At, out var d))
        return new BadRequestResult();
    if (dto.Email is null)
        return new BadRequestResult();
    if (dto.Quantity < 1)
        return new BadRequestResult();

    var reservations =
        await Repository.ReadReservations(d).ConfigureAwait(false);
    int reservedSeats = reservations.Sum(r => r.Quantity);
    if (10 < reservedSeats + dto.Quantity)
        return new StatusCodeResult(
            StatusCodes.Status500InternalServerError);

    var r =
        new Reservation(d, dto.Email, dto.Name ?? "", dto.Quantity);
    await Repository.Create(r).ConfigureAwait(false);

    return new NoContentResult();
}
```

6.2.5 WHEN DO YOU HAVE ENOUGH TESTS?

Did the refactoring leave a flank open? What if someone later changes the code back to using SingleOrDefault? All tests would still pass, but the implementation would be incorrect.

That's important question, but I'm not aware of any quantitative answer. I usually ask myself: *How likely is such a regression to happen?*

I generally assume benign intent from other programmers[3]. The tests are in place to prevent us from making the kind of mistakes that our brains tend to

---

3. This depends on context. Imagine an open-source project used for something important, such as security or control of hardware. If a contributor could sneak in malicious code, this could have a real impact. You might be wise to adopt a more paranoid stance under such circumstances.

make. So how likely is it, for example, that a programmer would change the call to Sum to a call to SingleOrDefault?

I don't consider it particularly likely, but if it happened, what would be the impact? We'd get unhandled exceptions in the production environment. Hopefully, we'd discover the issue quickly and fix it. In such a case, be sure to write an automated test that reproduces the defect. Any defect that makes it to production tautologically demonstrates that *that* particular error could happen. If it can happen once, it can happen again. Prevent a regression with a test.

In general, deciding whether you have enough tests is standard risk assessment. Weigh the probability of an adverse outcome with its impact. I don't know of a way to quantify neither probability nor impact, so figuring this out is still mostly an art.

6.3 CONCLUSION

In geometry (and geographical surveys) *triangulation* is a process to determine the location of a point. When used about test-driven development it's a loose metaphor.

When the process is used in geometry, the point in question already exists, but you don't know its position. That's the situation to the left in figure 6.4.

Figure 6.4 Test-driven development is like triangulation, except that the roles are reversed. In a geographical survey the point already exists and you must measure the points from where you triangulate to be able to calculate the position of the target. In test-driven development the System Under Test initially doesn't exist, but the measurements (in the form of tests) do.

When you test-drive a code base, the tests play the role of measurements. What's different is that when you add a test, it measures something that isn't there yet. That's the situation to the right in figure 6.4.

The more tests you add, the better you describe the System Under Test, just as the more measurements you take in a geographical survey, the more precisely can you determine the target's position. For this to work, though, you must shift your perspective substantially between each measurement.

You can use an interplay between the Transformation Priority Premise, the Devil's Advocate, and the Red Green Refactor process to arrive at a comprehensive 360° description of the desired behaviour without too many redundant test cases.

7 DECOMPOSITION

No one deliberately decides to write legacy code. Code bases gradually deteriorate.

Why is that? Everyone seems to understand that a file with thousands of lines of code is a bad idea; that methods spanning hundreds of lines are difficult to work with. Programmers suffer when they have to work with such code bases.

If everyone understands that, though, then why do they allow the situation to become so bad?

7.1 CODE ROT

Code gradually becomes more complicated because each change seems small, and no one pays attention to the overall quality. It doesn't happen overnight, but one day you realise that you've developed a legacy code base, and by then, it's too late to do anything about it.

At the beginning, a method has low complexity, but as you fix defects and add features, the complexity increases, as shown in figure 7.1. If you don't pay attention to, say, cyclomatic complexity, you pass seven without noticing it. You pass ten without noticing it. You pass fifteen and twenty without noticing it.

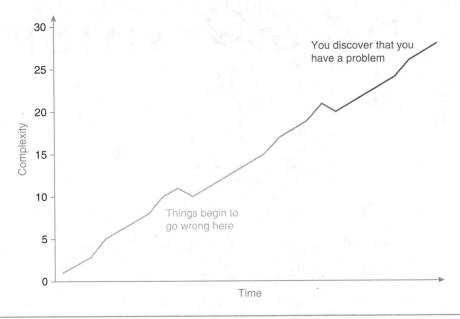

Figure 7.1 Gradual decay of a code base. Early on, things begin to go wrong as a complexity measure crosses a threshold. No one, however, pays attention to the metric, so you only discover that you have a problem much later, when the metric has become so great that it may be impossible to salvage.

One day you discover that you have a problem—not because you finally look at a metric, but because the code has now become so complicated that everyone notices. Alas, now it's too late to do anything about it.

Code rot sets in a little at a time; it works like boiling the proverbial frog.

7.1.1 THRESHOLDS

Agreeing on a threshold can help curb code rot. Institute a rule and monitor a metric. For example, you could agree to keep an eye on cyclomatic complexity. If it exceeds seven, you reject the change.

Such rules work because they can be used to counteract gradual decay. It's not the specific value seven that contributes to better code quality; it's the automatic activation of a rule based on a threshold. If you decide that the threshold should be ten instead, that'll also make a difference, but I find seven a good number, even if it's more symbolic than a strict limit. Recall from subsection 3.2.1 that seven is a token for your brain's working memory capacity.

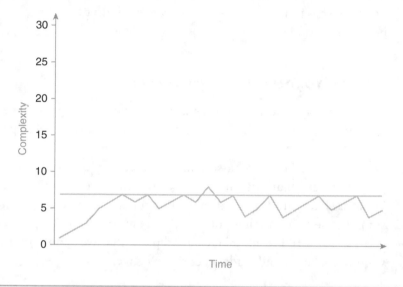

Figure 7.2 A threshold can help keep gradual decay in check.

Notice that figure 7.2 suggests that exceeding the threshold is still possible. Rules are in the way if you must rigidly obey them. Situations arise where breaking a rule is the best response. Once you've responded to the situation, however, find a way to bring the offending code back in line. Once a threshold is exceeded, you don't get any further warnings, and there's a risk that *that* particular code will gradually decay.

You could automate the process. Imagine running cyclomatic complexity analysis as part of a Continuous Integration build and rejecting changes that exceed a threshold. This is, in a way, a deliberate attempt to hack the management effect where you get what you measure. With emphasis on a metric like cyclomatic complexity, you and your colleagues will pay attention to it.

Be aware, however, of the law of unintended consequences[1]. Be careful with instituting hard rules.

I've had success with introducing threshold rules because they increase awareness. It can help a technical leader shift emphasis to the qualities that he or she wishes to improve. Once the team's mindset has changed, the rule itself becomes redundant.

7.1.2 CYCLOMATIC COMPLEXITY

You've already encountered the term cyclomatic complexity here and there in the book. It's one of the rare code metrics that I find useful in practice.

You'd expect a book about software engineering to be full of metrics. By now you've realised that this isn't the case. You can invent myriad code metrics[2], but most have little practical value. Preliminary research suggests that the simplest metric of all, lines of code, is the most pragmatic predictor of complexity [43]. I think that's a good point that we should return to, but I want to make sure all readers get the message.

The more lines of code, the worse the code base. Lines of code is only a productivity metric if you measure *lines of code deleted*. The more lines of code you add, the more code other people have to read and understand.

While lines of code may be a pragmatic indicator of complexity, cyclomatic complexity is useful for other reasons. It's a useful analysis tool because it not only informs you about complexity, but also guides you when it comes to unit testing.

---

1. For an entertaining introduction to the world of unintended consequences and perverse incentives, see *Freakonomics* [57] and *SuperFreakonomics* [58]. While the titles sound silly, as a university-educated economist, I can vouch for them.
2. See for example *Object-Oriented Metrics in Practice* [56].

Think of cyclomatic complexity as a measure of the number of pathways through a piece of code.

Even the simplest body of code affords a single pathway, so the minimum cyclomatic complexity is *1*. You can easily 'calculate' the cyclomatic complexity of a method or function. You start at 1, and then count how many times `if` and `for` occurs. For each of these keywords, you increment the number (which started at 1).

The specifics are language-dependent. The idea is to count branching and looping instructions. In C#, for example, you'd also have to include `foreach`, `while`, `do`, and each `case` in a `switch` block. In other languages, the keywords to count will differ.

What's the cyclomatic complexity of the `Post` method in the restaurant reservation system? Try to count all branching instructions in listing 6.9, starting with the number *1*.

Which number did you arrive at?

The cyclomatic complexity of listing 6.9 is *7*. Did you arrive at *6? 5?*

Here's how you arrive at 7. Remember to start with *1*. For each branching instruction you find, increment by 1. There are five `if` statements. *5* plus the starting number *1* is 6. The last one is harder to spot. It's the `??` null-coalescing operator which represents two alternative branches: one where `dto.Name` is null and one where it isn't. That's another branching instruction[3]. There's a total of seven pathways through the `Post` method.

Recall from section 3.2.1 that I use the number seven as a symbolic value that represents the limit of the brain's short-term memory. If you adopt a threshold of seven, the `Post` method in listing 6.9 is right at the limit. You could leave it

---

3. If you aren't used to thinking about C#'s null operators as branching instructions, this may not convince you, but maybe this will: Visual Studio's built-in code metrics calculator also arrives at a cyclomatic complexity of 7.

as is. That's fine, but has the consequence that if you need to add an eighth branch in the future, you should first refactor. Perhaps at that time, you don't have time to do that, so if you have time now, it might be better to do it prophylactically.

Hold that thought. We return to the `Post` method in section 7.2.2 to refactor it. Before we do that, however, I think we should cover some other guiding principles.

7.1.3   THE 80/24 RULE

What about the notion that lines of code is a simpler predictor for complexity?

We shouldn't forget about that. Don't write long methods. Write small blocks of code.

How small?

You can't give a universally good answer to that question. Among other things, it depends on the programming language in question. Some languages are much denser than others. The densest language I've ever programmed in is APL.

Most mainstream languages, however, seem to be verbose to approximately the same order of magnitude. When I write C# code, I become uncomfortable when my method size approaches 20 lines of code. C# is, however, a fairly wordy language, so it sometimes happens that I have to allow a method to grow larger. My limit is probably somewhere around 30 lines of code.

That's an arbitrary number, but if I have to quote one, it would be around that size. Since it's arbitrary anyway, let's make it 24, for reasons that I'll explain later.

The maximum line count of a method, then, should be 24.

To repeat the point from before, this depends on the language. I'd consider a 24-line Haskell or F# function to be so huge that if I received it as a pull request, I'd reject it on the grounds of size alone.

Most languages allow for flexibility in layout. For example, C-based languages use the ; character as a delimiter. This enables you to write more than one statement per line:

```
var foo = 32; var bar = foo + 10; Console.WriteLine(bar);
```

You could attempt to avoid the 24-line-height rule by writing wide lines. That would, however, defeat the purpose.

The purpose of writing small methods is to nudge yourself towards writing readable code; code that fits in your brain. The smaller, the better.

For completeness sake, let's institute a maximum line width as well. If there's any accepted industry standard for maximum line width, it's 80 characters. I've used that maximum for years, and it's a good maximum.

The 80-character limit has a long and venerable history, but what about the 24-line limit? While both are, ultimately, arbitrary, both fit the size of the popular VT100 terminal, which had a display resolution of 80 × 24 characters.

A box of 80 × 24 characters thus reproduces the size of an old terminal. Does that mean that I suggest you should write programs on terminals? No, people always misunderstand this. That should be the maximum size of a method[4]. On larger screens, you'd be able to see multiple small methods at the same time. For example, you could view a unit test and its target in a split screen configuration.

The exact sizes are arbitrary, but I think that there's something fundamentally right about such continuity with the past.

You can keep your line width in check with the help of code editors. Most development environments come with an option to paint vertical lines in the edit windows. You can, for example, put a line at the 80-character mark.

---

4. I feel the need to stress the point that this particular limit is arbitrary. The point is to have a threshold [97]. If your team is more comfortable with a 120 × 40 box, then that's fine, too. Just to prove the point, though, I wrote the entire example code base that accompanies this book using the 80 × 24 box as a threshold. It's possible, but I admit that it's a close fit for C#.

If you've been wondering why the code in this book is formatted as it is, one of the reasons is that it stays within the 80 character width limit.

Not only does the code in listing 6.9 have a cyclomatic complexity of 7, it's also exactly 24 lines high. That's one more reason to refactor it. It's right at the limit, and I don't think it's done yet.

7.2   CODE THAT FITS IN YOUR BRAIN

Your brain can only keep track of seven items at the same time. It's a good idea to take this into account when designing the architecture of the code base.

7.2.1   HEX FLOWER

When you look at a piece of code, your brain runs an emulator. It tries to interpret what the code will do when you execute it. If there's too much to keep track of, the code is no longer immediately comprehensible. It doesn't fit in your short-term memory. Instead, you must painstakingly work to commit the structure of the code to long-term memory. Legacy code is close at hand.

I posit the following rule, then:

> No more than seven things should be going on in a single piece of code.

There's more than one way to measure that, but one option is to use cyclomatic complexity. You could diagram the capacity of your short-term memory like figure 7.3.

Think of each of these circles as a 'memory slot' or 'register'. Each can hold a single chunk [80] of information.

If you squeeze the above bubbles together and also imagine that they're surrounded by other bubbles, the most compact representation is as figure 7.4.

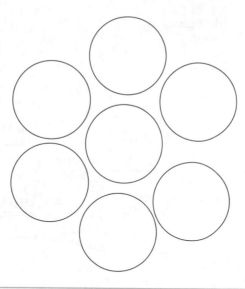

Figure 7.3 The capacity of human short-term memory illustrated as seven 'registers'.

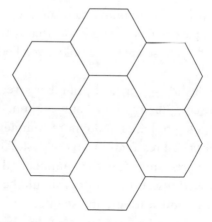

Figure 7.4 Seven 'registers' arranged in compact form. While hexagons could be arranged like this in an infinite grid, this particular shape looks like a stylised flower. For that reason, I'll refer to such diagrams as 'hex flowers'.

Conceptually, you should be able to describe what's going on in a piece of code by filling out the seven hexagons in that figure. What would the contents be for the code in listing 6.9?

It might look like figure 7.5.

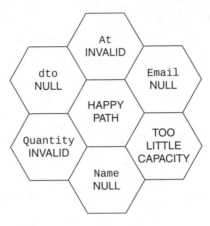

Figure 7.5 Hex flower diagram of the branches of the Post method in listing 6.9.

In each slot, I've plotted an outcome related to a branch in the code. From the cyclomatic complexity metric you know that listing 6.9 has seven pathways through the code. Those are the chunks I've filled into the hexagons.

All 'slots' are filled. If you treat the number seven as a hard limit[5], then you can't add more complexity to the Post method. The problem is that in the future, you're going to have to add more complex behaviour. For example, you may want to reject all reservations in the past. Also, the business rule only works for hipster restaurants with communal tables and single seatings. A more sophisticated reservation system should be able to handle tables of different sizes, second seatings, and so on.

You'll have to decompose the Post method to move forward.

7.2.2 COHESION

How, or where, should you decompose the Post method in listing 6.9?

---

5. The number seven isn't really a hard limit. Nothing in the line of reasoning presented here relies on that exact number, but the *visualisation*, on the other hand, does.

Perhaps it helps that the code is already organised into sections by a few blank lines[6]. There seems to be four sections; the first is a sequence of Guard Clauses [7]. This section is the best candidate for refactoring.

How can you tell?

The first section uses no instance members of the owning `ReservationsController` class. The second and third sections both use the `Repository` property. The fourth section is only a single return expression, so there's little to improve there.

That the second and third sections use an instance member doesn't preclude them from being extracted into helper methods, but the first section is more conspicuous. This relates to a central concept in object-oriented design: *cohesion*. I like the way that Kent Beck puts it:

> *"Things that change at the same rate belong together. Things that change at different rates belong apart."* [8]

Consider how instance fields of a class are used. Maximum cohesion is when all methods use all class fields. Minimum cohesion is when each method uses its own disjoint set of class fields.

Blocks of code that don't use any class fields at all look even more suspicious in that light. That's the reason I find that the best refactoring candidate is the first section of the code.

Your first attempt might resemble listing 7.1. This small method has only six lines of code and a cyclomatic complexity of 3. According to the metrics we've discussed so far, it looks great.

Notice, however, that it's marked static. This is necessary because a code analyser rule[7] has detected that it doesn't use any instance members. That could be a code smell. We'll return to that in a moment.

---

6. This book doesn't go into every little detail about how and why you lay out general source code, including how you should use blank lines. This is already covered in *Code Complete* [65]. I consider my use of blank lines to be consistent with it.
7. CA1822: Mark members as static.

Listing 7.1 Helper method to determine if a reservation DTO is valid.
(Restaurant/f8d1210/Restaurant.RestApi/ReservationsController.cs)

```
private static bool IsValid(ReservationDto dto)
{
    return DateTime.TryParse(dto.At, out _)
        && !(dto.Email is null)
        && 0 < dto.Quantity;
}
```

Did the introduction of the `IsValid` helper method improve the `Post` method? Listing 7.2 shows the result.

Listing 7.2 The `Post` method using the new `IsValid` helper method.
(Restaurant/f8d1210/Restaurant.RestApi/ReservationsController.cs)

```
public async Task<ActionResult> Post(ReservationDto dto)
{
    if (dto is null)
        throw new ArgumentNullException(nameof(dto));
    if (!IsValid(dto))
        return new BadRequestResult();

    var d = DateTime.Parse(dto.At!, CultureInfo.InvariantCulture);

    var reservations =
        await Repository.ReadReservations(d).ConfigureAwait(false);
    int reservedSeats = reservations.Sum(r => r.Quantity);
    if (10 < reservedSeats + dto.Quantity)
        return new StatusCodeResult(
            StatusCodes.Status500InternalServerError);

    var r =
        new Reservation(d, dto.Email!, dto.Name ?? "", dto.Quantity);
    await Repository.Create(r).ConfigureAwait(false);

    return new NoContentResult();
}
```

At first glance, that looks like an improvement. The line count is down to 22 and the cyclomatic complexity to 5.

Did it surprise you that cyclomatic complexity decreased?

After all, when you consider the combined behaviour of the Post method and its IsValid helper method, it hasn't changed. Shouldn't we count the complexity of IsValid into the complexity of the Post method?

That's a fair question, but it's not how the measure works. This way of viewing a method call represents both a danger and an opportunity. If you need to keep track of the details of how IsValid behaves, then nothing is gained. If, on the other hand, you can treat it as a single operation, then the corresponding hex flower (figure 7.6) looks better.

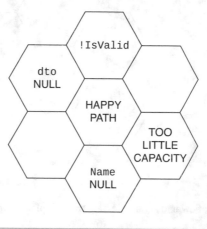

Figure 7.6 Hex flower diagram plotting the complexity of listing 7.2. Two empty 'registers' illustrate extra capacity of your short-term memory. In other words, the code fits in your brain.

Three fine-grained *chunks* have been replaced with a single slightly larger chunk.

> *"Short-term memory is measured in chunks [...] because each item can be a label that points to a much bigger information structure in long-term memory"* [80]

The key to such replacement is the ability to replace many things with one thing. You can do that if you can *abstract* the *essence* of the thing. Does that sound familiar?

That's Robert C. Martin's definition of *abstraction*:

> *"Abstraction is the elimination of the irrelevant and the amplification of the essential"* [60]

The `IsValid` method amplifies that it validates a Data Transfer Object while it eliminates the exact details about how it does that. We can draw another hexagonal short-term memory layout for it (figure 7.7).

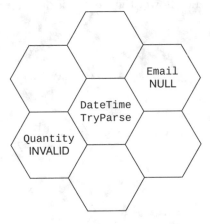

Figure 7.7 Hex flower diagram plotting the complexity of listing 7.1.

When you look at the code for `IsValid` you don't have to know anything about the surrounding context. The calling code doesn't influence the `IsValid` method, beyond passing an argument to it. Both `IsValid` and `Post` fit in your brain.

7.2.3   FEATURE ENVY

While complexity decreased with the above refactoring, the change introduced other problems.

The most evident problem is the code smell that the `IsValid` method is `static`[8]. It takes a `ReservationDto` parameter, but uses no instance members

---

8. It's not always a problem that a method is `static`, but in object-oriented design, it could be. It's worthwhile paying attention to your use of `static`.

of the ReservationsController class. That's a case of the Feature Envy [34] code smell. As *Refactoring* [34] suggests, try moving the method to the object it seems 'envious' of.

Listing 7.3 shows the method moved to the ReservationDto class. For now I decided to keep it internal, but I might consider changing that decision later.

Listing 7.3 IsValid method moved to the ReservationDto class. *(Restaurant/0551970/Restaurant.RestApi/ReservationDto.cs)*

```
internal bool IsValid
{
    get
    {
        return DateTime.TryParse(At, out _)
            && !(Email is null)
            && 0 < Quantity;
    }
}
```

I also chose to implement the member as a property[9] instead of a method. The previous method was 'envious' of the features of ReservationDto, but now that the member is a part of that class, it needs no further parameters. It could have been a method that took no input, but in this case a property seems like a better choice.

It's a simple operation without preconditions, and it can't throw exceptions. That fits the .NET framework guidelines' rules for property getters [23].

Listing 7.4 shows the part of the Post method where it checks whether the dto is valid.

Listing 7.4 Code fragment from the Post method. This is where it calls the IsValid method shown in listing 7.3. *(Restaurant/0551970/Restaurant.RestApi/ReservationsController.cs)*

```
if (!dto.IsValid)
    return new BadRequestResult();
```

---

9. A property is just C# syntactic sugar for a 'getter' (and/or 'setter') method.

All tests pass. Don't forget to commit the changes to Git and push them through your deployment pipeline [49].

7.2.4 LOST IN TRANSLATION

Even a small block of code can exhibit multiple problems. Fixing one issue doesn't guarantee that there are no more of them. That's the case with the Post method.

The C# compiler can no longer see that At and Email are guaranteed to be non-null. We have to tell it to turn off its static flow analysis for these references with the null-forgiving ! operator. Otherwise, the code doesn't compile. You're essentially suppressing the nullable-reference-types compiler feature. That's not a step in the right direction.

Another problem with listing 7.2 is that it effectively parses the At property twice—once in the IsValid method, and once again in the Post method.

It seems that too much is lost in the translation. It turns out that, after all, IsValid isn't a good abstraction. It eliminates too much and amplifies too little.

This is a typical problem with object-oriented validation. A member like IsValid produces a Boolean flag, but not all the information that downstream code might need—for example the parsed date. This compels other code to repeat the validation. The result is code duplication.

A better alternative is to capture the validated data. How do you represent validated data?

Recall the discussion about encapsulation in chapter 5. Objects should protect their invariants. That includes pre- and postconditions. A properly initialised object is guaranteed to be in a valid state—if it's not, encapsulation is broken because the constructor failed to check a precondition.

This is the motivation for a Domain Model. The classes that model the domain should capture its invariants. This is in contrast to Data Transfer Objects that model the messy interactions with the rest of the world.

In the restaurant reservation system, the domain model of a valid reservation already exists. It's the `Reservation` class, last glimpsed in listing 5.13. Return such an object instead.

7.2.5 PARSE, DON'T VALIDATE

Instead of an `IsValid` member that returns a Boolean value, translate Data Transfer Objects [33] to domain objects if the preconditions hold. Listing 7.5 shows an example.

Listing 7.5 The `Validate` method returns an encapsulated object. *(Restaurant/a0c39e2/Restaurant.RestApi/ReservationDto.cs)*

```
internal Reservation? Validate()
{
    if (!DateTime.TryParse(At, out var d))
        return null;
    if (Email is null)
        return null;
    if (Quantity < 1)
        return null;

    return new Reservation(d, Email, Name ?? "", Quantity);
}
```

The `Validate` method uses Guard Clauses [7] to check the preconditions of the `Reservation` class. This includes parsing the `At` string into a proper `DateTime` value. Only if all preconditions are fulfilled does it return a `Reservation` object. Otherwise, it returns null.

> **Maybe**
>
> Notice the method signature of the `Validate` method:
>
> ```
> internal Reservation? Validate()
> ```
>
> *(continues)*

The method's name and type is the first you see when you read code with which you're unfamiliar. If you can capture the *essence* of a method in the signature, then that's a good abstraction.

The `Validate` method's return type carries important information. Recall that the question mark indicates that the object may be null. That's important information when you're writing code calling the method. Not only that, but with C#'s nullable reference types feature turned on, the compiler is going to complain if you forget to handle the null case.

This is a relatively new feature in the realm of object-oriented languages. In previous versions of C# all objects could always be null. The same is still true for other object-oriented languages such as Java.

On the other hand, some languages (e.g. Haskell) have no null references, or go to great lengths to pretend that they don't exist (F#).

You can still model the presence and absence of values in these languages. You do that explicitly with a type called `Maybe` (in Haskell) or `Option` (in F#). You can easily port this notion to earlier versions of C# or other object-oriented languages. All you need is polymorphism and (preferably) generics [94].

If you did that, you could instead model the `Validate` method like this:

```
internal Maybe<Reservation> Validate()
```

The way the Maybe API works, callers would be forced to handle both cases: no reservation or exactly one reservation. Prior to C# 8's nullable reference types I've taught organisations to use Maybe objects instead of null. Developers quickly learn how much safer it makes their code.

If you can't use the nullable reference types feature of C#, declare null references to be illegal return values and use the Maybe container instead, when you want to indicate that a return value could be missing.

The calling code has to check whether the return value is null and act accordingly. Listing 7.6 shows how the Post method handles a null value.

Listing 7.6 The Post method calls the Validate method on the dto and branches on whether or not the returned value is null.
(Restaurant/a0c39e2/Restaurant.RestApi/ReservationsController.cs)

```
public async Task<ActionResult> Post(ReservationDto dto)
{
    if (dto is null)
        throw new ArgumentNullException(nameof(dto));

    Reservation? r = dto.Validate();
    if (r is null)
        return new BadRequestResult();

    var reservations = await Repository
        .ReadReservations(r.At)
        .ConfigureAwait(false);
    int reservedSeats = reservations.Sum(r => r.Quantity);
    if (10 < reservedSeats + r.Quantity)
        return new StatusCodeResult(
            StatusCodes.Status500InternalServerError);

    await Repository.Create(r).ConfigureAwait(false);

    return new NoContentResult();
}
```

Notice that this solves all the problems introduced by the static IsValid method shown in listing 7.1. The Post method doesn't have to suppress the compiler's static flow analyser, and it doesn't have to duplicate parsing the date.

The Post method's cyclomatic complexity is now down to 4. This fits in your brain, as figure 7.8 illustrates.

The Validate method is a better abstraction because it amplifies the essentials: does dto represent a valid reservation? It does that by *projecting* the input data into a stronger representation of the same data.

Alexis King calls this technique *parse, don't validate*.

"Consider: what is a parser? Really, a parser is just a function that consumes less-structured input and produces more-structured output. By its very nature, a parser is a partial function – some values in the domain do not correspond to any value in the range – so all parsers must have some notion of failure. Often, the input to a parser is text, but this is by no means a requirement" [54]

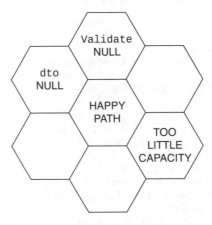

Figure 7.8 Hex flower diagram for the `Post` method shown in listing 7.6.

The `Validate` method is actually a parser: it takes the less-structured `ReservationDto` as input and produces the more-structured `Reservation` as output. Perhaps the `Validate` method ought to be named `Parse`, but I was concerned it might confuse readers with more narrow views on parsing.

7.2.6 FRACTAL ARCHITECTURE

Consider a diagram like figure 7.8 that depicts the `Post` method. Only four of the seven slots are occupied by chunks.

You know, however, that the chunk representing the `Validate` method amplifies the essentials while it eliminates some complexity. While you don't have to think about the complexity hidden by the chunk, it's still there, as suggested by figure 7.9.

You can zoom in on the `Validate` chunk. Figure 7.10 shows that the structure is the same.

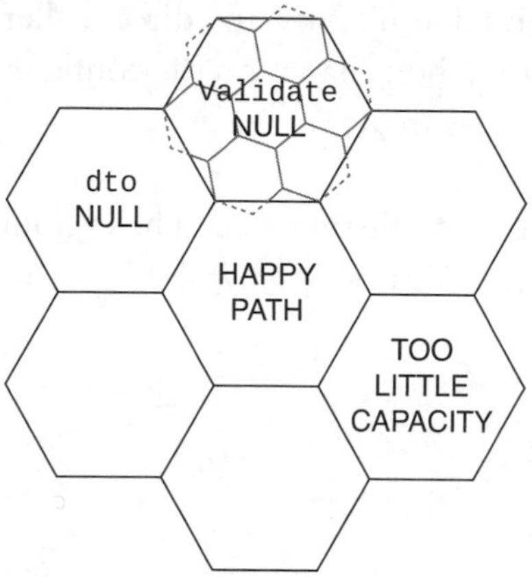

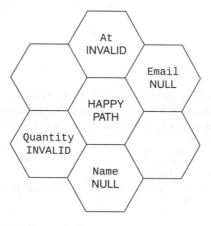

Figure 7.9 Hex flower hinting that each chunk can hide other complexity.

Figure 7.10 Hex flower for the `Validate` method shown in listing 7.5.

The cyclomatic complexity of the `Validate` method is 5, so if you use that as a yardstick for complexity, it makes sense to fill out five of the seven slots with chunks.

By now you'll have noticed that when you zoom in on a detail, it has the same hex flower shape as the caller. What happens if you zoom out?

The Post method doesn't have any direct callers. The ASP.NET framework calls Controller methods based on the configuration in the Startup class. How does that class measure up?

It hasn't changed since listing 4.20. The cyclomatic complexity of *the entire class* is as low as 5. You can easily plot it in the a hex flower like figure 7.11.

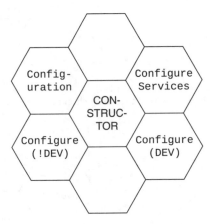

Figure 7.11 All complexity elements of the Startup class. Most class members have a cyclomatic complexity of *1*, so they take up only one hexagon. The Configure method has a cyclomatic complexity of 2, so it takes up two hexagons: one where IsDevelopment is true, and one where it's false.

Even the overall definition of the application fits in your brain. It should stay that way.

Imagine that you're a new team member, and this is the first time you're looking at the code base. A good place to start, if you're trying to understand how the application works, is the entry point. That's the Program class, which hasn't changed since listing 2.4. If you know ASP.NET you quickly realise that nothing unexpected is going on here. To understand the application, you should look at the Startup class.

When you open the Startup class, you're pleasantly surprised to learn that it fits in your brain. From the Configure method you quickly learn that the system uses ASP.NET's standard Model View Controller [33] system, as well as its regular routing engine.

From the `ConfigureServices` method you learn that the application reads a connection string from its configuration system and uses it to register a `SqlReservationsRepository` object with the framework's Dependency Injection Container [25]. This should suggest to you that the code uses Dependency Injection and a relational database.

This is a high-level view of the system. You don't learn any details, but you learn where to look if you're interested in details. If you want to know about the database implementation, you can navigate to the `SqlReservationsRepository` code. If you want to see how a particular HTTP request is handled, you find the associated Controller class.

When you navigate to those parts of the code base, you also learn that each class, or each method, fits in your brain at that level of abstraction. You can diagram the chunks of the code in a 'hex flower', as you've repeatedly seen throughout this chapter.

Regardless of the 'zoom level', the 'complexity structure' looks the same. This quality is reminiscent of mathematical fractals, which made me name this style of architecture *fractal architecture*. At all levels of abstraction, the code should fit in your brain.

In contrast to mathematical fractals, you can't keep zooming indefinitely in a code base. Sooner or later, you'll reach the highest level of resolution. That'll be methods that call none of your other code. For example, the methods in the `SqlReservationsRepository` class (see e.g. listing 4.19) don't call any other user code.

Another way to illustrate this style of architecture is as a tree, with the leaf nodes representing the highest level of resolution.

In general, you could illustrate an architecture that fits in your brain as a fractal tree, like in figure 7.12. At the trunk, your brain can handle up to seven chunks, represented by seven branches. At each branch, your brain can again handle seven more branches, and so on. A mathematical fractal tree is conceptually infinite, but when drawing it, you sooner or later have to stop rendering the branches.

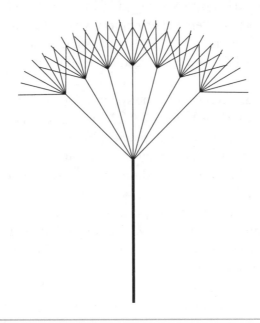

Figure 7.12 Seven-way fractal tree.

A fractal architecture is a way to organise code so that wherever you look, it fits in your brain. Lower-level details should be represented as a single abstract chunk, and higher-level details should be either irrelevant at that level of zoom, or otherwise explicitly visible as method parameters or injected dependencies. Keep in mind that *what you see is all there is* [51].

A fractal architecture doesn't happen by itself. You have to explicitly consider the complexity of each block of code you write. You can calculate cyclomatic complexity, keep an eye on lines of code, or count the number of variables involved in a method. Exactly how you evaluate complexity is less important than keeping it low.

Chapter 16 takes you on a tour of the finished example code base. The completed system is more complex than you've so far seen, but it still meets the requirements of a fractal architecture.

7.2.7 COUNT THE VARIABLES

As implied above, you can get another perspective on complexity by counting the number of variables in a method. I sometimes do that just to get another view on things.

If you decide to do that, make sure that you count all the involved objects. That includes local variables, method arguments, and class fields.

For example, the `Post` method in listing 7.6 involves five variables: `dto`, `r`, `reservations`, `Repository`, and `reservedSeats`. Three of those are local variables while `dto` is a parameter and `Repository` is a property (which is backed by an implicit, auto-generated class field). That's five things you have to keep track of. Your brain can do that, so this is fine.

I mostly do this when I consider if it's okay to add another parameter to a method. Are four parameters too many? It sounds like four parameters are well within the limit of seven, but if those four arguments interact with five local variables and three class fields, then too much is probably going on. One way out of such a situation is to introduce a Parameter Object [34].

Obviously, this type of complexity analysis doesn't work with interfaces or abstract methods, since there's no implementation.

7.3 CONCLUSION

Code bases aren't born as legacy code. They degrade over time. They accumulate cruft so gradually that it's difficult to notice.

High-quality code is like an unstable equilibrium, as pointed out by Brian Foote and Joseph Yoder:

> *"Ironically, comprehensibility can work against an artifact's preservation, by causing it to mutate more rapidly than artifacts that are harder to understand [...] An object with a clear interface and hard to understand internals may remain relatively intact." [28]*

You must actively prevent code from rotting. You can pay attention by measuring various metrics, such as lines of code, cyclomatic complexity, or just counting the variables.

I've no illusions about the universality of these metrics. They can be useful guides, but ultimately, you must use your own judgement. I find, however, that monitoring metrics like these can raise awareness of code rot.

When you combine metrics with aggressive thresholds, you establish a culture that actively pays attention to code quality. This tells you *when* to decompose a code block into smaller components.

Complexity metrics don't tell you which parts to decompose. This is a big subject that's already covered by many other books [60][27][34], but a few things to look for are cohesion, Feature Envy, and validation.

You should aim for an architecture of your code base so that regardless of where you look, the code fits in your head. At a high level, there's seven or fewer things going on. In the low-level code, there's at most seven things you have to keep track of. At the intermediary level, this still holds.

At every zoom level, the complexity of the code remains within humane bounds. This self-similarity at different levels of resolution looks enough like fractals that I call this *fractal architecture*.

It doesn't happen by itself, but if you can achieve it, the code is orders of magnitude easier to understand than legacy code because it'll mostly involve your short-term memory.

In chapter 16 you get a tour of the 'completed' code base, so that you can see how the concept of fractal architecture plays out in a realistic setting.

API DESIGN

8

When a block of code grows too complex, you should decompose it, as implied by figure 8.1. Chapter 7 discussed *where* to take things apart. In this chapter, you'll learn how to design the new parts.

Figure 8.1 Decompose a block of code into smaller blocks when it becomes too complex. How should the new blocks look? You'll learn some principles of API design in this chapter.

You can decompose code in many ways. There isn't a single correct way to do it, but there are more wrong ways than good ways. Staying on the narrow path of good API design requires skill and taste. Fortunately, the skill can be learned. Congruent with the theme of this book, you can apply heuristics to API design, as you will see in this chapter.

8.1   PRINCIPLES OF API DESIGN

The acronym API means *Application Programming Interface*, that is: an interface against which you can write client code. You have to be careful with these words, because their meanings are overloaded.

8.1.1   AFFORDANCE

How do you understand the word *interface?* You might think of it as a language keyword, as in listing 6.5. In the context of APIs, we use it in a broader sense. An interface is an *affordance*. It's the set of methods, values, functions, and objects you have at your disposal to interact with some other code. With good encapsulation, the interface is the set of operations that preserve the invariants of the objects involved. In other words, the operations guarantee that the object states are all valid.

An API enables you to interact with an encapsulated package of code, just like a door handle enables you to interact with a door. Donald A. Norman uses the term *affordance* to describe such a relationship.

> *"The term* affordance *refers to the relationship between a physical object and a person (or for that matter, any interacting agent, whether animal or human, or even machines and robots). An affordance is a relationship between the properties of an object and the capabilities of the agent that determine just how the object could possibly be used. A chair affords ("is for") support and, therefore, affords sitting. Most chairs can also be carried by a single person (they afford lifting), but some can only be lifted by a strong person or by a team of people. If young or relatively weak people cannot lift a chair, then for these people, the chair does not have that affordance, it does not afford lifting."* [71]

I find that this notion translates well to API design. An API like `IReservationsRepository` in listing 6.5 affords reading reservations related to a certain date, as well as adding a new reservation. You can only call the methods if you can supply the required input arguments. The relationship between client code and an API is akin to the relationship between caller and a properly encapsulated object. The object only affords its capabilities to client code that fulfils the required preconditions. If you have no `Reservation`, you can't call the `Create` method.

As Norman also writes:

"Every day we encounter thousands of objects, many of them new to us. Many of the new objects are similar to ones we already know, but many are unique, yet we manage quite well. How do we do this? Why is it that when we encounter many unusual natural objects, we know how to interact with them? Why is this true with many of the artificial human-made objects we encounter? The answer lies with a few basic principles. Some of the most important of these principles come from a consideration of affordances." [71]

When you encounter a chair for the first time, it's clear from the shape how you can use it. Office chairs come with extra capabilities: you can adjust their height, and so on. With some models, you can easily find the appropriate lever, while with other models, this is harder. All the levers look the same, and the one you thought would adjust the height instead adjusts the seat angle.

How does a an API advertise its affordances? When you're working with a compiled statically typed language, you can use the type system. Development environments can use type information to display the operations available on a given object, as you're typing, as shown in figure 8.2.

Figure 8.2 An IDE can show available methods on an object as you type. In Visual Studio this is called *IntelliSense*.

This offers a degree of discoverability called *dot-driven development*[1], because once you type the dot (period) after an object, you're presented with a selection of methods you can call.

8.1.2 POKA-YOKE

A common error is to design a Swiss Army knife. I've met many developers who think that a good API is one that enables as many activities as possible. Like a Swiss Army knife, such an API may collect many capabilities in one place, but none are as fit for their purpose as a specialised tool (figure 8.3). At the end of this design road lies the God Class[2].

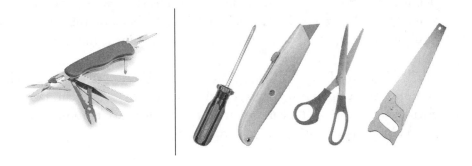

Figure 8.3 A Swiss Army knife can be handy in a bind, but is no substitute for proper tools. Figures not to scale.

Good interface design considers not only what's possible, but also what should be deliberately impossible—the affordances. The members exposed by an API advertise its capabilities, but the operations *not* supplied communicate what you're not supposed to do.

Design APIs so that it's difficult to misuse them. An important concept in lean software development is to *build quality in* [82]—that is, mistake-proof both

---

1. I first heard this term in a talk by Phil Trelford at the 2012 GOTO Copenhagen conference. I've found no earlier definition of the term.
2. *God Class* [15] is an antipattern that describes classes with dozens of members implemented in thousands of lines of code in a single file.

your artefacts and processes, instead of waiting until the end to detect and fix defects. In lean manufacturing this is known by the Japanese word *poka-yoke*, which means *mistake-proofing*. It translates well to software engineering [1].

Poka-yoke comes in two flavours: active and passive. Active mistake-proofing involves inspecting new artefacts as soon as they come into being. Test-driven development is the prime example [1]. You should run automated tests all the time.

I am, however, particularly enamoured with the notion of passive mistake-proofing. In the physical world you can find many examples of this. Cable connectors such as USB and HDMI can only be inserted the correct way. Height restriction barriers, as in figure 8.4, warn drivers that their vehicle is not going to fit. Such systems require no active inspection to work.

Figure 8.4 A height restriction barrier. Light-weight bars hang from chains. A truck too tall for what's up ahead will first hit these bars, with much noise but little damage.

Likewise, design APIs so that they *make illegal states unrepresentable* [69]. If a state is invalid, it's best to design the API so that it's impossible to express it in code. Capture the absence of a capability in the API's design, so that something that should be impossible doesn't even compile[3]. A compiler error gives you faster feedback than a runtime exception [99].

8.1.3 WRITE FOR READERS

If you recall your school days, you probably remember writing essays. Your teacher insisted that you should consider the context, *sender*, *receiver*, and so on. Recall that the *sender* is the person who ostensibly 'writes' the text, and the *receiver* is the person who reads it. Your teacher instructed you to explicitly consider the relationship between sender and receiver.

I've met more than one software developer who recall those days with loathing; who are happy that they are now programmers, literary analysis far behind them.

I've got bad news for you.

All this is still relevant in your professional life. There's a reason schools teach these skills. Sender and receiver matter when you compose an email. That relationship matters when you write documentation. And it matters when you write code.

Code is read more than it's written.

Write code for future readers. It may be yourself.

8.1.4 FAVOUR WELL-NAMED CODE OVER COMMENTS

You've probably heard that you should write clean code instead of comments [61]. Comments may deteriorate as the code evolves around them. What was once a correct comment becomes misleading as time passes. Ultimately, the only artefact you can trust is *the code*. Not the comments in the code, but the actual instructions and expressions that are compiled to working software. Listing 8.1 shows a typical example.

---

3. This is trivial to do in programming languages with *sum types*. These include Haskell and F#. In object-oriented design, the direct equivalent is the more verbose Visitor design pattern [107].

Listing 8.1 A comment explaining the intent of code. Don't do that. Replace it with a well-named method, as shown in listing 8.2.
(Restaurant/81b3348/Restaurant.RestApi/MaitreD.cs)

```
// Reject reservation if it's outside of opening hours
if (candidate.At.TimeOfDay < OpensAt ||
    LastSeating < candidate.At.TimeOfDay)
    return false;
```

If possible, replace the comment with a method with a helpful name [61], as in listing 8.2.

Listing 8.2 A method call replaces a comment. Compare with listing 8.1.
(Restaurant/f3cd960/Restaurant.RestApi/MaitreD.cs)

```
if (IsOutsideOfOpeningHours(candidate))
    return false;
```

Not all comments are bad [61], but favour well-named methods over comments.

8.1.5 X OUT NAMES

Don't rest on your laurels, though. Just as comments can grow stale and misleading over time, so can method names. Hopefully you pay more attention to method names than comments, but it still happens that someone changes the implementation of a method, but forgets to update the name.

Fortunately, with a statically typed language, you can use types to keep you honest. Design APIs so that they advertise their contracts with types. Consider the updated version of `IReservationsRepository` shown in listing 8.3. It has a third method named `ReadReservation`. It's a descriptive name, but is it sufficiently self-documenting?

One question I often find myself asking when I explore an unfamiliar API is: *Should I check the return value for null?* How do you communicate that in a durable and consistent way?

You could try to communicate with descriptive naming. For example, you might call the method `GetReservationOrNull`. This works, but is vulnerable

Listing 8.3 IReservationsRepository with an additional ReadReservation method compared to listing 6.5. *(Restaurant/ee3c786/Restaurant.RestApi/IReservationsRepository.cs)*

```
public interface IReservationsRepository
{
    Task Create(Reservation reservation);

    Task<IReadOnlyCollection<Reservation>> ReadReservations(
        DateTime dateTime);

    Task<Reservation?> ReadReservation(Guid id);
}
```

to changes in behaviour. You might later decide to change the API design so that null is no longer a valid return value, but forget to change the name.

Notice, however, that with C#'s nullable reference types feature, that information is already included in the method's type signature[4]. Its return type is Task<Reservation?>. Recall that the question mark indicates that the Reservation object could be null.

As an exercise in API design, try to *x out the method names* and see if you can still figure out what they do:

```
public interface IReservationsRepository
{
    Task Xxx(Reservation reservation);
    Task<IReadOnlyCollection<Reservation>> Xxx(DateTime dateTime);
    Task<Reservation?> Xxx(Guid id);
}
```

What does it look like Task Xxx(Reservation reservation) does? It takes a Reservation object as input, but it doesn't return anything[5]. Since there's no return value, it must perform some sort of side effect. What might it be?

---

4. If your language doesn't make the distinction between nullable and non-nullable reference types explicit, you can instead adopt the Maybe concept described on page 145. In that case, the signature of the ReadReservation method would be Task<Maybe<Reservation>> ReadReservation(Guid id).

5. Strictly speaking, it returns a Task, but that object contains no additional data. Regard Task as the asynchronous equivalent of void.

It could be that it saves the reservation. It might also conceivably transform it to an email and send it. It could log the information. This is where the defining object comes into play. When you know that the object that defines the method is called `IReservationsRepository`, the implied context is one of persistence. This enables you to eliminate logging and emailing as alternatives.

Still, it's not clear whether that method creates a new row in the database, or it updates an existing one. It might even do both. It's also technically possible that it deletes a row, although a better candidate signature for a delete operation would be `Task Xxx(Guid id)`.

What about `Task<IReadOnlyCollection<Reservation>> Xxx(DateTime dateTime)`? This method takes a date as input and returns a collection of reservations as output. It doesn't take much imagination to guess that this is a date-based query.

Finally, `Task<Reservation?> Xxx(Guid id)` takes an ID as input, and may or may not return a single reservation. That's unambiguously an ID-based lookup.

This technique works as long as objects afford only few interactions. The example has only three members, and they all have different types. When you combine method signatures with the name of the class or interface, you can often guess what a method does.

Notice, though, how it took more guesswork to reason about the anonymised `Create` method. Since there's effectively no return type, you have to reason about its intent based exclusively on the input type. With the queries, you have both input types and output types to hint at the method's intent.

X'ing out method names can be a useful exercise, because it helps you empathise with future readers of your code. You may think that the method name you just coined is descriptive and helpful, but it may not be to someone with a different context.

Names are still helpful, but you don't have to repeat what the types already state. This gives you room to tell the reader something he or she can't divine from the types.

Notice the importance of keeping the tools sharp, so to speak. This is another reason to favour specialised APIs over Swiss Army knives. When an object only exposes three or four methods, each method tends to have a type distinct from the other methods in that context. When you have dozens of methods on the same object, this is less likely to work well.

The method types are most likely to be helpful when the types alone disambiguate them from each other. If all methods return `string` or `int`, their types are less likely to be helpful. That's another reason to eschew stringly typed [3] APIs.

8.1.6   COMMAND QUERY SEPARATION

When you X out names, the role that static types can play comes into focus. Consider a method signature like `void Xxx()`. This tells you hardly anything about what the method does. All you can say is that it must have some sort of side effect, because it doesn't return anything, and what other reason for existence could it have?

Clearly, if you give the method a name, it's easier to guess what it does. It might be `void MoveToNextHoliday()` or `void Repaint()`. The possibilities are endless.

With a method structure like `void Xxx()`, the only way you can communicate with the reader is by choosing a good name. As you add types, you get more design options. Consider a signature like `void Xxx(Email x)`. It's still not clear exactly what's being done to the `Email` argument, but some side effect must be involved. What could it be?

An obvious side effect involving an email is to send it. It's hardly unambiguous, though. The method might also delete the email.

What's a side effect? It's when a procedure changes the state of something. This could be a local effect, like changing the state of an object, or a global effect, like changing the state of the application as a whole. This could include deleting a row from a database, editing a file on disk, repainting a graphical user interface, or sending an email.

The goal of good API design is to factor code so that it fits in our brains. Recall that the purpose of encapsulation is to hide implementation details. Thus, the code that implements a method could make use of local state changes, and you shouldn't regard those as side effects. Consider the helper method shown in listing 8.4.

Listing 8.4 A method with local state change, but no observable side effects. *(Restaurant/9c134dc/Restaurant.RestApi/MaitreD.cs)*

```
private IEnumerable<Table> Allocate(
    IEnumerable<Reservation> reservations)
{
    List<Table> availableTables = Tables.ToList();
    foreach (var r in reservations)
    {
        var table = availableTables.Find(t => t.Fits(r.Quantity));
        if (table is { })
        {
            availableTables.Remove(table);
            if (table.IsCommunal)
                availableTables.Add(table.Reserve(r.Quantity));
        }
    }

    return availableTables;
}
```

This method creates the local variable `availableTables`, which it then proceeds to modify before returning it. You might think that this counts as a side effect because the state of `availableTables` changes. On the other hand, the `Allocate` method doesn't change the state of the object that defines it, and it returns `availableTables` as a read-only collection[6].

When you write code that calls the `Allocate` method, all you need to know is that if you supply it a collection of reservations, you receive a collection of tables. As far as you're concerned, there's no side effect that you can observe.

Methods with side effects should return no data. In other words, their return type should be `void`. That makes it trivial to recognise them. When you see a

---

6. `IEnumerable<T>` is the standard .NET implementation of the Iterator [39] design pattern.

method that returns no data, you know that its *raison d'être* is to carry out a side effect. Such methods are called *Commands* [67].

To distinguish between procedures with and without side effects, then, methods that do return data should have no side effects. Thus, when you see a method signature like `IEnumerable<Table>` `Allocate(IEnumerable<Reservation> reservations)`, you ought to realise that it has no side effects because it has a return type. Such methods are called *Queries* [67][7].

It's much easier to reason about APIs if you keep Commands and Queries separate. Don't return data from methods with side effects, and don't cause side effects from methods that return data. If you follow that rule, you can distinguish between these two types of functions without having to read the implementation code.

This is known as *Command Query Separation* (CQS[8]). As most other techniques in this book, this isn't something that just happens automatically. The compiler doesn't need or enforce this rule[9], so it's your responsibility. You could make a checklist out of this rule, if need be.

As you saw in subsection 8.1.5, it's easier to reason about Queries than it is to reason about Commands, so favour Queries over Commands.

To be clear, it's trivially technically possible to write a method that both has a side effect and returns data. That's neither a Command nor a Query. The compiler doesn't care, but when you follow Command Query Separation, this combination isn't legal. You can always apply this principle, but it may require

---

7. Careful: a Query doesn't have to be a database query, although it can be. The distinction between Commands and Queries was made by Bertrand Meyer in or before 1988 [67]. At that time, relational databases weren't as pervasive as they are now, so the term *query* didn't come with as strong an association to database operations as may be the case today.
8. Be careful to not confuse CQS with CQRS (Command Query Responsibility Segregation). This is an *architectural style* that takes its terminology from CQS (hence the acronym resemblance), but takes the notion much further.
9. Unless the compiler is the Haskell or PureScript compiler.

some practice before you figure out how to deal with various knotty situations[10].

8.1.7 HIERARCHY OF COMMUNICATION

Just as comments can grow stale, so can names. It seems that there's a generalisable rule:

> Don't say anything with a comment that you can say with a method name. Don't say anything with a method name you can say with a type.

In priority, from most important to least important:

1. Guide the reader by giving APIs distinct types.
2. Guide the reader by giving methods helpful names.
3. Guide the reader by writing good comments.
4. Guide the reader by providing illustrative examples as automated tests.
5. Guide the reader by writing helpful commit messages in Git.
6. Guide the reader by writing good documentation.

The types are part of the compilation process. If you make a mistake with the types of your API, your code will likely not compile. None of the other alternatives for communicating with the reader has that quality.

Good method names are still part of the code base. You look at those every day. They're also a good way to communicate your intent to the reader.

There are matters that you can't easily communicate with good naming. These may include the *reason* you decide to write the implementation code in a particular way. That's still a legitimate reason to include a comment [61].

---

10. The thorniest problem people commonly run into is how to add a row to a database and return the generated ID to the caller. This, too, can be solved with adherence to CQS [95].

Likewise, there are considerations that relate to a particular *change* you make to the code. These should be documented as commit messages.

Finally, a few high-level questions are best answered by documentation. These include how to set up the development environment, or the overall mission of the code base. You can document such things in a readme file or another kind of documentation.

Notice that while I don't dismiss old-fashioned documentation, I consider it the least effective way to communicate with other developers. The code never grows stale. By definition, this is the only artefact that is always current. Everything else (names, comments, documentation) easily stagnates.

8.2 API DESIGN EXAMPLE

How do you apply such API design principles to code? What does it look like when used to solve a nontrivial problem? You'll see an example in this section.

The logic so far implemented in `ReservationsController` is trivial. Consider listing 7.6. The restaurant has a hard-coded capacity of ten seats. The decision rule doesn't take into account the size of each party of guests, so the implication is that all guests are seated at the same table. A typical configuration at hipster restaurants is bar-style seating with a view to the kitchen.

The logic in listing 7.6 also doesn't take into account the time of day of the reservation. The implication is that there's only a single seating per day.

Granted, I've dined at restaurants like that, but they are rare. Most places have more than one table, and they may have second seatings. This is when guests are allotted a given duration to finish their meal. If you've made a reservation for 18:30, someone else may have a reservation for your table for 21:00. You have $2\frac{1}{2}$ hours to finish your meal.

The reservation system should also take opening hours into account. If the restaurant opens at 18:00, a reservation for 17:30 should be rejected. Likewise, the system should reject reservations in the past.

All of that (table configurations, second seatings, and opening hours) should be configurable. These requirements clearly are complex enough that you'll have to factor the code to stay within the constraints suggested in this book. The cyclomatic complexity should be seven or less, the methods shouldn't be too big, or involve too many variables.

You'll need to delegate that business decision to a separate object.

8.2.1 MAÎTRE D'

Only two lines of code in listing 7.6 handle the business logic. These two lines of code are repeated in listing 8.5 for clarity.

Listing 8.5 The only two lines of code from listing 7.6 that actually make a business decision. *(Restaurant/a0c39e2/Restaurant.RestApi/ReservationsController.cs)*

```
int reservedSeats = reservations.Sum(r => r.Quantity);
if (10 < reservedSeats + r.Quantity)
```

With the new requirements, the decision is going to be significantly more complex. It makes sense to define a Domain Model [33]. What should you call the class? If you want to adopt a ubiquitous language [26] that the domain experts already speak, you could call it *maître d'*. In formal restaurants, the *maître d'hôtel* is the head waiter who oversees the guest area of a restaurant (as opposed to the *chef de cuisine*, who manages the kitchen).

Taking reservations and assigning tables is among a maître d's responsibilities. Adding a `MaitreD` class sounds like proper domain-driven design [26].

Contrary to previous chapters, I'll skip the iterative development to instead show you the results. If you're interested in the unit tests I wrote, and the small steps I took, they're all visible as commits in the Git repository that accompanies the book. You can see the `MaitreD` API I arrived at in listings 8.6 and 8.7. Take a moment to consider them. Which conclusions do you arrive at?

Listings 8.6 and 8.7 only show the publicly visible API. I've hidden the implementation code from you. This is the point of encapsulation. You should

Listing 8.6 The `MaitreD` constructor. Another overload that takes a `params` array also exists. *(Restaurant/62f3a56/Restaurant.RestApi/MaitreD.cs)*

```
public MaitreD(
    TimeOfDay opensAt,
    TimeOfDay lastSeating,
    TimeSpan seatingDuration,
    IEnumerable<Table> tables)
```

Listing 8.7 Signature of the `WillAccept` instance method on `MaitreD`. *(Restaurant/62f3a56/Restaurant.RestApi/MaitreD.cs)*

```
public bool WillAccept(
    DateTime now,
    IEnumerable<Reservation> existingReservations,
    Reservation candidate)
```

be able to interact with `MaitreD` objects without knowing implementation details. Can you?

How does one create a new `MaitreD` object? If you start typing `new MaitreD(`, as soon as you type the left bracket, your IDE will display what is needed in order to continue, as shown in figure 8.5. You'll need to supply `opensAt`, `lastSeating`, `seatingDuration`, and `tables` arguments. All are required. None can be null.

Figure 8.5 IDE displaying the requirements of a constructor, based on static type information.

Can you figure out what to do here? What should you put in place of `opensAt`? A `TimeOfDay` value is required. This is a custom type created for the purpose, but I hope that I made a good job naming it. If you wonder how to create instances of `TimeOfDay`, you can look at its public API. The `lastSeating` parameter works the same way.

Can you figure out what `seatingDuration` is for? I hope that this, too, is sufficiently self-explanatory.

What do you think the `tables` parameter is for? You've never seen the `Table` class before, so you'll have to learn the public API of that class as well. I'm going to skip further exegesis. The point isn't that *I* should talk you through the API. The point is to give you a sense for how to reason about an API.

You can put the `WillAccept` method in listing 8.7 through the same kind of analysis. If I've done my job well, it should be clear how to interact with it. If you give it the arguments it requires, it'll tell you whether it will accept the `candidate` reservation.

Does the method perform any side effects? It returns a value, so it looks like a Query. According to Command Query Separation, then, it must have no side effects. This is indeed the case. This means that you can call the method without worrying about what's going to happen. The only thing that's going to happen is that it'll use some CPU cycles and return a Boolean value.

8.2.2 INTERACTING WITH AN ENCAPSULATED OBJECT

You should be able to interact with a well-designed API without knowing the implementation details. Can you do that with a `MaitreD` object?

The `WillAccept` method requires three arguments. Refer to the method signature in listing 8.7. You'll need a valid instance of the `MaitreD` class, as well as a `DateTime` representing `now`, a collection of `existingReservations`, and the `candidate` reservation.

Assuming that the `ReservationsController` already has a valid `MaitreD` object, you can replace the two lines of code in listing 8.5 with a single call to `WillAccept`, as shown in listing 8.8. Despite the increased complexity of the total system, the size and complexity of the `Post` method remains low. All the new behaviour is in the `MaitreD` class.

Listing 8.8 You can replace the two lines of business logic shown in listing 8.5 with a single call to `WillAccept`. *(Restaurant/62f3a56/Restaurant.RestApi/ReservationsController.cs)*

```
if (!MaitreD.WillAccept(DateTime.Now, reservations, r))
```

The Post method of ReservationsController uses DateTime.Now to supply the now argument. It already has a collection of existing reservations from its injected Repository as well as the validated candidate reservation r (see listing 7.6). The conditional expression uses a Boolean negation (!) so that the Post method rejects the reservation when WillAccept returns false.

How is the MaitreD object in listing 8.8 defined? It's a read-only property initialised via the ReservationsController constructor, shown in listing 8.9.

Listing 8.9 ReservationsController **constructor.**
(Restaurant/62f3a56/Restaurant.RestApi/ReservationsController.cs)

```
public ReservationsController(
    IReservationsRepository repository,
    MaitreD maitreD)
{
    Repository = repository;
    MaitreD = maitreD;
}

public IReservationsRepository Repository { get; }
public MaitreD MaitreD { get; }
```

This looks like Constructor Injection [25], apart from the fact that MaitreD isn't a polymorphic dependency. Why did I decide to do it that way? Is it a good idea to take a formal dependency on MaitreD? Isn't it just an implementation detail?

Consider the alternative: pass all configuration values one-by-one via ReservationsController's constructor, as you can see in listing 8.10.

This seems like an odd design. Granted, ReservationsController no longer has an publicly visible dependency on MaitreD, but it's still there. If you change the constructor of MaitreD, you'll also have to change the constructor of ReservationsController. The design choice shown in listing 8.9 causes less maintenance overhead, because if you change the MaitreD constructor, you only have to edit the places where the injected MaitreD object is created.

Listing 8.10 ReservationsController constructor with exploded configuration values for MaitreD. **Compared to listing 8.9 this doesn't seem like a better alternative.** *(Restaurant/0bb8068/Restaurant.RestApi/ReservationsController.cs)*

```
public ReservationsController(
    IReservationsRepository repository,
    TimeOfDay opensAt,
    TimeOfDay lastSeating,
    TimeSpan seatingDuration,
    IEnumerable<Table> tables)
{
    Repository = repository;
    MaitreD =
        new MaitreD(opensAt, lastSeating, seatingDuration, tables);
}
```

This happens in the `Startup` class' `ConfigureServices` method, as shown in listing 8.11. `MaitreD` is an immutable class; once created, it can't change. This is by design. One of the many benefits of such a stateless service is that it's thread-safe, so that you can register it with Singleton lifetime [25].

Listing 8.11 Load restaurant settings from the application configuration and register a MaitreD object containing those values. The ToMaitreD method is shown in listing 8.12. *(Restaurant/62f3a56/Restaurant.RestApi/Startup.cs)*

```
var settings = new Settings.RestaurantSettings();
Configuration.Bind("Restaurant", settings);
services.AddSingleton(settings.ToMaitreD());
```

You can see the `ToMaitreD` method in listing 8.12. The `OpensAt`, `LastSeating`, `SeatingDuration`, and `Tables` properties belong to a `RestaurantSettings` object with poor encapsulation. Due to the way ASP.NET's configuration system works, you're expected to define configuration objects in such a way that they can be populated with values read from a file. In a sense, such objects are like Data Transfer Objects [33] (DTOs).

Contrary to DTOs that arrive as JSON documents while the service is running, there's little you can do if parsing of configuration values fails. In that case, the application can't start. For that reason, the `ToMaitreD` method doesn't check the values it passes to the `MaitreD` constructor. If the values are

Listing 8.12 The `ToMaitreD` method converts values read from the application configuration to a `MaitreD` object. *(Restaurant/62f3a56/Restaurant.RestApi/Settings/RestaurantSettings.cs)*

```
internal MaitreD ToMaitreD()
{
    return new MaitreD(
        OpensAt,
        LastSeating,
        SeatingDuration,
        Tables.Select(ts => ts.ToTable()));
}
```

invalid, the constructor will throw an exception and the application will crash, leaving a log entry on the server.

8.2.3 IMPLEMENTATION DETAILS

It's good to know that you can *use* a class like `MaitreD` without knowing all of the implementation details. Sometimes, however, your task involves changing the behaviour of an object. When that's your task, you'll need to go a level deeper in the fractal architecture. You'll have to read the code.

Listing 8.13 shows the `WillAccept` implementation. It stays within the bounds of humane code. Its cyclomatic complexity is 5, it has 20 lines of code, stays within 80 characters in width, and activates 7 objects.

It's not the whole implementation. The way to stay within the bounds of code that fits in your brain is to aggressively delegate pieces of the implementation to other parts. Take a moment to look at the code and see if you get the gist of it.

You've never seen the `Seating` class before. You don't know what the `Fits` method does. Still, hopefully you can get a sense of where to look next, depending on your motivation for looking at the code. If you need to change the way the method allocates tables, where would you look? If there's a bug in the seating overlap detection, where do you go next?

You could decide to look at the `Allocate` method. You've already seen it. It's in listing 8.4. When you look at that code, you can forget about the

Listing 8.13 The `WillAccept` method. *(Restaurant/62f3a56/Restaurant.RestApi/MaitreD.cs)*

```
public bool WillAccept(
    DateTime now,
    IEnumerable<Reservation> existingReservations,
    Reservation candidate)
{
    if (existingReservations is null)
        throw new ArgumentNullException(nameof(existingReservations));
    if (candidate is null)
        throw new ArgumentNullException(nameof(candidate));
    if (candidate.At < now)
        return false;
    if (IsOutsideOfOpeningHours(candidate))
        return false;

    var seating = new Seating(SeatingDuration, candidate);
    var relevantReservations =
        existingReservations.Where(seating.Overlaps);
    var availableTables = Allocate(relevantReservations);
    return availableTables.Any(t => t.Fits(candidate.Quantity));
}
```

`WillAccept` method. Looking at `Allocate` is another zoom-in operation in the fractal architecture. Remember that *what you see is all there is* [51]. What you need to know should be right there in the code.

The `Allocate` method does a good job of that. It activates six objects. Apart from the object property `Tables`, all are declared and used inside the method. This means that you don't need to keep in your head any other context that impacts how the method works. It fits in your brain.

It still delegates some of its implementation to other objects. It calls `Reserve` on `table`, and the `Fits` method makes another appearance. If you're curious about the `Fits` method, you could go and look at that as well. You can see it in listing 8.14.

It's not even close to the limits of our brains' capacity, but it still abstracts two chunks (`Seats` and `quantity`) into one. It represents yet another zoom-in operation in the fractal architecture. When you read the source code of `Fits`, you only need to keep track of `Seats` and `quantity`. You don't have to care

Listing 8.14 The `Fits` method. `Seats` is a read-only `int` property. (*Restaurant/62f3a56/Restaurant.RestApi/Table.cs*)

```
internal bool Fits(int quantity)
{
    return quantity <= Seats;
}
```

about the code that *calls* the `Fits` method in order to understand how it works. It fits in your brain.

I haven't shown you the `Reserve` method, or the `Seating` class, but they follow the same design principles. All implementations respect our cognitive constraints. All are Queries. If you're interested in these implementation details, you can consult the Git repository that accompanies the book.

8.3 CONCLUSION

Write code for readers. As Martin Fowler put it:

> *"Any fool can write code that a computer can understand. Good programmers write code that humans can understand."* [34]

Obviously, the code must result in working software, but that's the low bar. That's what Fowler means by 'code that a computer can understand.' It's not a sufficiently high bar. For code to be sustainable, you must write it so that humans understand it.

Encapsulation is an important part of this endeavour. It involves designing APIs so that the implementation details are irrelevant. Recall Robert C. Martin's definition of *abstraction*:

> *"Abstraction is the elimination of the irrelevant and the amplification of the essential"* [60]

The implementation details should stay irrelevant until you actually need to change them. Thus, design APIs so that they afford reasoning about them from the outside. This chapter covered some fundamental design principles that help push API design in that direction.

TEAMWORK

When I was young, I loathed teamwork. I could usually complete school assignments faster by working by myself than in a group. I felt that other group members stole my thunder, and I resented having to argue for my way of doing things when I 'knew' I was right.

I don't think that I would have much liked my younger self.

Thinking back on it, I may have self-selected into a vocation that looked promising to a person with limited interest in social interaction. I think I have that in common with quite a few other programmers.

The bad news is that as a software developer, you rarely work alone.

You work in a software development team with other programmers, product owners, managers, operations specialists, designers, etc. This is no different from the 'real' engineers discussed in subsection 1.3.4. They also work in teams.

A major part of being an engineer is to follow various processes. In this chapter, you'll learn about some beneficial processes for software engineering. Use these processes to help yourself and your team mates more readily understand the code.

A word of warning: Don't confuse process with outcome. Like checklists, following a processes improves the chance of success. The most important part of any process, however, is to understand the underlying motivation for it. When you understand why a particular process is beneficial, you know when to follow it, and when to deviate from it. In the end, it's the outcome that matters.

Keep in mind, though, that outcomes can be positive or negative. As discussed in subsection 3.1.2, it's impractical to measure the direct outcomes of your actions. They could have immediate positive effects now, but net negative impact over six months. For example, technical debt accrues over time.

A process works as a proxy for the actual effect you're aiming for. It's not a guarantee that all will go well, but it helps.

9.1 Git

Most software development organisations now use Git instead of other version control systems such as CVS or Subversion. Despite its distributed nature, you typically use it with a centralised service such as GitHub, Azure DevOps Services, Stash, GitLab, etc.

Such services come with additional capabilities like work item management, statistics, or automatic backups. Managers often consider these services essential, but don't give the actual source control features much thought.

Likewise, most software developers I've met think of Git as a way to integrate their code with the rest of their team's code base. They give little thought to how they interact with it.

Used in this way, Git is almost an afterthought. That's a wasted opportunity. Use Git tactically.

9.1.1 Commit Messages

When you make a commit, you should write a commit message. For most programmers, this is an obstacle to be cleared as easily as possible. You have to write *something*, but while Git rejects empty commit messages, it'll accept anything else.

People typically write *what's* in the commit, and then nothing more. Examples include *"FirstName Added"*, *"No empty saga"*, or *"Handle CustomerUpdated Added"*[1]. That's not as helpful as it could be.

Consider the hierarchy of communication described in subsection 8.1.7. Anything you write and persist is a message to the future, for you and your team members. On the other hand, focus on *communication* over writing. You don't have to spend much time explaining what changed in a commit. The commit diff already contains that information.

> Focus on *communication* over writing.

Believe it or not, a standard for Git commit messages exists. It's known as the *50/72 rule*, and it's not an official standard, but rather a de-facto standard based on experience with the tool [81].

- Write a summary in the imperative, no wider than 50 characters.
- If you add more text, leave the second line blank.
- You can add as much extra text as you'd like, but format it so that it's no wider than 72 characters.

These rules are based on how various Git features work. For example, if you want to see a list of commits, you can use `git log --oneline`:

```
$ git log --oneline
8fa3e47 (HEAD) Make /reservations URL segment lowercase
fbf74ae Return IDs from database in range query
033388a Return 404 Not Found for non-guid id
0f97b34 Return 404 Not Found for absent reservation
ee3c786 Read existing reservation
62f3a56 Introduce TimeOfDay struct
```

Such a list shows the summary line from each commit, but none of the rest of the commit message. Even if *you* don't use Git from the command line,

---

1. These are real, slightly anonymised examples.

someone else might. Additionally, some graphical user interfaces that make Git more friendly actually interoperate with the Git command-line API. There'll be less friction if you follow the 50/72 rule.

The summary serves as a headline or a chapter title. It enables you to navigate the history of the repository. Thus, it's an exception from the rule that you don't need to explain *what* changed in the commit.

Write the summary in the imperative mood. While there isn't a strong force behind this particular rule, it's a convention. For years, I wrote my commit messages in the past tense while following the formatting rules of the 50/72 rule, and that gave me no problems. I did it because I found it more natural to describe the work I'd just performed in the past tense, and no one had told me about the rule of using imperative mood. Once I learned about that rule, I reluctantly changed my ways, none the worse for wear.

Usually, the imperative form is shorter than the past-tense form. For example, 'return' is shorter than 'returned'. This, at least, gives you a slight advantage when you struggle to fit a summary into 50 characters.

You don't have to write more than the summary, and often, if the commit is small and self-explanatory, that's all I do.

Proper Prose

When you write emails, code comments, replies to bug reports, exception messages, or commit notes, you no longer have to play by the rules of a compiler or interpreter. I think that instead, you should play by the rules of grammar.

Too many programmers seem to believe that if it isn't code, it doesn't matter. When it comes to prose, anything goes. Here's a few examples:

- *"if we needed it back its on source control. but I doubt its comming back it is a legal issue."* Marvel at the disregard for basic punctuation.

- *"Thanks Paulo for your incite!"* What sort of unlawful behaviour did Paulo *insight?*
- *"To menus open at the same time"* What happens if *tree* or *for* menus are open at the same time?

Some people are dyslexic or don't have English as their first language; they are excused. But if you *can*, please write proper prose.

Have you ever tried to do a text-based search for an email, in an issue-tracking system, or even in commit messages, only to be unable to find something you just *know* ought to be there? After much wasted time, you discover that the reason you couldn't find the thing was because the word you were searching for was misspelled.

Apart from such waste of time, slipshod prose also looks unprofessional and slows down the reader. It also gives the reader an impression that you're less intelligent and capable than you are. Don't cause that friction. write good

When is a commit self-explanatory? As often as code is. That is, less frequently than you think. If in doubt, add more context.

The commit diff already contains information about *what changed*, and the code itself is the artefact that controls how the software behaves. There's no reason to repeat that information in the commit message.

While you can find answers to questions about *what* and *how* elsewhere, a commit message is often the best place to explain *why* a change was made, or why it took that form. Here's a short example:

```
Introduce TimeOfDay struct

This makes the roles of the constructor parameters to MaitreD clearer.
A large part of the TimeOfDay type was autogenerated by Visual Studio.
```

The message answers two questions:

- Why was the `TimeOfDay` type introduced?
- Why does it look like most of the code wasn't driven by tests?

You can find many other examples of commit messages that answer *why* questions in the code repository that accompanies the book.

Struggling to understand the rationale behind code may be the highest-ranked problem in software development [24], so it's important to make it clear.

9.1.2 CONTINUOUS INTEGRATION

Continuous Integration is already established in most software development organisations. Except that it isn't.

While everyone seems to 'know' that Continuous Integration is a proper software engineering practice, most confuse it with having a Continuous Integration server. Such a server is a fine thing to have, but doesn't guarantee that you do Continuous Integration.

Continuous Integration is a *practice*. It's a way to work. You do what it says on the tin: you *continually integrate* your code with the code that your colleagues are working on.

Integration means *merging*, and you shouldn't take the word *continuous* too literally. The point, though, is to frequently share your code with everyone else. How frequently? As a rule of thumb, at least every four hours[2].

I've met quite a few developers who'd tell me that the reason that Git is so great is that it solves the problem of 'merge hell'. Ironically, it doesn't. It does, however, foster a workflow different from centralised source control system workflows.

---

2. More frequent integration would be even better. At the limit, you could integrate every time you've made a change and all tests pass.

The underlying problem with merge hell is the same as any other kind of concurrent work on a shared resource. It's the same problem as with database transactions. You have more than one client that wishes to modify a shared resource. With source control, the resource is code rather than database rows, but the problem is the same.

You can solve this problem in a few ways. Databases have historically offered transactions as a solution. This involves taking locks on resources. Visual SourceSafe also worked that way. As soon as you changed a bit in a file, SourceSafe would mark that file as checked out, and no one else could edit it until it got checked in again.

Sometimes, people would go home for the day, leaving files checked out. This effectively prevented other people working at other schedules from doing anything with that file. Pessimistic locking doesn't scale well.

Optimistic locking tends to be a more scalable tactic, as long as contention is unlikely [55]. Before you start modifying a resource, you take a snapshot[3] of it. Then you edit it. When you want to save your changes, you compare the current state with the snapshot, as illustrated in figure 9.1. If you can tell that the resource didn't change since you began modifying it, you can safely save your changes.

Even if the resource was edited, you may be able to merge the two changes. If a database row was edited, but different columns were changed, you could still apply your changes. If you're editing a code file, merging is possible if your colleague changed a different part of the file than you did[4].

If, however, you're both editing the same line of code at the same time, you have a merge conflict. How do you avoid that? In the same way that you do with optimistic locking. You can't *guarantee* that it'll never happen, but you can make it unlikely. The shorter the time you spend editing the code, the less likely it is that someone else made a change to the same part at the same time.

---

3. You can also use a hash or a database-generated row version.
4. There's no guarantee that the merged result makes sense, though.

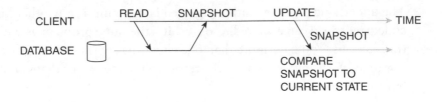

Figure 9.1 Optimistic locking. A client first reads the current version of a resource from the database. While it edits the resource, it also retains a copy of the snapshot. When it wishes to update the resource, it also sends the snapshot copy along for the ride. The database compares the snapshot with the current state of the resource. Only if the snapshot matches the current state does the update complete.

You may have heard that Continuous Integration means 'running on trunk'. Some people seem to take that so literally that they don't create branches in Git. Instead, they write everything on *master*.

The only thing you accomplish by doing that is to demonstrate that you haven't understood what the problem is. The problem is *concurrency*—not the name of the Git branch on which you're working. Unless you're doing mob programming[5] with all your colleagues, there's always a risk that one of your coworkers is editing the same line of code that you are.

Decrease that risk. Make small changes, and merge as often as you can. I recommend that you integrate *at least* every four hours. It's a somewhat arbitrary period; I picked it because it represents approximately half a day's work. You shouldn't sit on something for more than half a day before you share it with the rest of your team. Otherwise, your local Git repositories are going to diverge, and the result with be merge hell.

If you can't complete a feature in four hours, then hide it behind a feature flag[6] and integrate the code anyway [49].

9.1.3 SMALL COMMITS

There's much variance in programming. Sometimes, you can produce a lot of code in four hours. At other times, half a day goes by without a single line of working code. Trying to replicate or understand a bug can take hours.

---

5. For details about mob programming, see subsection 9.2.2.
6. See section 10.1 for more details.

Learning how to use an unfamiliar API may require days of research. Sometimes, it turns out that you'll have to scrap the code you spent a couple of hours writing. All of that is normal.

A major benefit of Git is the *manoeuvrability* that it provides; that it enables you to experiment, as illustrated by figure 9.2. Try out some code. If it works, commit it. If not, reset. This works best if you make many small commits. If the last commit you made was a small one, it means that throwing it away only discards the code that you actually want to get rid of.

Figure 9.2 When you make many small commits, mistakes are cheap. You can even commit the mistakes and abandon them on side branches, if it should turn out that you need them later. The yeah branch looks promising. Once you've reached a good checkpoint on that branch, integrate it with master.

Manoeuvrability

The more volatile your environment, the more precious the ability to react to unforeseen events. Git gives you tactical manoeuvrability.

Manoeuvrability is a military concept from combat aviation that captures how quickly you can exchange kinetic and potential energy; how fast you can gain and shed momentum [74]. How good you are at turning on a dime.

It's not only about being fast. It's about being able to change direction and accelerate. This is also useful in software development.

At the tactical level, Git gives you excellent manoeuvrability. You can be in the middle of something, but if you realise that you actually need to be

(continues)

doing something else, you can easily stash your changes and begin anew. If you're in doubt about whether a particular refactoring will improve the code, then try it out. If you think the change improves things, commit it; if not, reset[a].

It's not just a version control system; it's a tactical advantage.

---

[a]Or, even better, commit it to a new branch. You don't have to share that branch with anyone; it'll just stay on your hard drive. Who knows, what looked useless today could be useful in the future. If nothing else, if someone in the future suggests the same refactoring that you just tried, you can always show them: *"I already tried that; here's the result."*

Git is a distributed version control system. Until you share your changes with other people or systems, the commits are only on your local hard drive. This means that you can edit your commit history before you push it.

I relish the ability to edit local Git branches before I push them. Not that I find it necessary to hide my mistakes or appear supernaturally prescient, but because it liberates me to experiment and still enables me to leave behind a coherent commit trail.

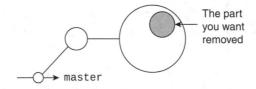

Figure 9.3 When you make coarse-grained commits, it can be hard to later undo only parts of them. Here, a commit contains some code that you'd like to undo, but it's an integral part of that Death Star commit, which also contains code that you'd like to keep.

If you make coarse-grained commits, you can't easily manipulate your code's history. You may regret some changes you made, but when they're bundled with unrelated edits in a single big commit, as in figure 9.3, you can't easily undo only the changes you wish to get rid of.

Your commit history should be a series of snapshots of working software. Don't commit code that doesn't work. On the other hand, every time your code successfully builds, then commit it. Make micro-commits [78].

- Rename a symbol; commit
- Extract a method; commit
- Inline a method; commit
- Add a test and make it pass; commit
- Add a Guard Clause; commit
- Fix the way code is formatted; commit
- Add a comment; commit
- Delete redundant code; commit
- Fix a typo; commit

In practice, you can't make all commits small. The example Git repository that accompanies this book has lots of micro-commit examples, but you'll also be able to find the occasional larger commit.

The more small commits you have, the easier you can change your mind.

After a couple of hours, you may have tried lots of things that you then abandoned. The result may be only a handful of small, good commits. Clean up your local branch and integrate it with *master*.

9.2 COLLECTIVE CODE OWNERSHIP

Is there a part of your code base that only Irina works on? What happens when she goes on vacation? What happens when she's sick? What happens if she quits?

You can organise code ownership in multiple ways, but if a single person 'owns' a part of the code base, you're vulnerable to team changes. Every owner becomes a critical resource – a single point of failure. It also makes refactoring harder. You can't easily rename a method if one developer owns the method and another programmer owns the code that calls the method [30].

By sharing the code, you increase the bus factor. Ideally, there should be no part of the code base where only one person dares to go.

> ## Bus Factor
>
> How many team members can be hit by a bus before development halts?
>
> You want that number to be as high as possible. If it's *1*, it means that if only *one* team member is out of commission, development flounders.
>
> Some people dislike the morbid connotation of the term, and instead prefer to ask: Can the team survive if Vera wins the lottery and quits? The notion is then named the *lottery factor*, but the idea is the same.
>
> Regardless of what you call it, the point is to raise awareness that circumstances change. Team members come and go. In addition to winning the lottery, or getting hit by a bus, people get reassigned, or they simply quit their job for a myriad of reasons.
>
> The point isn't to actually *measure* any factor, but to organise work so that no single person is indispensable.

When you have more than one programmer on a team, people tend to specialise. Some developers prefer user-interface programming, while others thrive with back-end development. Collective code ownership doesn't prohibit specialisation, but as figure 9.4 illustrates, it favours overlap of responsibilities.

I avoid user-interface development if I can, but if there's only one other user-interface programmer on my team, I ought to take responsibility for that part of the code base as well. As soon as there's more than one team member who handles the user interface, I may decide that it's in good hands. This enables me to focus on parts closer to my heart.

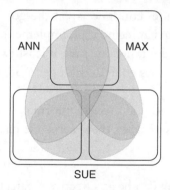

Figure 9.4 Three developers (Ann, Max, and Sue) work on a code base. Ann prefers working on the left and top module (e.g. HTTP API and Domain Model). Max favours the top and right module, while Sue likes the two bottom modules best. All share a part of the code base with another team member.

As argued in chapter 3, the code is the only artefact that matters. Collective code ownership entails, then, that you must constantly answer the following question in the affirmative:

Does the team contain more than one person comfortable working with a particular part of the code?

In other words, at least two active maintainers of the code base should approve the changes.

You can do this in formal and informal ways, including pair programming and code reviews. The key is that any code change involves more than one person.

9.2.1 PAIR PROGRAMMING

Pair programming [5] involves two software developers collaborating in real time on the same problem. There are several styles of pair programming [12], but they all share the feature that collaboration happens in real time.

The process includes continuous, on-the-go code reviews [12]. Code produced by a pair represents agreement on implementation details. The resulting commits already contain code that at least two persons are comfortable with. As approval processes go, it doesn't get more informal than that.

I've seen teams who find this *too* informal. They add notes about co-authors in commit messages or when they merge the changes into master. This is entirely optional.

Pair programming can be an effective means to achieve collective code ownership.

> *"Consistent pairing makes sure that every line of code was touched or seen by at least 2 people. This increases the chances that anyone on the team feels comfortable changing the code almost anywhere. It also makes the codebase more consistent than it would be with single coders only.*
>
> *Pair programming alone does not guarantee you achieve collective code ownership. You need to make sure that you also rotate people through different pairs and areas of the code, to prevent knowledge silos."* [12]

It's almost as if pair programming comes with real-time code review and informal approval process as a side effect. It's a low-latency sort of review. Since you're already two team members working on the code, you don't have to wait for anyone else to later approve the changes.

Even so, not everyone likes pair programming. As a typical introvert [16], I personally find the activity exhausting. It also leaves little room for contemplation, and it requires synchronisation of schedules.

I don't insist that all teams pair-program, but it's hard to argue against the above benefits[7]. Regardless, it's hardly practical or desirable to do it all the time [12]. You can mix pair programming with other processes in this chapter to arrive at a mix that suits your particular organisation.

---

7. There's also some evidence that it's an efficient way to work [116].

9.2.2 MOB PROGRAMMING

If two programmers working together on a problem is good, then three developers working together must be even better. And what about four people? Five?

If you can hijack a conference room or another space where a group of people can write code in collaboration, you can engage in mob programming[8].

It's hard enough to convince management (or even your fellow developers) that pair programming is productive. The knee-jerk reaction is that two people working on the same problem must exhibit half the productivity of two people working concurrently on two separate problems. It's even harder to convince naysayers that three or more people working on the same problem doesn't represent a drop in productivity.

I hope that, since you've made it so far into the book, you're convinced that productivity is unrelated to how fast someone types on a keyboard.

There's likely a point of diminishing returns. Imagine trying to mob-program with 50 people. The majority would have little to contribute, or, alternatively, nothing would get done if you had to achieve group consensus.

It seems, though, that there's a sweet spot for small groups.

Mob programming isn't my default modus operandi, but I find it useful in certain circumstances.

I've used it with great success as a programming coach. In one engagement, I spent two to three days a week with a few other programmers, helping them apply test-driven development practices to their production code bases. After a few months of that, I went on vacation. Meanwhile those programmers kept going with test-driven development. Mob programming is great for knowledge transfer.

---

8. I dislike the term *mob programming*, since *a mob*, to me, is an unthinking horde. *Ensemble programming* [84] might be a better term.

Since it involves more than one person collaborating on a single set of code changes, you get all the review and approval benefits from mob programming that pair programming gives you.

Try it, if possible. Use it if you like it.

9.2.3   CODE REVIEW LATENCY

As Laurent Bossavit convincingly argues, most 'common knowledge' in software development is more myth than reality [13]. Only a few practices have documented effects. A code review is one such practice [20].

It's one of the most effective ways to find defects in code [65], yet most organisations don't use it. A prevalent reason is that people feel that it slows down development.

It's true that a code review can introduce latency into the development process. It is, however, a mistake to believe that development is more efficient if most bugs remain undetected until much later.

In most organisations I've helped, a piece of work (typically termed a *feature*) is handled by a single developer. When that programmer declares the work *done*, no further vetting takes place.

Various organisations have different definitions of *done*. Some operate with the catchphrase *done done* to imply that the work is only done when the feature is complete and available for use in the production system.

As you learned in subsection 3.1.2, a too myopic focus on delivering 'value' may overlook problems arising from pushing a rickety, erratic, spurious feature to production.

Figure 9.5 illustrates a situation where you declare a feature done. Later, a defect is found. At that time, you're working on something else. Fixing the bug isn't part of the plan. Your team may decide to remedy the situation, but since it's unplanned work, it strains your capacity. Either you work overtime, or you miss the deadline on other features.

Figure 9.5 Many organisations don't perform code reviews. When a developer declares a feature done, a long time may pass before a bug is discovered. This leads to unplanned work.

Missed deadlines encourage crunch mode: a combination of working long hours and weekends with constant firefighting. There's never time to do things 'right' because there's always a new unanticipated problem that you have to deal with. This is a vicious circle.

With code reviews you can effectively detect problems before you declare the work done. Preventing defects becomes part of the process instead of part of the problem.

The problem with typical approaches is illustrated by figure 9.6. A developer submits a piece of work for review. Then much time passes before the review takes place.

Figure 9.6 How not to do code reviews: let much time pass between completion of a feature and the review. (The smaller boxes to the right of the review indicate improvements based on the initial review, and a subsequent review of the improvements.)

Figure 9.7 illustrates an obvious solution to the problem. Reduce the wait time. Make code reviews part of the daily rhythm of the organisation.

Figure 9.7 Reduce the wait time between feature completion and code review. A review will typically spark some improvements, and a smaller review of those improvements. These activities are indicated by the smaller boxes to the right of the review.

Most people already have a routine that they follow. You should make code reviews part of that routine. You can do that on an individual level, or you can structure your team around a daily rhythm. Many teams already have a daily stand-up. Such a regularly occurring event creates an anchor around which the day revolves. Typically, lunchtime is another natural break in work.

Consider, for example, setting aside half an hour each morning, as well as half an hour after lunch[9], for reviews.

Keep in mind that you should make only small sets of changes. Sets that represent less than half a day's work. If you do that, and all team members review those small changes twice a day, the maximum wait time will be around four hours.

9.2.4   REJECTING A CHANGE SET

I once helped a development organisation transition from developers working in isolated silos with little cooperation to collective code ownership. One practice I wanted to teach them was taking small steps.

Soon, I received a pull request from a remote developer I hadn't heard from in a couple of weeks. It was massive. Thousands of lines to review, distributed over fifty files.

I didn't review it. I immediately rejected it on the grounds of being too big[10]. Then I worked with the entire team, showing them how to make small changes. I never again received a pull request of that size.

Every time you perform a code review, saying *no* should be a real option. A code review is worth nothing if it's only a rubber stamp.

---

9. You could also set aside half an hour *before* lunch, as well as before you go home for the day, but you'd be more likely to skip the activities because you'd be in the middle of doing something else.

10. I had the support of management to do this. Sometimes, consultants are permitted to do things regular employees aren't. Unfair, yes, but true.

I often see people submit a big change for review. A big change set represents days (or weeks) of work. Reviewing a big change set takes a long time [78]. Such a review can often drag on for days while the author tries to address your myriad concerns.

Either that, or you give up and accept the changes because you have other work to do.

Don't do that. Reject big change sets.

Reviewers are often reluctant to reject a change set that represents days of work. This is a common problem known as the *sunk cost fallacy* [51]. True, your colleague has already spent much time making the changes, but if you think that you'll have to waste more time maintaining a poor design, then the choice is clear. Cut your losses. The time your colleague wasted is already lost. Don't waste more time on badly organised code.

Rejecting days or weeks of work hurts. Rejecting a few hours of work is more palatable. That's one more reason to make small changes that represent half a day's work.

Besides, a code review that takes more than an hour isn't effective [20].

9.2.5 CODE REVIEWS

The most fundamental question that a code review should answer is this:

Will I be okay maintaining this?

That's really it[11]. You can assume, I think, that the author will be happy to maintain his or her own code. If you're also ready to maintain it, then you're two persons, and you're on the way to collective code ownership.

---

11. To be fair, you shouldn't forget an even more important and basic question: *Does the change address a valid concern?* Sometimes, you misunderstand your assignment. I've done that. We all do that. It's worth keeping that question in mind during a code review. It *can* be a cause to reject a change, but I don't consider it the prime focus of a *code* review.

What should you look for in a code review?

The most important criterion is whether the code is *readable*. Does it fit in your brain?

Keep in mind that documentation (if it even exists) is typically stale, comments can be misleading, and so on. Ultimately, the only artefact you can trust is the code. The day you have to maintain it, the author may no longer be around.

Some people conduct reviews by sitting together. The author guides the reviewer through the changes. This is undesirable:

- The reviewer is unable to judge whether the code is readable on its own merits.
- The author may be able to fast-talk the reviewer into overlooking problematic practices.

Code reviews should be conducted by the reviewer *reading* the code at his or her own pace. The author just wrote the code, so he or she isn't in a position to evaluate whether the code is readable. That's the reason he or she shouldn't be actively involved in the code reading.

While rejection should be a real option, your job as a reviewer isn't to hurt the author or to prove your own superiority. It's to reach an agreement on how to move forward.

Nitpicking typically isn't helpful, so don't worry too much about code formatting or variable names[12]. Consider whether the code fits in your brain. Are methods too long or too complex?

Cory House suggests things to look for [47]:

- Does the code work as intended?
- Is the intent clear?

---

12. You can always change the formatting later, or fix a typo in a variable name. As long as a fix doesn't constitute a breaking change, don't let it drag out the review. On the other hand, typos in public APIs *should* be addressed, because fixing them would constitute breaking changes.

- Is there needless duplication?
- Could existing code have solved this?
- Could this be simpler?
- Are the tests comprehensive and clear?

This isn't an exhaustive list, but it gives you an idea what to look for.

The outcome of a code review typically isn't a binary accept/reject decision. Instead, a review produces a list of suggestions that the author and the reviewer can use to engage in a dialogue. While the author should be absent from the actual code reading, friendly interpersonal interaction can help speed up the rest of the process.

You'll typically agree on some improvements. The author goes back to implement them, and submits the new changes for a repeat review, as illustrated in figure 9.7. This is an iterative process. Subsequent reviews tend to be quicker. Soon, you reach consensus and integrate the changes.

All team members should be authors, and all team members should review other team members' code. Being a reviewer is neither a privilege nor a burden reserved for the elect few.

Not only does that stimulate collective code ownership, but it also encourages everyone to conduct reviews in a civilised manner.

9.2.6 Pull Requests

Online Git services such as GitHub, Azure DevOps Services, etc. support *GitHub flow*[13], which is a lightweight team workflow where you create branches on your local machine, but use the centralised service to handle merges.

When you wish to merge a branch into `master`, you can issue a *pull request*. This represents an appeal for your changes to be integrated with the `master` branch.

---

13. Not to be confused with *Git flow*.

In many team settings, you typically have sufficient permissions to complete the merge yourself. Nevertheless, you should make it a team policy that someone else must review and sign off on the changes. This is just another way to perform a code review.

When you *create* a pull request, keep the rules for working with Git in mind. Specifically [91]:

- Make each pull request as small as possible. That's smaller than you think.
- Do only one thing in each pull request. If you want to do multiple things, put them in separate pull requests.
- Avoid reformatting, unless that's the only thing the pull request does.
- Make sure the code builds.
- Make sure all tests pass.
- Add tests of new behaviour.
- Write proper commit messages.

When you *review* a pull request, all the points about performing a code review apply. In addition, GitHub flow is an asynchronous workflow, so you'll typically be doing the review by writing. Keep in mind that tone and intent is easily lost in writing. You may mean no harm with a particular phrasing, but the recipient may read it in a way that hurts. Be extra polite and use emojis to indicate your friendly attitude.

As a reviewer, you should take the time it takes to do a proper review. Keep in mind that if the pull request is too big, it's better to decline it[14] than rubber-stamp approve it.

If you decide to take on the review, work *with* the author to make improvements. Don't just point out things you don't like; offer concrete alternatives. Remember to cheer when you see something you like. Pull down the code and run it on your own machine [113].

---

14. Beginners often submit oversized pull requests because they don't know how to split their work into smaller parts. That's what *code that fits in your brain* is all about, but it's not something that everyone knows how to do from day one. Help your colleagues with that.

9.3 CONCLUSION

Every team member has a few strong skills. It's only natural that you gravitate towards the part of the code base that best suits you. If everyone does that, it may engender a sense of ownership. That's fine as long as it remains *weak code ownership* [30]. This is when a piece of code has a 'natural' owner or main developer, but everyone is allowed to make changes to it.

You should promote collective code ownership by processes that call for more than a single person being responsible for every change to the code base. You can do this informally with pair or mob programming, or more formally with code reviews.

As subsection 1.3.4 discussed, 'real' engineers work in teams, and they sign off on each others' work [40]. Having more than one pair of eyes on everything that goes on is one of the most engineering-like practices you can adopt in software development.

SUSTAINABILITY II

Part I was about getting up to speed. The structure revolved around an example code base accelerating from zero (no code) to a deployed feature.

Once you have a deployed feature, you have a working system. One feature, however, is hardly enough. You'll have to add more. Along the way, you'll discover that, despite your best efforts, the software has bugs.

It's no fun accelerating from zero to great speed only to hit a wall. Once you've achieved velocity, you want to maintain it.

Part II focuses on keeping a good cruising speed. How do you add new features to an existing code base? How do you troubleshoot? What about cross-cutting concerns? What about performance?

Part II discusses such topics, with an emphasis on augmenting existing code. The examples come from the same code base as in part I, but are sampled from a wider range of commits.

If you want to follow along in the Git repository, I left that part of it more honest; that is, less polished. I haven't tried to hide my mistakes, so you'll see commits that undo the work of previous commits, etc.

I've written extensive commit messages whenever I felt that a commit contained something worth pointing out. If you will, the log is a little narrative by itself. It might be worthwhile to read as a kind of appendix.

10 AUGMENTING CODE

The reality of professional software development is that you mostly work with existing code. The previous chapters had much to say about beginning a new code base, and how to go from zero to a working system as efficiently as possible. Greenfield development comes with its own set of challenges, but they're different from the problems typically associated with making changes to an existing code base.

You'll mostly be editing production code. Even if you do test-driven development, you'll mostly be *adding* new tests, while you'll often have to *change* existing production code.

The process of changing the structure of existing code without changing its behaviour is called *refactoring*. Other resources [34][53][27] already cover that ground, so I don't intend to regurgitate that material here. Instead, I'll focus on how to add new behaviour to a code base.

Informally, I tend to think of addition of behaviour as roughly falling into three buckets:

- Completely new functionality
- Enhancements to existing behaviour
- Bug-fixing

You'll learn about bug-fixing in chapter 12, while this chapter covers the other two cases. Completely new behaviour is, in many ways, the easiest kind of change to make, so let's start there.

10.1 FEATURE FLAGS

When your task is to add a completely new feature, most of the code you'll be writing will be *new* code; code that you add to the code base, rather than changes made to the existing code base.

Perhaps there's existing code infrastructure that you can leverage, and perhaps you'll have to make modifications to it before you can add the new feature, but for the most part, adding a new feature is smooth sailing. The biggest challenge that you're likely to encounter[1] is sticking to the practice of Continuous Integration.

As you learned in subsection 9.1.2, as a rule of thumb, you should merge your code with the *master* branch *at least* twice a day. In other words, you can, at most, work on something for four hours before you ought to integrate it. What if you can't complete an entire feature in four hours?

Most people are uncomfortable with merging incomplete features into *master*, particularly if their team also practices Continuous Deployment. That would imply that incomplete features are deployed to the production system. Surely, that's undesirable.

The solution is to distinguish between the feature itself and the code that implements it. You *can* deploy 'incomplete code' to your production system, as long as the behaviour that it implements is unavailable. Hide the functionality behind a feature flag [49].

10.1.1 CALENDAR FLAG

Here's an example from the restaurant code base. Once I was done with the functionality to make a reservation, I wanted to add a *calendar* feature to the

---

1. Apart from, of course, that the feature itself may be difficult to implement.

system. This should enable a client to browse a month or a day to view how many remaining seats are available. This can be used by a user interface to display whether or not a date is even open for additional reservations, and so on.

Adding calendars is a complex undertaking. You need to enable navigation from month to month, calculate the maximum number of remaining seats for a given time slot, and so on. It's unlikely you can do all of that in four hours; I couldn't[2].

Before I started this work, the REST API's 'home' resource responded with the JSON representation shown in listing 10.1.

Listing 10.1 Sample HTTP interaction with the REST API's 'home' resource. When you GET the 'index' page /, you receive a JSON array of links. As you can tell from the localhost part of the URL, I took this example from running the system on my development machine. When requesting the resource from the deployed system, the URL identifies a proper host name.

```
GET / HTTP/1.1

HTTP/1.1 200 OK
Content-Type: application/json
{
  "links": [
    {
      "rel": "urn:reservations",
      "href": "http://localhost:53568/reservations"
    }
  ]
}
```

The system is a true RESTful API that uses hypermedia controls (i.e. *links*) [2] rather than OpenAPI (née Swagger) or the like. A client wishing to make a reservation requests the only documented URL of the API (the 'home'

---

2. If you examine the example code base, you can compare the commit that starts this work with the commit that ends it. Close to two months separate those two! Okay, so in between, I had a four-week summer vacation, did some other work for paying clients, et cetera. By a rough estimate, though, the entire work may still represent between one and two weeks of work. It definitely wasn't done in four hours!

resource) and looks for a link with the relationship type `"urn:reservations"`. The actual URL should be opaque to the client.

Before I started working on the calendar feature, the code that generated the response in listing 10.1 looked like listing 10.2.

Listing 10.2 The code responsible for generating the output shown in listing 10.1. `CreateReservationsLink` is a private helper method. *(Restaurant/b6fcfb5/Restaurant.RestApi/HomeController.cs)*

```
public IActionResult Get()
{
    return Ok(new HomeDto { Links = new[]
    {
        CreateReservationsLink()
    } });
}
```

When I started working on the calendar feature, I soon realised that it'd take me more than four hours, so I introduced a feature flag [49]. It enabled me to write the `Get` method as shown in listing 10.3.

Listing 10.3 Generation of calendar links hidden behind a feature flag. By default, the `enableCalendar` flag is false, which results in output identical to that shown in listing 10.1. Compared with the code in listing 10.2 the highlighted lines implement the new feature. *(Restaurant/cbfa7b8/Restaurant.RestApi/HomeController.cs)*

```
public IActionResult Get()
{
    var links = new List<LinkDto>();
    links.Add(CreateReservationsLink());
    if (enableCalendar)
    {
        links.Add(CreateYearLink());
        links.Add(CreateMonthLink());
        links.Add(CreateDayLink());
    }
    return Ok(new HomeDto { Links = links.ToArray() });
}
```

The `enableCalendar` variable is a Boolean value (a *flag*) that ultimately originates from a configuration file. In the context of listing 10.3, it's a class field supplied via the Controller's constructor, as shown in listing 10.4.

Listing 10.4 HomeController constructor receiving a feature flag.
(Restaurant/cbfa7b8/Restaurant.RestApi/HomeController.cs)

```
private readonly bool enableCalendar;

public HomeController(CalendarFlag calendarFlag)
{
    if (calendarFlag is null)
        throw new ArgumentNullException(nameof(calendarFlag));

    enableCalendar = calendarFlag.Enabled;
}
```

The CalendarFlag class is just a wrapper around a Boolean value. The wrapper is conceptually redundant, but is required because of a technical detail: The built-in ASP.NET Dependency Injection Container is responsible for composing classes with their dependencies, and it refuses to consider a value type[3] a dependency. As a workaround for this issue, I introduced the CalendarFlag wrapper[4].

When the system starts, it reads various values from its configuration system. It uses those values to configure the appropriate services. Listing 10.5 shows how it reads the EnableCalendar value and configures the CalendarFlag 'service'.

Listing 10.5 Configuring the feature flag based on its configuration value.
(Restaurant/cbfa7b8/Restaurant.RestApi/Startup.cs)

```
var calendarEnabled = new CalendarFlag(
    Configuration.GetValue<bool>("EnableCalendar"));
services.AddSingleton(calendarEnabled);
```

---

3. In C# known as a struct.

4. I could live with this workaround because I knew that it was only going to be temporary. Once the feature is fully implemented, you can delete its feature flag. An alternative to introducing wrapper classes for primitive dependencies is to dispense with the built-in Dependency Injection Container altogether. I'd be inclined to do this in a code base if I had to maintain it for years, but I acknowledge that this comes with its own set of advantages and disadvantages. I don't want to fight that battle here, but you can read how to do that in ASP.NET in Steven van Deursen's and my book *Dependency Injection Principles, Practices, and Patterns* [25].

If the "EnableCalendar" configuration value is missing, the GetValue method returns the default value, which for Boolean values in .NET is false. So I simply didn't configure the feature, which meant that I could keep merging and deploying to production without exposing that behaviour.

In the automated integration tests, however, I overrode the configuration to turn on the feature. Listing 10.6 shows how. This means that I could still use integration tests to drive the behaviour of the new feature.

Listing 10.6 Overriding the feature flag configuration for testing purposes. The highlighted lines are new compared to listing 4.22.
(Restaurant/cbfa7b8/Restaurant.RestApi.Tests/RestaurantApiFactory.cs)

```
protected override void ConfigureWebHost(IWebHostBuilder builder)
{
    if (builder is null)
        throw new ArgumentNullException(nameof(builder));

    builder.ConfigureServices(services =>
    {
        services.RemoveAll<IReservationsRepository>();
        services.AddSingleton<IReservationsRepository>(
            new FakeDatabase());

        services.RemoveAll<CalendarFlag>();
        services.AddSingleton(new CalendarFlag(true));
    });
}
```

Additionally, when I wanted to perform some exploratory testing by interacting with the new calendar feature in a more ad hoc fashion, I could set the "EnableCalendar" flag to true in my local configuration file, and the behaviour would also light up.

Once, after weeks of work, I was finally able to complete the feature and turn it on in production. I deleted the CalendarFlag class. That caused all the conditional code that relied on the flag to no longer compile. After that, it was basically a matter of *leaning on the compiler* [27] to simplify all the places where the flag was used. Deleting code is always so satisfying, because it means that there's less code to maintain.

The 'home' resource now responds with the output shown in listing 10.7.

Listing 10.7 Sample HTTP interaction with the REST API's 'home' resource, now with calendar links. Compare with listing 10.1.

```
GET / HTTP/1.1

HTTP/1.1 200 OK
Content-Type: application/json
{
  "links": [
    {
      "rel": "urn:reservations",
      "href": "http://localhost:53568/reservations"
    },
    {
      "rel": "urn:year",
      "href": "http://localhost:53568/calendar/2020"
    },
    {
      "rel": "urn:month",
      "href": "http://localhost:53568/calendar/2020/10"
    },
    {
      "rel": "urn:day",
      "href": "http://localhost:53568/calendar/2020/10/20"
    }
  ]
}
```

In this example, you've seen how to use a feature flag to hide a feature until it's fully implemented. This example is based on a REST API, where it's easy to hide incomplete behaviour: just don't surface the new capability as a link. In other types of applications, you could use the flag to hide the corresponding user interface elements, and so on.

10.2 THE STRANGLER PATTERN

When you add a new feature, you can often do that by appending new code to the existing code base. Enhancing existing features is something else.

I once led an effort to *refactor towards deeper insight* [26]. My colleague and I had identified that the key to implementing a new feature would require changing a fundamental class in our code base.

While such an insight rarely arrives at an opportune time, we wanted to make the change, and our manager allowed it.

A week later, our code still didn't compile.

I'd hoped that I could make the change to the class in question and then *lean on the compiler* [27] to identify the call sites that needed modification. The problem was that there was an abundance of compilation errors, and fixing them wasn't a simple question of search-and-replace.

My manager finally took me aside to let me know that he wasn't satisfied with the situation. I could only concur.

After a mild dressing down, he allowed me to continue the work, and a few more days of heroic[5] effort saw the work completed.

That's a failure I don't intend to repeat.

As Kent Beck puts it:

> *"for each desired change, make the change easy (warning: this may be hard), then make the easy change"* [6]

I *did* try to make the change easy, but failed to realise just how hard it would be. It doesn't have to be that hard, though. Follow a simple rule of thumb:

For any significant change, don't make it in-place; make it side-by-side.

This is also known as the Strangler pattern [35]. Despite its name, it has nothing to do with violence, but is named after the *strangler fig*, a vine that grows around a 'host' tree and over years may strangle it by stealing both light

---

5. To be clear, heroism isn't an engineering practice. It's too unpredictable, and also stimulates the development of sunk cost fallacies. Try to do without it.

and water. At that time, the vine has grown strong enough to support itself. Left is a new, hollow tree approximately the size and shape of the old, dead tree, as illustrated by figure 10.1.

Figure 10.1 Stages of strangler fig lifetime. To the left is a tree, in the middle the original tree has been girdled by the strangler fig, and to the right, only the strangler fig remains.

Martin Fowler originally described the pattern in the context of large-scale architecture, as a way to gradually replace a legacy system with a newer system. I've found it to be useful at almost any scale.

In object-oriented programming you can apply the pattern both at the method level and the class level. At the method level, you first add a new method, gradually move callers over, and finally delete the old method. At the class level, you first add a new class, gradually move callers over, and finally delete the old class.

You'll see examples of both, starting at the method level.

10.2.1 METHOD-LEVEL STRANGLER

When I was implementing the calendar feature discussed in section 10.1, I needed a way to read reservations for multiple dates. The current incarnation of the `IReservationsRepository` interface, however, looked as in listing 10.8. The `ReadReservations` method took a single `DateTime` as input, and returned all the reservations for that date.

Listing 10.8 The `IReservationsRepository` interface with a `ReadReservations` method focused on a single date. *(Restaurant/53c6417/Restaurant.RestApi/IReservationsRepository.cs)*

```
public interface IReservationsRepository
{
    Task Create(Reservation reservation);

    Task<IReadOnlyCollection<Reservation>> ReadReservations(
        DateTime dateTime);

    Task<Reservation?> ReadReservation(Guid id);

    Task Update(Reservation reservation);

    Task Delete(Guid id);
}
```

I needed a method that would return reservations for a range of dates. Your reaction to such a requirement might be to add a new method overload and leave it at that. Technically, that's possible, but think of the maintenance tax. When you add more code, you have more code to maintain. An extra method on an interface means that you'll have to maintain it on all implementers, too.

I'd rather prefer replacing the old `ReadReservations` method with a new method. This is possible, because reading reservations for a range of dates instead of a single date actually weakens the preconditions. You can view the current method as a special case, where the range is just a single date.

If much of your code already calls the current method, however, making the change in one fell swoop might be overreaching. Instead, add the new method first, gradually migrate call sites, and finally delete the old method. Listing 10.9 shows the `IReservationsRepository` interface with the new method added.

When you add a new method like that, the code fails to compile until you add it to all classes that implement the interface. The restaurant reservation code base only has two implementers: `SqlReservationsRepository` and `FakeDatabase`. I added the implementation to both classes in the same commit, but that's all I had to do. Even with the SQL implementation, that represents perhaps five to ten minutes of work.

Listing 10.9 The IReservationsRepository interface with an additional ReadReservations method focused on a range of dates. The highlighted lines are new compared to listing 10.8. *(Restaurant/fa29d2f/Restaurant.RestApi/IReservationsRepository.cs)*

```
public interface IReservationsRepository
{
    Task Create(Reservation reservation);

    Task<IReadOnlyCollection<Reservation>> ReadReservations(
        DateTime dateTime);

    Task<IReadOnlyCollection<Reservation>> ReadReservations(
        DateTime min, DateTime max);

    Task<Reservation?> ReadReservation(Guid id);

    Task Update(Reservation reservation);

    Task Delete(Guid id);
}
```

Alternatively, I could also have added the new ReadReservations overload to both SqlReservationsRepository and FakeDatabase, but left them throwing a NotImplementedException. Then, in following commits, I could have used test-driven development to flush out the desired behaviour. At every point during this process, I'd have a set of commits that I could merge with *master*.

Yet another option would be to first add methods with identical signatures to the concrete classes, and only after all those are in place, add the method to the interface.

In any case, you can *incrementally* develop the new method, because at this point, no code is using it.

When the new method is firmly in place, you can edit the call sites, *one at a time*. In this way, you can take as much time as you need. You can merge with *master* at any time during this process, even if that means deploying to production. Listing 10.10 shows a code fragment that now calls the new overload.

Listing 10.10 Code fragment calling the new ReadReservations overload. The two first highlighted lines are new, while the last highlighted line was edited to call the new method instead of the original ReadReservations method. *(Restaurant/0944d86/Restaurant.RestApi/ReservationsController.cs)*

```
var min = res.At.Date;
var max = min.AddDays(1).AddTicks(-1);
var reservations = await Repository
    .ReadReservations(min, max)
    .ConfigureAwait(false);
```

I changed the calling code one call site at a time, and committed to Git after each change. After a few commits, I was done; there were no more code calling the original ReadReservations method.

Finally, I could delete the original ReadReservations method, leaving the IReservationsRepository interface as shown in listing 10.11.

Listing 10.11 The IReservationsRepository interface once the Strangler process has completed. The original ReadReservations method is gone; only the new version remains. Compare with listings 10.8 and 10.9. *(Restaurant/bcffd6b/Restaurant.RestApi/IReservationsRepository.cs)*

```
public interface IReservationsRepository
{
    Task Create(Reservation reservation);

    Task<IReadOnlyCollection<Reservation>> ReadReservations(
        DateTime min, DateTime max);

    Task<Reservation?> ReadReservation(Guid id);

    Task Update(Reservation reservation);

    Task Delete(Guid id);
}
```

When you delete a method from an interface, remember to also remove it from all implementing classes. The compiler isn't going to complain if you let them stay, but that's a maintenance burden you don't need to take on.

10.2.2 CLASS-LEVEL STRANGLER

You can also apply the Strangler pattern on the class level. If you have a class that you'd like to refactor, but you're concerned that it'll take too long to change it in place, you can add a new class, move callers over one by one, and finally delete the old class.

You can find a few examples of that in the online restaurant reservation code base. In one case, I found that I'd over-engineered a feature[6]. I needed to model the allocation of reservations to tables at a given time, so I'd added a generic Occurrence<T> class that could associate *any* type of object with a time. Listing 10.12 shows its constructor and properties to give you a sense of it.

Listing 10.12 Constructor and properties of the Occurrence<T> class. This class associates any type of object with a time. It turned out, however, that this was over-engineered. (*Restaurant/4c9e781/Restaurant.RestApi/Occurrence.cs*)

```
public Occurrence(DateTime at, T value)
{
    At = at;
    Value = value;
}

public DateTime At { get; }
public T Value { get; }
```

After I'd implemented the features where I needed the Occurrence<T> class, I realised that I didn't really need it to be generic. All the code that used the object contained a collection of tables with associated reservations.

Generics do make code slightly more complex. While I find them useful in the right circumstance, they also make things more abstract. For example, I had a method with the signature shown in listing 10.13.

---

6. Yes, even when I try my best to follow all practices that I present in this book, I, too, err. Despite admonitions to do the simplest thing that could possibly work [22], I occasionally make things too complicated because 'I'm certainly going to need it later'. Hitting yourself over the head for your errors, however, isn't productive. When you realise your mistake, just acknowledge and correct it.

Listing 10.13 A method returning a triple-nested generic type. Too abstract? *(Restaurant/4c9e781/Restaurant.RestApi/MaitreD.cs)*

```
public IEnumerable<Occurrence<IEnumerable<Table>>> Schedule(
    IEnumerable<Reservation> reservations)
```

Consider the advice from subsection 8.1.5. By looking at the types, can you figure out what the `Schedule` method does? How do you think about a type like `IEnumerable<Occurrence<IEnumerable<Table>>>`?

Wouldn't the method be easier to understand if it had the signature shown in listing 10.14?

Listing 10.14 A method returning a collection of `TimeSlot` objects. It's the same method as shown in listing 10.13, but with a more concrete return type. *(Restaurant/7213b97/Restaurant.RestApi/MaitreD.cs)*

```
public IEnumerable<TimeSlot> Schedule(
    IEnumerable<Reservation> reservations)
```

`IEnumerable<TimeSlot>` seems like a more palatable return type, so I wanted to refactor from the `Occurrence<T>` class to such a `TimeSlot` class.

There was already enough code that used `Occurrence<T>` that I didn't feel comfortable that I could perform such a refactoring in a brief enough time span. Instead, I decided to use the Strangler pattern: first add the new `TimeSlot` class, then migrate callers one by one, and finally delete the `Occurrence<T>` class.

I first added the `TimeSlot` class to the code base. Listing 10.15 shows its constructor and properties so that you can get a sense of how it looks.

As soon as I'd added this class I could commit it to Git and merge it with the *master* branch. That didn't break any functionality.

I could then start to migrate code from using `Occurrence<T>` to use `TimeSlot`. I started with some helper methods, like the one shown in listing 10.16.

Listing 10.15 Constructor and properties of the `TimeSlot` class. *(Restaurant/4c9e781/Restaurant.RestApi/TimeSlot.cs)*

```
public TimeSlot(DateTime at, IReadOnlyCollection<Table> tables)
{
    At = at;
    Tables = tables;
}

public DateTime At { get; }
public IReadOnlyCollection<Table> Tables { get; }
```

Listing 10.16 Signature of a helper method that takes an `Occurrence` parameter. Compare with listing 10.17. *(Restaurant/4c9e781/Restaurant.RestApi/ScheduleController.cs)*

```
private TimeDto MakeEntry(Occurrence<IEnumerable<Table>> occurrence)
```

Instead of taking an `Occurrence<IEnumerable<Table>>` parameter I wanted to change it to take a `TimeSlot` parameter, as shown in listing 10.17.

Listing 10.17 Signature of a helper method that takes a `TimeSlot` parameter. Compare with listing 10.16. *(Restaurant/0030962/Restaurant.RestApi/ScheduleController.cs)*

```
private static TimeDto MakeEntry(TimeSlot timeSlot)
```

The code that *called* this `MakeEntry` helper method was itself a helper method that received an `IEnumerable<Occurrence<IEnumerable<Table>>>` argument, and I wanted to gradually migrate callers. I realised that I could do that if I added the temporary conversion method in listing 10.18. This method supports the conversion between the old class and the new class. Once I completed the Strangler migration I deleted it together with the class itself.

I also had to migrate the `Schedule` method in listing 10.13 to the version in listing 10.14. Since I had multiple callers, I wanted to migrate each caller separately, committing to Git between each change. This meant that I needed the two versions of `Schedule` to exist side by side for a limited time. That's not strictly possible because they differ only in their return type, and C# doesn't support return-type overloading.

Listing 10.18 Temporary conversion method from `Occurrence` to `TimeSlot`.
(Restaurant/0030962/Restaurant.RestApi/Occurrence.cs)

```
internal static TimeSlot ToTimeSlot(
    this Occurrence<IEnumerable<Table>> source)
{
    return new TimeSlot(source.At, source.Value.ToList());
}
```

To get around that issue, I first used the Rename Method [34] refactoring to rename the original `Schedule` method to `ScheduleOcc`[7]. I then copied and pasted it, changed its return type and changed the new method's name back to `Schedule`. I now had the original method called `ScheduleOcc` and the new method with a better return type, but no callers. Again, this is a point where you can commit your changes and merge with *master*.

With two methods, I could now migrate callers one at a time, checking my changes into Git for each method. Again, this is work that you can do gradually without getting in the way of other work that you or your team mates perform. Once all callers called the new `Schedule` method, I deleted the `ScheduleOcc` method.

The `Schedule` method wasn't the only method that returned data that used `Occurrence<T>`, but I could migrate the other methods to `TimeSlot` using the same technique.

When I finally had completed the migration, I deleted the `Occurrence<T>` class, including the conversion helper method in listing 10.18.

During this process, I was never more than five minutes from being able to do a commit, and all commits left the system in a consistent state that could be integrated and deployed.

10.3 VERSIONING

Do yourself a favour: Read the Semantic Versioning specification [83]. Yes, all of it. It takes less than fifteen minutes. In short, it uses a *major.minor.patch*

---

7. *Occ* for *Occurrence*.

scheme. You only increment the *major* version when you introduce breaking changes; incrementing the *minor* version indicates the introduction of a new feature, and a *patch* version incrementation indicates a bug fix.

Even if you don't decide to adopt Semantic Versioning, I believe that it'll help you think more clearly about breaking and nonbreaking changes.

If you're developing and maintaining a monolithic application with no API, breaking changes may not matter, but as soon as other code depends on your code, it does.

This is true regardless of where that depending code lives. Obviously, backwards compatibility is crucial if you have external, paying customers who depend on your API. But even if the system that depends on your code is 'just' another code base in your organisation, it still pays to think about compatibility.

Every time you break compatibility, you'll need to coordinate with your callers. Sometimes, this happens reactively, as in *"your latest change broke our code!"* It'd be better if you can give clients advance warning.

Things run smoother, though, if you can avoid breaking changes. In Semantic Versioning, this means staying on the same major version for a long time. This may take a little time getting used to.

I once maintained an open-source library that stayed on major version *3* for more than four years! The last version *3* release was *3.51.0*. Apparently, we added 51 new features during those four years, but since we didn't break compatibility, we didn't increment the major version.

10.3.1 ADVANCE WARNING

If you *must* break compatibility, be deliberate about it. If you can, warn users in advance. Consider the hierarchy of communication discussed in subsection 8.1.7 to figure out which communications channel will work best.

For example, some languages enable you to deprecate methods with an annotation. In .NET this is called [Obsolete], in Java @Deprecated. Listing 10.19 shows an example. This'll cause the C# compiler to emit a compiler warning for all code that calls that method.

Listing 10.19 Deprecated method. The [Obsolete] attribute marks the method as deprecated, as well as giving a hint about what to do instead. *(Restaurant/4c9e781/Restaurant.RestApi/CalendarController.cs)*

```
[Obsolete("Use Get method with restaurant ID.")]
[HttpGet("calendar/{year}/{month}")]
public Task<ActionResult> LegacyGet(int year, int month)
```

If you realise that you *must* break compatibility, consider if you can bundle more than one breaking change into a single release. This isn't always a good idea, but it sometimes can be. Every time you introduce a breaking change, you force client developers to deal with it. If you have multiple smaller breaking changes, it might make client developers' lives easier if you bundle them into a single release.

On the other hand, it's probably not a good idea to release multiple breaking changes if each of them forces client developers into massive rework. Exercise some judgment; this is, after all, the *art* of software engineering.

10.4 Conclusion

You work in existing code bases. As you add new features, or enhance the ones already there, or fix bugs, you make changes to existing code. Take care that you do so in small steps.

If you're working on a feature that takes a long time to implement, it might be tempting to develop it on a feature branch. Don't do that; it'll lead to merge hell. Instead, hide the feature behind a feature flag and integrate often [49].

When you want to make a sizeable refactoring, consider using the Strangler pattern. Instead of performing the edit in situ, change the code by letting the new and the old ways co-exist for a while. This enables you to gradually migrate callers a little at a time. You can even do this as a maintenance task that you interleave with other work. Only when the migration is complete do you delete the old method or class.

If the method or class is part of a published object-oriented API, deleting a method or class may constitute a breaking change. In such a case, you'll need to explicitly consider versioning. First deprecate the old API to warn users about the impending change, and only delete the deprecated API when releasing a new major version.

11 EDITING UNIT TESTS

Few code bases are bootstrapped with the practices covered in the first part of the book. They have long methods, high degrees of complexity, poor encapsulation, and little automated test coverage. We call such code bases *legacy code*. There's already a great book about *Working Effectively with Legacy Code* [27], so I don't intend to repeat its lessons here.

11.1 REFACTORING UNIT TESTS

If you have a trustworthy automated test suite, you can apply many of the lessons from *Refactoring* [34]. That book discusses how to change the structure of existing code without changing its behaviour. Many of the techniques described in it are built into modern IDEs, such as renaming, extracting helper methods, moving code around, and so on. I don't wish to spend too much time on that topic, either, because it, too, is covered in greater depth by other sources [34].

11.1.1   CHANGING THE SAFETY NET

While *Refactoring* [34] explains how to change the structure of production code, given the safety net of an automated test suite, *xUnit Test Patterns* [66] comes with the subtitle *Refactoring Test Code*[1].

Test code is code you write to gather confidence that your production code works. As I've argued in this book, it's easy to make mistakes when writing code. How do you know that your test code is mistake-free, then?

You don't, but some of the practices outlined earlier improves your chances. When you use tests as a driver for your production code, you're entering into a sort of double-entry bookkeeping [63] where the tests keep the production code in place, and the production code provides feedback about the tests.

Another mechanism that should instil trust is if you've been following the Red Green Refactor checklist. When you see a test fail, you know that it actually verifies something you want to verify. If you never edit the test, you can trust it to keep doing that.

What happens if you edit test code?

The more you edit test code, the less you can trust it. The backbone of refactoring, however, is a test suite:

> *"to refactor, the essential precondition is [...] solid tests"* [34]

Formally speaking, then, you can't refactor unit tests.

In practice, you're going to have to edit unit test code. You should realise, however, that contrary to production code, there's no safety net. Modify tests carefully; move deliberately.

---

1. Although, to be fair, it's more a book about design patterns than about refactoring.

11.1.2 ADDING NEW TEST CODE

In test code, the safest edits you can make is to append new code. Obviously, you can add entirely new tests; that doesn't diminish the trustworthiness of existing tests.

Clearly, adding an entirely new test class may be the most isolated edit you can make, but you can also append new test methods to an existing test class. Each test method is supposed to be independent of all other test methods, so adding a new method shouldn't affect existing tests.

You can also append test cases to a parametrised test. If, for example, you have the test cases shown in listing 11.1, you can add another line of code, as shown in listing 11.2. That's hardly dangerous.

Listing 11.1 A parametrised test method with three test cases. Listing 11.2 shows the updated code after I added a new test case. *(Restaurant/b789ef1/Restaurant.RestApi.Tests/ReservationsTests.cs)*

```
[Theory]
[InlineData(null, "j@example.net", "Jay Xerxes", 1)]
[InlineData("not a date", "w@example.edu", "Wk Hd", 8)]
[InlineData("2023-11-30 20:01", null, "Thora", 19)]
public async Task PostInvalidReservation(
```

Listing 11.2 A test method with a new test case appended, compared to listing 11.1. The line added is highlighted. *(Restaurant/745dbf5/Restaurant.RestApi.Tests/ReservationsTests.cs)*

```
[Theory]
[InlineData(null, "j@example.net", "Jay Xerxes", 1)]
[InlineData("not a date", "w@example.edu", "Wk Hd", 8)]
[InlineData("2023-11-30 20:01", null, "Thora", 19)]
[InlineData("2022-01-02 12:10", "3@example.org", "3 Beard", 0)]
public async Task PostInvalidReservation(
```

You can also add assertions to existing tests. Listing 11.3 shows a single assertion in a unit test, while listing 11.4 shows the same test after I added two more assertions.

Listing 11.3 A single assertion in a test method. Listing 11.4 shows the updated code after I added more assertions. *(Restaurant/36f8e0f/Restaurant.RestApi.Tests/ReservationsTests.cs)*

```
Assert.Equal(
    HttpStatusCode.InternalServerError,
    response.StatusCode);
```

Listing 11.4 Verification phase after I added two more assertions, compared to listing 11.3. The lines added are highlighted. *(Restaurant/0ab2792/Restaurant.RestApi.Tests/ReservationsTests.cs)*

```
Assert.Equal(
    HttpStatusCode.InternalServerError,
    response.StatusCode);
Assert.NotNull(response.Content);
var content = await response.Content.ReadAsStringAsync();
Assert.Contains(
    "tables",
    content,
    StringComparison.OrdinalIgnoreCase);
```

These two examples are taken from a test case that verifies what happens if you try to overbook the restaurant. In listing 11.3, the test only verifies that the HTTP response is `500 Internal Server Error`[2]. The two new assertions verify that the HTTP response includes a clue to what might be wrong, such as the message `No tables available`.

I often run into programmers who've learned that a test method may only contain a single assertion; that having multiple assertions is called Assertion Roulette. I find that too simplistic. You can view appending new assertions as a strengthening of postconditions. With the assertion in listing 11.3 any `500 Internal Server Error` response would pass the test. That would include a 'real' error, such as a missing connection string. This could lead to false negatives, since a general error could go unnoticed.

Adding more assertions strengthens the postconditions. Any old `500 Internal Server Error` will no longer do. The HTTP response must also come with content, and that content must, at least, contain the string `"tables"`.

---

2. Still a controversial design decision. See the footnote on page 116 for more details.

This strikes me as reminiscent of the Liskov Substitution Principle [60]. There are many ways to express it, but in one variation, we say that subtypes may weaken preconditions and strengthen postconditions, but not the other way around. You can think of of subtyping as an ordering, and you can think of time in the same way, as illustrated by figure 11.1. Just like a subtype depends on its supertype, a point in time 'depends' on previous points in time. Going forward in time, you're allowed to strengthen the postconditions of a system, just like a subtype is allowed to strengthen the postcondition of a supertype.

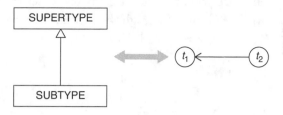

Figure 11.1 A type hierarchy forms a directed graph, as indicated by the arrow from *subtype* to *supertype*. Time, too, forms a directed graph, as indicated by the arrow from t_2 to t_1. Both present a way to order elements.

Think of it another way, adding new tests or assertions is fine; deleting tests or assertions would weaken the guarantees of the system. You probably don't want that; herein lie regression bugs and breaking changes.

11.1.3 SEPARATE REFACTORING OF TEST AND PRODUCTION CODE

Many code changes are 'safe' if you perform them correctly. Some of the refactorings described in *Refactoring* [34] are now included in modern IDEs. The most basic are various rename operations such as *Rename Variable* and *Rename Method*. Others include *Extract Method* or *Move Method*.

Such refactorings tend to be 'safe' in the sense that you can be confident that they aren't going to change the behaviour of the code. This also applies to test code. Use those refactorings with confidence in your production and test code alike.

Other changes are more risky[3]. When you perform such changes in your production code, a good test suite will alert you to any problems. If you make such changes in your test code, there's no safety net.

Or rather, that's not quite true ....

The test code and the production code are coupled to each other, as figure 11.2 illustrates. If you introduce a bug in the production code, *but didn't change the tests*, the tests may alert you to the problem. There's no guarantee that this will happen, since you may not have any test cases that will expose the defect you just introduced, but you might be lucky. Furthermore, if the bug is a regression, you ought to already have a test of that scenario in place.

Figure 11.2 Test code and production code are coupled.

Likewise, if you edit the test code *without changing the production code*, a mistake may manifest as a failing test. Again, there's no guarantee that this will happen. You could, for example, first use the *Extract Method* to turn a set of assertions into a helper method. This is in itself a 'safe' refactoring. Imagine, however, that you now go look for other occurrences of that set of assertions and replace them with a call to the new helper method. That isn't as safe, because you could make a mistake. Perhaps you replace a small *variation* of the assertion set with a call to the helper method. If that variation, however, implied a stronger set of postconditions, you've just inadvertently weakened the tests.

While such mistakes are difficult to guard against, other mistakes will be immediately apparent. If, instead of weakening postconditions, you accidentally strengthen them too much, tests may fail. You may then inspect the failing test cases and realise that you made a mistake.

---

3. *Add Parameter*, for example.

For this reason, *when* you need to refactor your test code, try to do it without touching the production code.

You can think of this rule as jumping from production code to test code and back to production code, as illustrated by figure 11.3.

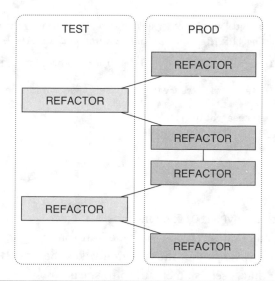

Figure 11.3 Refactor test code apart from production code. Commit each refactoring separately. It's safer to refactor production code, so you can refactor it more often than test code. Other, safer changes, such as renaming a method, may touch both test and production code; those kinds of changes are not shown in this figure.

As an example, I was working on the restaurant code base to add email capabilities. I'd already implemented the behaviour that when you make a reservation, the system should send you a confirmation email.

Interaction with the external world is best modelled as a polymorphic type, and I favour interfaces like the one shown in listing 11.5 over base classes.

To unit test that the system sends an email under the right circumstances, I added the Test Spy [66] shown in listing 11.6 to keep an eye on indirect output [66].

Listing 11.5 Initial iteration of the IPostOffice interface.
(Restaurant/b85ab3e/Restaurant.RestApi/IPostOffice.cs)

```
public interface IPostOffice
{
    Task EmailReservationCreated(Reservation reservation);
}
```

Listing 11.6 Initial version of SpyPostOffice, implementing the version of IPostOffice shown in listing 11.5. *(Restaurant/b85ab3e/Restaurant.RestApi.Tests/SpyPostOffice.cs)*

```
public class SpyPostOffice : Collection<Reservation>, IPostOffice
{
    public Task EmailReservationCreated(Reservation reservation)
    {
        Add(reservation);
        return Task.CompletedTask;
    }
}
```

Notice that SpyPostOffice inherits from a collection base class. This enables the implementation to Add the reservation to itself. A test can use this behaviour to verify that the system invokes the EmailReservationCreated method; that it sends an email, so to speak.

A test can create an instance of SpyPostOffice, pass it to constructors or methods that take an IPostOffice argument, exercise the System Under Test [66], and then inspect its state, as implied by listing 11.7.

Listing 11.7 Assert that the expected reservation is in the postOffice collection. The postOffice variable is a SpyPostOffice object. *(Restaurant/b85ab3e/Restaurant.RestApi.Tests/ReservationsTests.cs)*

```
Assert.Contains(expected, postOffice);
```

With that behaviour firmly in place, I started on a related feature. The system should also send an email when you delete a reservation. I added a new method to the IPostOffice interface, as shown in listing 11.8.

Listing 11.8 Second iteration of the `IPostOffice` interface. The highlighted line indicates the new method, compared to listing 11.5. *(Restaurant/1811c8e/Restaurant.RestApi/IPostOffice.cs)*

```
public interface IPostOffice
{
    Task EmailReservationCreated(Reservation reservation);

    Task EmailReservationDeleted(Reservation reservation);
}
```

Since I'd added a new method to the `IPostOffice` interface, I also had to implement that method in the `SpyPostOffice` class. Since both the `EmailReservationCreated` and `EmailReservationDeleted` methods take a `Reservation` argument, I could just `Add` the `reservation` to the Test Spy [66] itself.

But as I started writing a unit test for the new behaviour, I realised that while I could write an assertion like the one in listing 11.7, I could only verify that the Test Spy [66] contained the `expected` reservation. I couldn't verify how it got there; whether the spy added it via the `EmailReservationCreated` or the `EmailReservationDeleted` method.

I had to improve the 'sensitivity' of `SpyPostOffice` in order to be able to do that.

I'd already embarked on a set of changes that touched the production code. The `IPostOffice` interface is part of the production code, and there was also a production implementation of it (called `SmtpPostOffice`). I was in the process of making changes to the production code, and all of a sudden, I realised that I had to refactor the test code.

This is one of the many reasons that Git is such a game changer, even for individual development. It's an example of the *manoeuvrability* that it offers. I simply stashed[4] my changes and independently edited the `SpyPostOffice` class. You can see the result in listing 11.9.

---

4. `git stash` saves your dirty files in a 'hidden' commit and resets the repository to HEAD. Once you're done with whatever else you wanted to do, you can retrieve that commit with `git stash pop`.

Listing 11.9 Refactored `SpyPostOffice` (fragment). The `Observation` class is a nested class, which isn't shown. It just holds an `Event` and a `Reservation`. *(Restaurant/b587eef/Restaurant.RestApi.Tests/SpyPostOffice.cs)*

```
internal class SpyPostOffice :
    Collection<SpyPostOffice.Observation>, IPostOffice
{
    public Task EmailReservationCreated(Reservation reservation)
    {
        Add(new Observation(Event.Created, reservation));
        return Task.CompletedTask;
    }

    internal enum Event
    {
        Created = 0
    }
```

I introduced a nested `Observation` class to keep track of *both* the type of interaction and the reservation itself. I also changed the base class to a collection of observations.

This broke some of my tests, because an assertion like the one shown in listing 11.7 would look for a `Reservation` object in a collection of `Observation` objects. That didn't type-check, so I had to massage the test in place, too.

I managed to do that without touching the production code. When I was done, all tests still passed. That's no guarantee that I didn't make a mistake while refactoring, but at least it eliminates a category of errors[5].

Once I had refactored the test code, I popped the stashed changes and continued where I'd left off. Listing 11.10 shows the updated `SpyPostOffice`.

While these changes also involved editing the test code, they were safer because they were only additions. I didn't have to refactor existing test code.

---

5. That the changes to the tests inadvertently strengthened some preconditions.

Listing 11.10 Updated `SpyPostOffice`. It now implements the version of `IPostOffice` shown in listing 11.8. *(Restaurant/1811c8e/Restaurant.RestApi.Tests/SpyPostOffice.cs)*

```
internal class SpyPostOffice :
    Collection<SpyPostOffice.Observation>, IPostOffice
{
    public Task EmailReservationCreated(Reservation reservation)
    {
        Add(new Observation(Event.Created, reservation));
        return Task.CompletedTask;
    }

    public Task EmailReservationDeleted(Reservation reservation)
    {
        Add(new Observation(Event.Deleted, reservation));
        return Task.CompletedTask;
    }

    internal enum Event
    {
        Created = 0,
        Deleted = 1
    }
}
```

11.2 See Tests Fail

If you *must* edit both test and production code at the same time, consider verifying the tests by making them fail deliberately, if only temporarily.

It's surprisingly easy to write tautological assertions [105]. These are assertions that never fail, even if the production code is faulty.

Don't trust a test that you haven't seen fail. If you changed a test, you can temporarily change the System Under Test to make the test fail. Perhaps comment out some production code, or return a hard-coded value. Then run the test you edited and verify that with the temporary sabotage in place, the test fails.

Once more, Git offers manoeuvrability. If you have to change both tests and production code at the same time, you can stage your changes and only then sabotage the System Under Test. Once you've seen the test fail, you can discard the changes in your working directory and commit the staged changes.

11.3 CONCLUSION

Be careful editing unit test code; there's no safety net.

Some changes are relatively safe. Adding new tests, new assertions, or new test cases tends to be safe. Applying refactorings built into your IDE also tends to be safe.

Other changes to test code are less safe, but may still be desirable. Test code is code that you have to maintain. It's as important that it fits in your brain as production code does. Sometimes, then, you should refactor test code to improve its internal structure.

You may, for example, want to address duplication by extracting helper methods. When you do that, make sure that you edit only the test code, and that you don't touch the production code. Check such changes to test code into Git as separate commits. This doesn't *guarantee* that you didn't make mistakes in the test code, but it improves your chances.

12 TROUBLESHOOTING

Professional software development consists of more than feature development. There are also meetings, time reports, compliance activities, and ... defects.

You run into errors and problems all the time. Your code doesn't compile, the software doesn't do what it's supposed to, it runs too slowly, et cetera.

The better you get at solving problems, the more productive you are. Most of your troubleshooting skills may be based on "the shifting sands of individual experience" [4], but there *are* techniques that you can apply.

This chapter presents some of them.

12.1 UNDERSTANDING

The best advice I can think of is this:

> Try to understand what's going on.

If you don't understand why something doesn't work[1], then make understanding it a priority. I've witnessed a fair amount of 'programming by coincidence' [50]: throw enough code at the wall to see what sticks. When it looks as though the code works, developers move on to the next task. Either they don't understand why the code works, or they may fail to understand that it doesn't, really.

If you understand the code from the beginning, chances are that it'll be easier to troubleshoot.

12.1.1   SCIENTIFIC METHOD

When a problem manifests, most people jump straight into troubleshooting mode. They want to *address* the problem. For people who program by coincidence [50], addressing a problem typically involves trying various incantations that may have worked before on a similar problem. If the first magic spell doesn't work, they move on to the next. This can involve restarting a service, rebooting a computer, running a tool with elevated privileges, changing small pieces of code, calling poorly-understood routines, etc. When it looks like the problem has disappeared, they call it a day without trying to understand why [50].

Needless to say, this isn't an effective way to deal with problems.

Your first reaction to a problem should be to understand why it's happening. If you have absolutely no idea, ask for help. Usually, though, you already have some inclination of what the problem may be. In that case, adopt a variation of the scientific method [82]:

- Make a prediction. This is called a *hypothesis*.
- Perform the experiment.
- Compare outcome to prediction. Repeat until you understand what's going on.

---

1. Or, if you don't understand why something *does* work.

Don't be intimidated by the term 'scientific method'. You don't have to don a lab coat or design a randomised controlled double-blind trial. But *do* try to come up with a falsifiable hypothesis. This might simply be a prediction, such as *"if I reboot the machine, the problem goes away,"* or *"if I call this function, the return value will be 42."*

The difference between this technique and 'programming by coincidence' is that the goal of going through these motions isn't to address the problem. The goal is to understand it.

A typical experiment could be a unit test, with a hypothesis that if you run it, it'll fail. See subsection 12.2.1 for more details.

12.1.2 SIMPLIFY

Consider if *removing* some code can make a problem go away.

The most common reaction to a problem is to add more code to address it. The unspoken line of reasoning seems to be that the system 'works', and the problem is just an aberration. Thus, the reasoning goes, if the problem is a special case, it should be solved with more code to handle that special case.

This may occasionally be the case, but it's more likely that the problem is a manifestation of an underlying implementation error. You'd be surprised how often you can solve problems by *simplifying* the code.

I've seen plenty of examples of such an 'action bias' in our industry. People who solve problems I never have because I work hard to keep my code simple:

• People develop complex Dependency Injection Containers [25] instead of just composing object graphs in code.

• People develop complicated 'mock object libraries' instead of writing mostly pure functions.

• People create elaborate package restore schemes instead of just checking dependencies into source control.

- People use advanced diff tools instead of merging more frequently.

- People use convoluted object-relational mappers (ORMs) instead of learning (and maintaining) a bit of SQL.

I could go on.

To be fair, coming up with a simpler solution is *hard*. For example, it took me a decade of erecting increasingly more elaborate contraptions in object-oriented code before I found simpler solutions. It turns out that many things that are difficult in traditional object-oriented programming are simple in functional programming. Once I learned about some of these concepts, I found ways to use them in object-oriented contexts, too.

The point is that a catchphrase like KISS[2] is useless in itself, because *how* does one keep things simple?

You often have to be *smart* to keep it simple[3], but look for simplicity anyway. Consider if there's a way you can solve the problem by *deleting* code.

12.1.3 RUBBER DUCKING

Before we discuss some specific problem-solving practices, I want to share some general techniques. It's not unusual to be stuck on a problem. How do you get unstuck?

You may be staring at a problem with no clue as to how to proceed. As the above advice goes, your first priority should be to understand the problem. What do you do if you're drawing a blank?

If you don't manage your time, you can be stuck with a problem for a long time, so *do* manage your time. Time-box the process. For example, set aside 25 minutes to look at the problem. If, after the time is up, you've made no progress, take a break.

---

2. Keep It Simple, Stupid.

3. Rich Hickey discusses simplicity in *Simple Made Easy* [45]. I owe much of my perspective on simplicity to that talk.

When you take a break, physically remove yourself from the computer. Go get a cup of coffee. Something happens in your brain when you get out of your chair and away from the screen. After a couple of minutes away from the problem, you'll likely begin to think about something else. Perhaps you meet a colleague as you're moving about. Perhaps you discover that the coffee machine needs a refill. Whatever it is, it temporarily takes your mind off the problem. That's often enough to give you a fresh perspective.

I've lost count of the number of times I return to a problem after a stroll, only to realise that I've been thinking about it the wrong way.

If walking about for a few minutes isn't enough, try asking for help. If you have a colleague to bother, do that.

I've experienced this often enough: I start explaining the problem, but halfway in, I break off in mid-sentence: *"Never mind, I've just gotten an idea!"*

The mere act of explaining a problem tends to produce new insight.

If you don't have a colleague, you may try explaining the problem to a rubber duck, such as the one shown in figure 12.1.

Figure 12.1 A rubber duck. Talk to it. It'll solve your problems.

It doesn't really have to be a rubber duck, but the technique is known as *rubber ducking* because one programmer actually did use one [50].

Instead of using a rubber duck, I typically begin writing a question on the Stack Overflow Q&A site. More often than not, I realise what the problem is before I'm done formulating the question[4].

And if realisation *doesn't* come, I have a written question that I can publish.

12.2 DEFECTS

I once started in a new job in a small software startup. I soon asked my co-workers if they'd like to use test-driven development. They hadn't used it before, but they were keen on learning new things. After I'd shown them the ropes, they decided that they liked it.

A few months after we'd adopted test-driven development, the CEO came by to talk to me. He mentioned in passing that he'd noticed that since we'd started using tests, defects in the wild had significantly dropped.

That still makes me proud to this day. The shift in quality was so dramatic that the CEO had noticed. Not by running numbers or doing a complex analysis, but simply because it was so significant that it called attention to itself.

You can reduce the number of defects, but you can't eliminate them. But do yourself a favour: don't let them accumulate.

> The ideal number of defects is zero.

Zero bugs isn't as unrealistic as it sounds. In lean software development, this is known as *building quality in* [82]. Don't push defects in front of you to 'deal with them later'. In software development, *later* is *never*.

---

4. When that happens, I *don't* succumb to the sunk cost fallacy. Even if I've spent time writing the question, I usually delete it because I deem that it's not, after all, of general interest.

When a bug appears, make it a priority to address it. Stop what you're doing[5] and fix the defect instead.

12.2.1 Reproduce Defects as Tests

Initially, you may not even understand what the problem is, but when you think that you do, perform an experiment: The understanding should enable you to formulate a hypothesis, which again enables you to design an experiment.

Such an experiment may be an automated test. The hypothesis is that when you run the test, it'll *fail*. When you actually do run the test, if it *does* fail, you've validated the hypothesis. As a bonus, you also have a failing test that reproduces the defect, and that will later serve as a regression test.

If, on the other hand, the test succeeds, the experiment failed. This means that your hypothesis was wrong. You'll need to revise it so that you can design a new experiment. You may need to repeat this process more than once.

When you finally have a failing test, 'all' you have to do is to make it pass. This can occasionally be difficult, but in my experience, it usually isn't. The hard part of addressing a defect is understanding and reproducing it.

I'll show you an example from the online restaurant reservation system. While I was doing some exploratory testing I noticed something odd when I updated a reservation. Listing 12.1 shows an example of the issue. Can you spot the problem?

The problem is that the email property holds the name, and vice versa. It seems that I accidentally switched them around somewhere. That's the initial hypothesis, but it may take a little investigation to figure out *where*.

Have I not been following test-driven development? Then how could this happen?

---

5. Isn't it wonderful that with Git you can simply stash your current work?

Listing 12.1 Updating a reservation with a PUT request. A defect is manifest in this interaction. Can you spot it?

```
PUT /reservations/21b4fa1975064414bee402bbe09090ec HTTP/1.1
Content-Type: application/json
{
  "at": "2022-03-02 19:45",
  "email": "pan@example.com",
  "name": "Phil Anders",
  "quantity": 2
}

HTTP/1.1 200 OK
Content-Type: application/json; charset=utf-8
{
  "id": "21b4fa1975064414bee402bbe09090ec",
  "at": "2022-03-02T19:45:00.0000000",
  "email": "Phil Anders",
  "name": "pan@example.com",
  "quantity": 2
}
```

This could happen because I'd implemented `SqlReservationsRepository`[6] as a Humble Object [66]. This is an object so simple that you may decide not to test it. I often use the rule of thumb that if the cyclomatic complexity is *1*, a test (also with a cyclomatic complexity of *1*) may not be warranted.

Even so, you can still make mistakes even when the cyclomatic complexity is *1*. Listing 12.2 shows the offending code. Can you spot the problem?

Given that you already know what the problem is, you can probably guess that the `Reservation` constructor expects the `email` argument before the `name`. Since both parameters are declared as `string`, though, the compiler doesn't complain if you accidentally swap them. This is another example of stringly typed code [3], which we should avoid[7].

---

6. See for example listing 4.19.
7. One way to avoid stringly typed code is to introduce `Email` and `Name` classes that wrap their respective `string` values. This prevents some cases of accidentally swapping these two arguments, but as it turned out when I did it, it wasn't entirely foolproof. You can consult the example code's Git repository if you're interested in the details. The bottom line was that I felt that an integration test was warranted.

Listing 12.2 The offending code fragment that causes the defect shown in listing 12.1. Can you spot the programmer error?
(Restaurant/d7b74f1/Restaurant.RestApi/SqlReservationsRepository.cs)

```
using var rdr =
    await cmd.ExecuteReaderAsync().ConfigureAwait(false);
if (!rdr.Read())
    return null;

return new Reservation(
    id,
    (DateTime)rdr["At"],
    (string)rdr["Name"],
    (string)rdr["Email"],
    (int)rdr["Quantity"]);
```

It's easy enough to address the defect, but if I can make the mistake once, I can make it again. Thus, I want to prevent a regression. Before fixing the code, write a failing test that reproduces the bug. Listing 12.3 shows the test I wrote. It's an integration test that verifies that if you update a reservation in the database and subsequently read it, you should receive a reservation equal to the one you saved. That's a reasonable expectation, and it reproduces the error because the `ReadReservation` method swaps `name` and `email`, as shown in listing 12.2.

That `PutAndReadRoundTrip` test is an integration test that involves the database. This is new. So far in this book, all tests have been running without external dependencies. Involving the database is worth a detour.

12.2.2 SLOW TESTS

Bridging the gap between a programming language's perspective on data and a relational database is error-prone[8], so why not test such code?

In this subsection, you'll see an outline of how to do that, but there's a problem: such tests tend to be slow. They tend to be orders of magnitudes slower than in-process tests.

---

8. Proponents of object-relational mappers (ORMs) might argue that this makes the case for such a tool. As I've stated elsewhere in this book, I consider ORMs a waste of time: they create more problems than they solve. If you disagree, then feel free to skip this subsection.

Listing 12.3 Integration test of `SqlReservationsRepository`.
(Restaurant/645186b/Restaurant.RestApi.SqlIntegrationTests/SqlReservationsRepositoryTests.cs)

```
[Theory]
[InlineData("2032-01-01 01:12", "z@example.net", "z", "Zet", 4)]
[InlineData("2084-04-21 23:21", "q@example.gov", "q", "Quu", 9)]
public async Task PutAndReadRoundTrip(
    string date,
    string email,
    string name,
    string newName,
    int quantity)
{
    var r = new Reservation(
        Guid.NewGuid(),
        DateTime.Parse(date, CultureInfo.InvariantCulture),
        new Email(email),
        new Name(name),
        quantity);
    var connectionString = ConnectionStrings.Reservations;
    var sut = new SqlReservationsRepository(connectionString);
    await sut.Create(r);

    var expected = r.WithName(new Name(newName));
    await sut.Update(expected);
    var actual = await sut.ReadReservation(expected.Id);

    Assert.Equal(expected, actual);
}
```

The time it takes to execute a test suite matters, particularly for developer tests that you continually run. When you refactor with the test suite as a safety net, it doesn't work if it takes half an hour to run all tests. When you follow the Red Green Refactor process for test-driven development, it doesn't work if running the tests takes five minutes.

The maximum time for such a test suite should be ten seconds. If it's much longer than that, you'll lose focus. You'll be tempted to look at your email, Twitter, or Facebook while the tests run.

You can easily eat into such a ten-second budget if you involve a database. Therefore, move such tests to a second stage of tests. There are many ways you can do this, but a pragmatic way is to simply create a *second* Visual Studio solution to exist side-by-side with the day-to-day solution. When you do that, remember to also update the build script to run this new solution instead, as shown in listing 12.4.

Listing 12.4 Build script running all tests. The `Build.sln` file contains both unit and integration tests that use the database. Compare with listing 4.2. *(Restaurant/645186b/build.sh)*

```
#!/usr/bin/env bash
dotnet test Build.sln --configuration Release
```

The `Build.sln` file contains the production code, the unit test code, as well as integration tests that use the database. I do day-to-day work that doesn't involve the database in another Visual Studio solution called `Restaurant.sln`. That solution only contains the production code and the unit tests, so running all tests in that context is much faster.

The test in listing 12.3 is part of the integration test code, so only runs when I run the build script, or if I explicitly choose to work in the `Build.sln` solution instead of in `Restaurant.sln`. It's sometimes practical to do that, if I need to perform a refactoring that involves the database code.

I don't want to go into too much detail about how the test in listing 12.3 works, because it's specific to how .NET interacts with SQL Server. If you're interested in the details, they're all available in the accompanying example code base, but briefly, all the integration tests are adorned with a `[UseDatabase]` attribute. This is a custom attribute that hooks into the xUnit.net unit testing framework to run some code before and after each test case. Thus, each test case is surrounded with behaviour like this:

1. Create a new database and run all DDL[9] scripts against it.
2. Run the test.
3. Tear down the database.

---

9. Data Definition Language, typically a subset of SQL. See listing 4.18 for an example.

Yes, each test *creates a new database* only to delete it again some milliseconds later[10]. That *is* slow, which is why you don't want such tests to run all the time.

Defer slow tests to a second stage of your build pipeline. You can do it as outlined above, or by defining new steps that only run on your Continuous Integration server.

12.2.3   NON-DETERMINISTIC DEFECTS

After running the restaurant reservation system for some time, the restaurant's maître d' files a bug: once in a while, the system seems to allow overbooking. She can't deliberately reproduce the problem, but the state of the reservations database can't be denied. Some days contain more reservations than the business logic shown in listing 12.5 allows. What's going on?

You peruse the application logs[11] and finally figure it out. Overbooking is a possible race condition. If a day is approaching capacity and two reservations arrive simultaneously, the `ReadReservations` method might return the same set of rows to both threads, indicating that a reservation is possible. As figure 12.2 shows, each thread determines that it can accept the reservation, so it adds a new row to the table of reservations.

This is clearly a defect, so you should reproduce it with a test. The problem is, however, that this behaviour isn't deterministic. Automated tests are supposed to be deterministic, aren't they?

It is, indeed, best if tests are deterministic, but do entertain, for a moment, the notion that nondeterminism may be acceptable. In which way could this be?

---

10. Whenever I explain this approach to integration testing with a database, I'm invariably met with the reaction that one can, instead, test by rolling back transactions. Yes, except that this means that you can't test database transaction behaviour. Also, using transaction rollback *may* be faster, but have you measured? I have, once, and found no significant difference. See also section 15.1 for my general position on performance optimisation.
11. See subsection 13.2.1.

Tests can fail in two ways: A test may indicate a failure where none is; this is called a false positive. A test may also fail to indicate an actual error; this is called a false negative.

Listing 12.5 Apparently, there's a bug in this code that allows overbooking. What could be the problem? *(Restaurant/dd05589/Restaurant.RestApi/ReservationsController.cs)*

```
[HttpPost]
public async Task<ActionResult> Post(ReservationDto dto)
{
    if (dto is null)
        throw new ArgumentNullException(nameof(dto));

    var id = dto.ParseId() ?? Guid.NewGuid();
    Reservation? r = dto.Validate(id);
    if (r is null)
        return new BadRequestResult();

    var reservations = await Repository
        .ReadReservations(r.At)
        .ConfigureAwait(false);
    if (!MaitreD.WillAccept(DateTime.Now, reservations, r))
        return NoTables500InternalServerError();

    await Repository.Create(r).ConfigureAwait(false);
    await PostOffice.EmailReservationCreated(r).ConfigureAwait(false);

    return Reservation201Created(r);
}
```

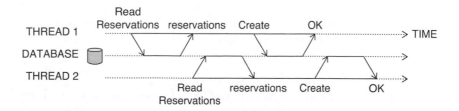

Figure 12.2 A race condition between two threads (e.g. two HTTP clients) concurrently trying to make a reservation.

False positives are problematic because they introduce noise, and thereby decrease the signal-to-noise ratio of the test suite. If you have a test suite that often fails for no apparent reason, you stop paying attention to it [31].

False negatives aren't quite as bad. Too many false negatives could decrease your trust in a test suite, but they introduce no noise. Thus, at least, you know that if a test suite is failing, there *is* a problem.

One way to deal with the race condition in the reservation system, then, is to reproduce it as the non-deterministic test in listing 12.6.

Listing 12.6 Non-deterministic test that reproduces a race condition.
(Restaurant/98ab6b5/Restaurant.RestApi.SqlIntegrationTests/ConcurrencyTests.cs)

```
[Fact]
public async Task NoOverbookingRace()
{
    var start = DateTimeOffset.UtcNow;
    var timeOut = TimeSpan.FromSeconds(30);
    var i = 0;
    while (DateTimeOffset.UtcNow - start < timeOut)
        await PostTwoConcurrentLiminalReservations(
            start.DateTime.AddDays(++i));
}
```

This test method is only an orchestrator of the actual unit test. It keeps running the `PostTwoConcurrentLiminalReservations` method in listing 12.7 for 30 seconds, over and over again, to see if it fails. The assumption, or hope, is that if it can run for 30 seconds without failing, the system may actually have the correct behaviour.

There's no guarantee that this is the case. If the race condition is as scarce as hen's teeth, this test could produce a false negative. That's not my experience, though.

When I wrote this test, it only ran for a few seconds before failing. That gives me some confidence that the 30-second timeout is a sufficiently safe margin, but I admit that I'm guessing; it's another example of the art of software engineering.

It turned out that the system had the same bug when updating existing reservations (as opposed to creating new ones), so I also wrote a similar test for that case.

Listing 12.7 The actual test method orchestrated by the code in listing 12.6. It attempts to post two concurrent reservations. The state of the system is that it's almost sold out (the capacity of the restaurant is ten, but nine seats are already reserved), so only one of those reservations should be accepted.
(Restaurant/98ab6b5/Restaurant.RestApi.SqlIntegrationTests/ConcurrencyTests.cs)

```
private static async Task PostTwoConcurrentLiminalReservations(
    DateTime date)
{
    date = date.Date.AddHours(18.5);
    using var service = new RestaurantService();
    var initialResp =
        await service.PostReservation(new ReservationDtoBuilder()
            .WithDate(date)
            .WithQuantity(9)
            .Build());
    initialResp.EnsureSuccessStatusCode();

    var task1 = service.PostReservation(new ReservationDtoBuilder()
        .WithDate(date)
        .WithQuantity(1)
        .Build());
    var task2 = service.PostReservation(new ReservationDtoBuilder()
        .WithDate(date)
        .WithQuantity(1)
        .Build());
    var actual = await Task.WhenAll(task1, task2);

    Assert.Single(actual, msg => msg.IsSuccessStatusCode);
    Assert.Single(
        actual,
        msg => msg.StatusCode == HttpStatusCode.InternalServerError);
}
```

These tests are examples of slow tests that ought to be included only as second-stage tests as discussed in subsection 12.2.2.

There are various ways you can address a defect like the one discussed here. You can reach for the Unit of Work [33] design pattern. You can also deal with the issue at the architectural level, by introducing a durable queue with a single-threaded writer that consumes the messages from it. In any case, you need to serialise the reads and the writes involved in the operation.

I chose to go for a pragmatic solution: use .NET's lightweight transactions, as shown in listing 12.8. Surrounding the critical part of the Post method with a

TransactionScope effectively serialises[12] the reads and writes. That solves the problem.

Listing 12.8 The critical part of the Post method is now surrounded with a TransactionScope, which serialises the read and write methods. The highlighted code is new compared to listing 12.5. *(Restaurant/98ab6b5/Restaurant.RestApi/ReservationsController.cs)*

```
using var scope = new TransactionScope(
    TransactionScopeAsyncFlowOption.Enabled);
var reservations = await Repository
    .ReadReservations(r.At)
    .ConfigureAwait(false);
if (!MaitreD.WillAccept(DateTime.Now, reservations, r))
    return NoTables500InternalServerError();

await Repository.Create(r).ConfigureAwait(false);
await PostOffice.EmailReservationCreated(r).ConfigureAwait(false);
scope.Complete();
```

In my experience, most defects can be reproduced as deterministic tests, but there's a residual that eludes this ideal. Multithreaded code infamously falls into that category. Of two evils, I prefer nondeterministic tests over no test coverage at all. Such tests will often have to run until they time out in order to give you confidence that they've sufficiently exercised the test case in question. You should, therefore, put them in a second stage of tests that only runs on demand and as part of your deployment pipeline.

12.3 BISECTION

Some defects can be elusive. When I developed the restaurant system I ran into one that took me most of a day to understand. After wasting hours following several false leads, I finally realised that I couldn't crack the nut only by staring long enough at the code. I had to use a *method*.

---

12. *Serialisability*, here, refers to making sure that database transactions behave as though they were serialised one after another [55]. It has nothing to do with converting objects to and from JSON or XML.

Fortunately, such a method exists. We can call it *bisection* for lack of a better word. In all its simplicity, it works like this:

1. Find a way to detect or reproduce the problem.
2. Remove half of the code.
3. If the problem is still present, repeat from step 2. If the problem goes away, restore the code you removed, and remove the other half. Again, repeat from step 2.
4. Keep going until you've whittled down the code that reproduces the problem to a size so small that you understand what's going on.

You can use an automated test to detect the problem, or use some ad hoc way to detect whether the problem is present or absent. The exact way you do this doesn't matter for the technique, but I find that an automated test is often the easiest way to go about it, because of the repetition involved.

I often use this technique when I *rubber duck* by writing a question on Stack Overflow. Good questions on Stack Overflow should come with a *minimal working example*. In most cases I find that the process of producing the minimal working example is so illuminating that I get unstuck before I have a chance to post the question.

12.3.1 Bisection with Git

You can also use the bisection technique with Git to identify the commit that introduced the defect. I ultimately used that with the problem I ran into.

I'd added a secure resource to the REST API to list the schedule for a particular day. A restaurant's maître d' can make a GET request against that resource to see the schedule for the day, including all reservations and who arrives when. The schedule includes names and emails of guests, so it shouldn't be available without authentication and authorisation[13].

This particular resource demands that a client presents a valid JSON Web Token (JWT). I'd developed this security feature with test-driven development and I had enough tests to feel safe.

---

13. For an example of what this looks like, see subsection 15.2.5.

Then one day, as I was interacting with the deployed REST API, I could no longer access this resource! I first thought that I'd supplied an invalid JWT, so I wasted hours troubleshooting that. Dead end.

It finally dawned on me that this security feature *had* worked. I'd interacted with the deployed REST API earlier and seen it work. At one time it worked, and now it didn't. In between these two known states a commit must have introduced the defect. If I could identify that particular code change, I might have a better chance of understanding the problem.

Unfortunately, there was some 130 commits between those two extremes.

Fortunately, I'd found an easy way to detect the problem, if given a commit.

This meant that I could use Git's `bisect` feature to identify the exact commit that caused the problem.

Git can run an automated bisection for you if you have an automated way to detect the problem. Usually, you don't. When you bisect, you're looking for a commit that introduced a defect that *went unnoticed at the time*. This means that even if you have an automated test suite, the tests didn't catch that bug.

For that reason, Git can also bisect your commits in an interactive session. You start such a session with `git bisect start`, as shown in listing 12.9.

Listing 12.9 The start of a Git bisect session. I ran it from Bash, but you can run it in any shell where you use Git. I've edited the terminal output by removing irrelevant data that Bash tends to show, so that it fits on the page.

```
~/Restaurant ((56a7092...))
$ git bisect start

~/Restaurant ((56a7092...)|BISECTING)
```

This starts an interactive session, which you can tell from the Git integration in Bash (it says `BISECTING`). If the current commit exhibits the defect you're investigating, you mark it as shown in listing 12.10

Listing 12.10 Marking a commit as bad in a bisect session.

```
$ git bisect bad

~/Restaurant ((56a7092...)|BISECTING)
```

If you don't provide a commit ID, Git is going to assume that you meant the current commit (in this case `56a7092`).

You now tell it about a commit ID that you know is good. This is the other extreme of the range of commits you're investigating. Listing 12.11 shows how that's done.

Listing 12.11 Marking a commit as good in a bisect session. I've trimmed the output a little to make it fit on the page.

```
$ git bisect good 58fc950
Bisecting: 75 revisions left to test after this (roughly 6 steps)
[3035c14...] Use InMemoryRestaurantDatabase in a test

~/Restaurant ((3035c14...)|BISECTING)
```

Notice that Git is already telling you how many iterations to expect. You can also see that it checked out a new commit (`3035c14`) for you. That's the half-way commit.

You now have to check whether or not the defect is present in this commit. You can run an automated test, start the system, or any other way you've identified to answer that question.

In my particular case, the half-way commit didn't have the defect, so I told Git, as shown in listing 12.12.

Listing 12.12 Marking the half-way commit as good in a bisect session. I've trimmed the output a little to make it fit on the page.

```
$ git bisect good
Bisecting: 37 revisions left to test after this (roughly 5 steps)
[aa69259...] Delete Either API

~/Restaurant ((aa69259...)|BISECTING)
```

Again, Git estimates how many more steps are left and checks out a new commit (aa69259).

Listing 12.13 Finding the commit responsible for the defect, using a Git bisect session.

```
$ git bisect bad
Bisecting: 18 revisions left to test after this (roughly 4 steps)
[75f3c56...] Delete redundant Test Data Builders

~/Restaurant ((75f3c56...)|BISECTING)
$ git bisect good
Bisecting: 9 revisions left to test after this (roughly 3 steps)
[8f93562...] Extract WillAcceptUpdate helper method

~/Restaurant ((8f93562...)|BISECTING)
$ git bisect good
Bisecting: 4 revisions left to test after this (roughly 2 steps)
[1c6fae1...] Extract ConfigureClock helper method

~/Restaurant ((1c6fae1...)|BISECTING)
$ git bisect good
Bisecting: 2 revisions left to test after this (roughly 1 step)
[8e1f1ce] Compact code

~/Restaurant ((8e1f1ce...)|BISECTING)
$ git bisect good
Bisecting: 0 revisions left to test after this (roughly 1 step)
[2563131] Extract CreateTokenValidationParameters method

~/Restaurant ((2563131...)|BISECTING)
$ git bisect bad
Bisecting: 0 revisions left to test after this (roughly 0 steps)
[fa0caeb...] Move Configure method up

~/Restaurant ((fa0caeb...)|BISECTING)
$ git bisect good
2563131c2d06af8e48f1df2dccbf85e9fc8ddafc is the first bad commit
commit 2563131c2d06af8e48f1df2dccbf85e9fc8ddafc
Author: Mark Seemann <mark@example.com>
Date:   Wed Sep 16 07:15:12 2020 +0200

    Extract CreateTokenValidationParameters method

Restaurant.RestApi/Startup.cs | 32 +++++++++++++++++++++-------------
1 file changed, 19 insertions(+), 13 deletions(-)

~/Restaurant ((fa0caeb...)|BISECTING)
```

I repeated the process for each step, marking the commit as either good or bad, depending on whether or not my verification step passed. This is shown in listing 12.13.

After just eight iterations, Git found the commit responsible for the defect. Notice that the last step tells you which commit is the 'first bad commit'.

Once I saw the contents of the commit, I immediately knew what the problem was and could easily fix it. I'm not going to tire you with a detailed description of the error, or how I fixed it. If you're interested, I wrote a blog post [101] with all the details, and you can also peruse the Git repository that accompanies the book.

The bottom line is that bisection is a potent technique for finding and isolating the source of an error. You can use it with or without Git.

12.4 CONCLUSION

There's a significant degree of personal experience involved in troubleshooting. I once worked in a team where a unit test failed on one developer's machine, while it passed on another programmer's laptop. The exact same test, the same code, the same Git commit.

We could have just shrugged and found a workaround, but we all knew that making the symptom go away without understanding the root cause tends to be a myopic strategy. The two developers worked together for maybe half an hour to reduce the problem to a minimal working example. Essentially, it boiled down to string comparison.

On the machine where the test failed, a comparison of strings would consider "aa" less than "bb", and "bb" less than "cc". That seems fine, doesn't it?

On the machine where the test *succeeded*, however, "bb" was still less than "cc", but "aa" was *greater than* "bb". What's going on?

At this point, I got involved, took one look at the repro and asked both developers what their 'default culture' was. In .NET, the 'default culture' is an

Ambient Context [25] that knows about culture-specific formatting rules, sort order, and so on.

As I expected, the machine that considered `"aa"` greater than `"bb"` was running with the Danish default culture, whereas the other machine used US English. The Danish alphabet has three extra letters (Æ, Ø, and Å) after Z, but the Å used to be spelled *Aa* in the old days, and since that spelling still exists in proper nouns, the *aa* combination is considered to be equivalent to *å*. Å being the last letter in the alphabet is considered greater than B.

It took me less than a minute to figure out what the problem was, because I'd run into enough problems with Danish sort orders earlier in my career. That's still the *shifting sands of individual experience*—the art of software engineering.

I'd never been able to identify the problem if my colleagues hadn't first used a methodology like bisection to reduce the problem to a simple symptom. Being able to produce a minimal working example is a superpower in software troubleshooting.

Notice what I *haven't* discussed in this chapter: debugging.

Too many people rely exclusively on debugging for troubleshooting. While I do occasionally use the debugger, I find the combination of the scientific method, automated testing, and bisection more efficient. Learn and use these more universal practices, because you can't use debugging tools in your production environment.

SEPARATION OF CONCERNS

Imagine changing your application's database schema and as a result, the font size increases in the emails that the system sends.

Why would the email template font size depend on the database schema? Good question. It ought not to.

In general, don't put business logic in your user interface. Don't put data import and export code in your security code. This principle is known as *separation of concerns*. It aligns with Kent Beck's aphorism:

> *"Things that change at the same rate belong together. Things that change at different rates belong apart."* [8]

An overarching theme of this book is that code should fit in your head. As subsections 7.1.3 and 7.2.7 argues, keep code blocks small and isolated. Keeping things apart is important.

Chapter 7 was mostly about principles and thresholds for decomposition. Why and when should you decompose bigger blocks of code into smaller ones? Chapter 7 didn't talk much about *how* to decompose.

In this chapter, I'll attempt to address that question.

13.1 COMPOSITION

Composition and decomposition are intricately connected. Ultimately, the purpose of writing code is to develop working software. You can't arbitrarily tear things apart. While decomposition is important, as figure 13.1 illustrates, you must be able to recompose what you decomposed.

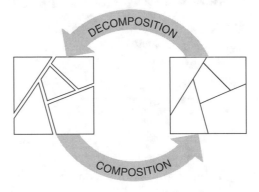

Figure 13.1 Decomposition is intimately related to composition. Decompose so that you can compose working software from the parts.

Thus, models of composition are illustrative. There's more than one way to compose software components[1] together, and they aren't equally good. I may as well drop the bomb right away: object-oriented composition has problems.

13.1.1 NESTED COMPOSITION

Ultimately, software interacts with the real world. It paints pixels on the screen, saves data in databases, sends emails, posts on social media, controls industrial robots, et cetera. All of these are what we in the context of Command Query Separation call *side effects*.

---

1. I use the term *component* loosely. It could mean *object*, *module*, *library*, *widget*, or something else. Some programming languages and platforms come with specific notions of what a *component* might be, but these typically aren't compatible with another language's notion. Like *unit test* or *mock*, the term is vague.

Since side effects are software's raison d'être, it seems only natural to model composition around them. This is how most people tend to approach object-oriented design. You model *actions*.

Object-oriented composition tends to focus on composing side effects together. The Composite [39] design pattern may be the paragon of this style of composition, but most of the patterns in *Design Patterns* [39] rely heavily on composition of side effects.

As illustrated in figure 13.2, this style of composition relies on nesting objects in other objects, or side effects in other side effects. Since your goal should be code that fits in your head, this is a problem.

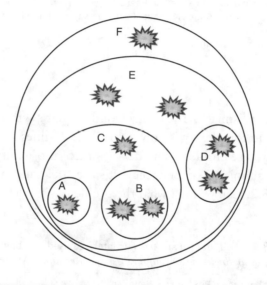

Figure 13.2 The typical composition of objects (or, rather, methods on objects) is nesting. The more you compose, the less the composition fits in your brain. In this figure, each star indicates a side effect that you care about. Object *A* encapsulates one side effect, and object *B* two. Object *C* composes *A* and *B*, but also adds a fourth side effect. That's already four side effects that you need to keep in mind when trying to understand the code. This easily gets out of hand: object *E* composes a total of eight side effects, and *F* nine. Those don't fit well in your brain.

To illustrate how this is problematic, I'm going to do something that I've so far abstained from doing. I'll show you *bad* code. Don't write code like listings 13.1 or 13.3.

Listing 13.1 Bad code: A Controller action interacting with a nested composition. Listing 13.6 shows a better alternative. *(Restaurant/b3dd0fe/Restaurant.RestApi/ReservationsController.cs)*

```
public IRestaurantManager Manager { get; }

public async Task<ActionResult> Post(ReservationDto dto)
{
    if (dto is null)
        throw new ArgumentNullException(nameof(dto));

    Reservation? r = dto.Validate();
    if (r is null)
        return new BadRequestResult();

    var isAccepted =
        await Manager.Check(r).ConfigureAwait(false);
    if (!isAccepted)
        return new StatusCodeResult(
            StatusCodes.Status500InternalServerError);

    return new NoContentResult();
}
```

Looking at listing 13.1 you may wonder what's wrong with it. After all, its cyclomatic complexity is only 4, there are 17 lines of code, and only 4 objects activated. The problem is hidden by one of those four objects: the `Manager`, which is an injected dependency. It's the `IRestaurantManager` interface in listing 13.2. Can you tell what the problem is?

Listing 13.2 The `IRestaurantManager` interface used in listing 13.1 and implemented in listing 13.3. *(Restaurant/b3dd0fe/Restaurant.RestApi/IRestaurantManager.cs)*

```
public interface IRestaurantManager
{
    Task<bool> Check(Reservation reservation);
}
```

Try doing the exercise of X'ing out the method name. If you do, you're left with `Task<bool> Xxx(Reservation reservation)`, which looks like an asynchronous predicate. This must be a method that checks if something about a reservation is true or false. But if you look at listing 13.1 in that light, the `Post` method only uses the Boolean value to decide which HTTP status code to return.

Did the programmer forget to *save* the reservation in the database?

Probably not. You decide to look at the implementation of `IRestaurantManager` in listing 13.3. It does a bit of validation and then calls `Manager.TrySave`.

Listing 13.3 Bad code: The implementation of the `IRestaurantManager` interface looks like it has a side effect. *(Restaurant/b3dd0fe/Restaurant.RestApi/RestaurantManager.cs)*

```
public async Task<bool> Check(Reservation reservation)
{
    if (reservation is null)
        throw new ArgumentNullException(nameof(reservation));

    if (reservation.At < DateTime.Now)
        return false;
    if (reservation.At.TimeOfDay < OpensAt)
        return false;
    if (LastSeating < reservation.At.TimeOfDay)
        return false;

    return await Manager.TrySave(reservation).ConfigureAwait(false);
}
```

If you continue to pull at this particular string of spaghetti, you'll ultimately discover that `Manager.TrySave` *both* saves the reservation in the database *and* returns a Boolean value. Based on what you've learned so far in this book, what's wrong with that?

It violates the Command Query Separation principle. While the method *looks* like a Query, it has a side effect. Why is this a problem?

Recall Robert C. Martin's definition:

> *"Abstraction is the elimination of the irrelevant and the amplification of the essential"* [60]

By hiding a side effect in a Query, I've *eliminated* something essential. In other words, more is going on in listing 13.1 than meets the eye. The cyclomatic complexity may be as low as 4, but there's a hidden fifth action that you ought to be aware of.

Granted, five chunks still fit in your brain, but that single hidden interaction is an extra 14 percent towards the budget of seven. It doesn't take many hidden side effects before the code no longer fits in your head.

13.1.2   SEQUENTIAL COMPOSITION

While nested composition is problematic, it isn't the only way to compose things. You can also compose behaviour by chaining it together, as illustrated in figure 13.3.

Figure 13.3 Sequential composition of two functions. The output from Where becomes the input to Allocate.

In the terminology of Command Query Separation, Commands cause trouble. Queries, on the other hand, tend to cause little trouble. They return data which you can use as input for other Queries.

The entire restaurant example code base is written with that principle in mind. Consider the WillAccept method in listing 8.13. After all the Guard Clauses [7] it first creates a new instance of the Seating class. You can think of a constructor as a Query under the condition that it has no side effects[2].

The next line of code filters the existingReservations using the Overlaps method in listing 13.4 as a predicate. The built-in Where method is a Query, and so is Overlaps.

The relevantReservations collection is the output of one Query, but becomes the input to the next Query: Allocate, shown in listing 13.5.

---

2. Constructors really, really shouldn't have side effects!

Listing 13.4 Overlaps method. This is a Query, since it has no side effects and returns data. *(Restaurant/e9a5587/Restaurant.RestApi/Seating.cs)*

```
internal bool Overlaps(Reservation other)
{
    var otherSeating = new Seating(SeatingDuration, other);
    return Start < otherSeating.End && otherSeating.Start < End;
}
```

Listing 13.5 Allocate method – another Query. *(Restaurant/e9a5587/Restaurant.RestApi/MaitreD.cs)*

```
private IEnumerable<Table> Allocate(
    IEnumerable<Reservation> reservations)
{
    List<Table> availableTables = Tables.ToList();
    foreach (var r in reservations)
    {
        var table = availableTables.Find(t => t.Fits(r.Quantity));
        if (table is { })
        {
            availableTables.Remove(table);
            if (table.IsCommunal)
                availableTables.Add(table.Reserve(r.Quantity));
        }
    }

    return availableTables;
}
```

Finally, the `WillAccept` method returns whether there's `Any` table among the `availableTables` that `Fits` the `candidate.Quantity`. The `Any` method is another built-in Query, and `Fits` shown in listing 8.14 is a predicate.

Compared to figure 13.3, you can say that the `Seating` constructor, `seating.Overlaps`, `Allocate`, and `Fits` are sequentially composed.

None of these methods have side effects, which means that once `WillAccept` returns its Boolean value, you can forget about how it reached that result. It truly eliminates the irrelevant and amplifies the essential.

13.1.3 REFERENTIAL TRANSPARENCY

There's a remaining issue that Command Query Separation fails to address: predictability. While a Query has no side effects that your brain has to keep track of, it could still surprise you if you get a new return value every time you call it – even with the same input.

This may not be quite as bad as side effects, but it'll still tax your brain. What happens if we institute an extra rule on top of Command Query Separation? The rule that Queries must be deterministic?

This would mean that a Query can't rely on random number generators, GUID creation, the time of day, day of the month, or any other data from the environment. That would include the contents of files and databases. That sounds restrictive, so what's the benefit?

A *deterministic* method *without side effects* is *referentially transparent*. It's also known as a *pure function*. Such functions have some very desirable qualities.

One of these qualities is that pure functions readily compose. If the output of one function fits as the input for another, you can sequentially compose them. Always. There are deep mathematical reasons for that[3], but suffice it to say that composition is ingrained into the fabric that pure functions are made of.

Another quality is that you can replace a pure function call with its result. The function call is *equal* to the output. The only difference between the result and the function call is the time it takes to get it.

Think about that in terms of Robert C. Martin's definition of *abstraction*. Once a pure function returns, the result is all you have to care about. How the function arrived at the result is an implementation detail. Referentially transparent functions eliminate the irrelevant and amplify the essential. As

---

3. One perspective is offered by category theory, on which functional programming languages like Haskell draw heavily. For a great introduction for programmers, see Bartosz Milewski's *Category Theory for Programmers* [68].

figure 13.4 illustrates, they collapse arbitrary complexity to a single result; a single chunk that fits in your brain.

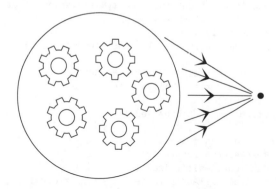

Figure 13.4 Pure function (left) collapsing to its result (right). Regardless of complexity, a referentially transparent function call can be replaced by its output. Thus, once you know what the output is, that's the only thing you need to keep track of as you read and interpret the calling code.

On the other hand, if you want to know how the function works, you zoom in on its implementation, in the spirit of fractal architecture. That might be the WillAccept method in listing 8.13. This method is, in fact, not just a Query, it's a pure function. When you look at the source code of that function, you've zoomed in on it, and the surrounding context is irrelevant. It operates exclusively on its input arguments and immutable class fields.

When you zoom out again, the entire function collapses into its result. It's the only thing your brain needs to keep track of.

What about all the nondeterministic behaviour and side effects? Where do they go?

Push all of that to the edge of the system; your Main method, your Controllers, your message handlers, et cetera. For example, consider listing 13.6 as a superior alternative to listing 13.1.

To be clear, the Post method itself isn't referentially transparent. It creates a new GUID (nondeterminism), queries the database (nondeterminism), gets the

Listing 13.6 Sequentially composed `Post` method. Contrast with listing 13.1.
(Restaurant/e9a5587/Restaurant.RestApi/ReservationsController.cs)

```
[HttpPost]
public async Task<ActionResult> Post(ReservationDto dto)
{
    if (dto is null)
        throw new ArgumentNullException(nameof(dto));

    var id = dto.ParseId() ?? Guid.NewGuid();
    Reservation? r = dto.Validate(id);
    if (r is null)
        return new BadRequestResult();

    var reservations = await Repository
        .ReadReservations(r.At)
        .ConfigureAwait(false);
    if (!MaitreD.WillAccept(DateTime.Now, reservations, r))
        return NoTables500InternalServerError();

    await Repository.Create(r).ConfigureAwait(false);

    return Reservation201Created(r);
}
```

current date and time (nondeterminism), and conditionally saves the reservation in the database (side effect).

Once it has collected all the data, it calls the pure `WillAccept` function. Only if `WillAccept` returns `true` does the `Post` method allow the side effect to happen.

Keep nondeterministic Queries and behaviour with side effects close to the edge of the system and write complex logic as pure functions. This style of programming is known as *functional core, imperative shell* [11], because programming with mostly pure functions is the realm of functional programming.

Do yourself a favour and learn functional programming[4]. It fits better in your head.

---

4. To learn functional programming I recommend that you try learning a proper functional programming language. Haskell is best, but the learning curve is steep. Find one that fits your preferences. Most of what you learn about functional programming you can carry back to improve your object-oriented code bases. The entire example code base for this book is written in the *functional core, imperative shell* style, even though it's written in the ostensibly object-oriented language C#.

13.2 CROSS-CUTTING CONCERNS

There's a set of concerns that tend to cut across disparate features. Not surprisingly, they're called *cross-cutting concerns*. They include [25]:

- Logging
- Performance monitoring
- Auditing
- Metering
- Instrumentation
- Caching
- Fault tolerance
- Security

You may not need all of these, but once you need one, that particular concern tends to apply to many features.

For example, if you find that you'll need to add a Circuit Breaker [73] to your web service calls, you probably need to do it everywhere you invoke that web service. Or, if you need to cache your database queries, you need to do that consistently.

In my experience, cross-cutting concerns have one thing in common: They're best implemented with the Decorator [39] design pattern. Let me show you an example.

13.2.1 LOGGING

Most of the items in the above list are variations on logging, in the sense that they involve writing data to some sort of log. Performance monitoring writes performance measurements to a performance log, auditing writes audit data to an audit trail, metering writes usage data to what will eventually become an invoice, and instrumentation writes debug information to a log.

You'll likely only need to implement a subset of the above cross-cutting concerns. Whether you need them depends on the requirements of the system.

You *should*, however, add a minimum of logging to your system. Your software will run into unforeseen circumstances when in use. It may crash or exhibit defects. In order to troubleshoot problems, you'll need to understand them. Logs give you invaluable insight into a running system.

As a minimum, you should make sure that all unhandled exceptions are logged. You may not need to take explicit action for that to happen. For example, ASP.NET automatically logs unhandled exceptions on both Windows and Microsoft Azure.

Keep an eye on the log. The ideal number of unhandled exceptions is zero. If you see an exception in the log, treat it as a defect. See section 12.2 for details.

While some defects are run-time crashes, others manifest as incorrect behaviour. The system keeps running while behaving incorrectly. You saw a few examples in section 12.2: The system allowed overbooking, and email address and name were swapped. You'll need more logs than just those unhandled exceptions to understand what's going on.

13.2.2 DECORATOR

The Decorator design pattern is also sometimes called *Russian dolls* after the traditional Russian matryoshka dolls that nest inside of each other, shown in figure 13.5.

Like the dolls, polymorphic objects can also nest inside each other. It's a great way to add unrelated functionality to an existing implementation. As an example, you'll see how to add logging to the database access interface in listing 13.7.

The code base already contains a class that implements the interface. It's called `SqlReservationsRepository`, and it performs the work of reading from and writing to the underlying SQL Server database. While you want to log what this class does, you should separate these concerns. Don't edit `SqlReservationsRepository` just to add logging. Add a Decorator. Listing 13.8 shows the class declaration and constructor. Notice that while it

Figure 13.5 Russian matryoshka dolls that can nest inside each other are often used as a metaphor for the Decorator design pattern.

Listing 13.7 Yet another version of the IReservationsRepository interface, this time with multi-tenant support. See for example listings 10.11 or 8.3 for other variations. *(Restaurant/3bfaa4b/Restaurant.RestApi/IReservationsRepository.cs)*

```
public interface IReservationsRepository
{
    Task Create(int restaurantId, Reservation reservation);

    Task<IReadOnlyCollection<Reservation>> ReadReservations(
        int restaurantId, DateTime min, DateTime max);

    Task<Reservation?> ReadReservation(Guid id);

    Task Update(Reservation reservation);

    Task Delete(Guid id);
}
```

implements the IReservationsRepository interface, it also wraps another IReservationsRepository object.

Since it implements the interface, it must implement all the methods. This is always possible, because it can trivially call the same method on Inner. Each method, however, gives the Decorator an opportunity to intercept the method call. As an example, listing 13.9 shows how it logs around the ReadReservation method.

Listing 13.8 The class declaration and constructor for the LoggingReservationsRepository Decorator. *(Restaurant/3bfaa4b/Restaurant.RestApi/LoggingReservationsRepository.cs)*

```
public sealed class LoggingReservationsRepository : IReservationsRepository
{
    public LoggingReservationsRepository(
        ILogger<LoggingReservationsRepository> logger,
        IReservationsRepository inner)
    {
        Logger = logger;
        Inner = inner;
    }

    public ILogger<LoggingReservationsRepository> Logger { get; }
    public IReservationsRepository Inner { get; }
```

Listing 13.9 The decorated ReadReservation method.
(Restaurant/3bfaa4b/Restaurant.RestApi/LoggingReservationsRepository.cs)

```
public async Task<Reservation?> ReadReservation(Guid id)
{
    var output = await Inner.ReadReservation(id).ConfigureAwait(false);
    Logger.LogInformation(
        "{method}(id: {id}) => {output}",
        nameof(ReadReservation),
        id,
        JsonSerializer.Serialize(output?.ToDto()));
    return output;
}
```

It first calls ReadReservation on the Inner implementation to get the output. Before returning the output it logs that the method was called, using the injected Logger. Listing 13.10 shows a typical log entry produced by that code.

The other methods of LoggingReservationsRepository work the same way. They call the Inner implementation, log the result, and return.

You have to configure ASP.NET's built-in Dependency Injection Container to use the Decorator around the 'real' implementation. Listing 13.11 shows how. Some Dependency Injection Containers natively know about the Decorator design pattern, but the built-in one doesn't. Fortunately, you can register services with a lambda expression to get around that limitation.

Listing 13.10 Example of a log entry produced by listing 13.9. The actual log entry is a single, wide line. I've edited it for readability by adding line breaks and a bit of indentation.

```
2020-11-12 16:48:29.441 +00:00 [Information]
Ploeh.Samples.Restaurants.RestApi.LoggingReservationsRepository:
ReadReservation(id: 55a1957b-f85e-41a0-9f1f-6b052f8dcafd) =>
{
  "Id":"55a1957bf85e41a09f1f6b052f8dcafd",
  "At":"2021-05-14T20:30:00.0000000",
  "Email":"elboughs@example.org",
  "Name":"Elle Burroughs",
  "Quantity":5
}
```

Listing 13.11 Configuring a Decorator with the ASP.NET framework. *(Restaurant/3bfaa4b/Restaurant.RestApi/Startup.cs)*

```
var connStr = Configuration.GetConnectionString("Restaurant");
services.AddSingleton<IReservationsRepository>(sp =>
{
    var logger =
        sp.GetService<ILogger<LoggingReservationsRepository>>();
    return new LoggingReservationsRepository(
        logger,
        new SqlReservationsRepository(connStr));
});
```

The example restaurant reservation system has other dependencies than `IReservationsRepository`. For example, it also sends emails, using an `IPostOffice` interface. To log these interactions, it uses a `LoggingPostOffice` Decorator equivalent to `LoggingReservationsRepository`.

You can address most cross-cutting concerns with Decorators. For caching you can implement a Decorator that first tries to read from a cache. Only if the value is not in the cache does it read the underlying data store, in which case it updates the cache before returning. This is known as a *read-through cache*.

When it comes to fault tolerance my previous book [25] contains a Circuit Breaker [73] example. It's also possible to address security concerns with Decorators, but most frameworks come with built-in security features, and it's better to use those. See subsection 15.2.5 for an example.

13.2.3 WHAT TO LOG

I once worked with a team that had found just the right amount of logging. We were developing and maintaining a suite of REST APIs. Each API would log details[5] of each HTTP request and the HTTP response it returned. It would also log all database interactions, including input arguments and the entire result set returned by the database.

I don't recall that there was a single defect that we couldn't track down and understand. It was just the right amount of logging.

Most development organisations log too much. Particularly when it comes to instrumentation, I often see examples of 'overlogging'. When logging is done to support future troubleshooting, you can't predict what you're going to need, so it's better to log too much data than too little. Or, at least, that's the rationale for 'overlogging'.

It'd be even better to log *only* what you need. Not too little, not too much, but just the right amount of logging. Obviously, we should call this *Goldilogs*.

How do you know what to log? How do you know that you've logged everything that you'll need, when you don't know your future needs?

The key is repeatability. Just like you should be able to reproduce builds and repeat deployments, you should also be able to reproduce execution.

If you can replay what happened when a problem manifested itself, you can troubleshoot it. You need to log just enough data to enable you to repeat execution. How do you identify that data?

Consider a line of code such as listing 13.12. Would you log that?

Listing 13.12 Would you log this statement?

```
int z = x + y;
```

---

5. Except sensitive information like JSON Web Tokens, which we redacted.

It might make sense to log what x and y are, particularly if these values are run-time values (e.g. entered by a user, the result of a web service call, etc.). You might do something like listing 13.13.

Listing 13.13 Logging input values might make sense.

```
Log.Debug($"Adding {x} and {y}.");
int z = x + y;
```

Would you ever log the result, though, as in listing 13.14?

Listing 13.14 Does it make sense to log the output of addition?

```
Log.Debug($"Adding {x} and {y}.");
int z = x + y;
Log.Debug($"Result of addition: {z}");
```

There's no reason to log the result of the calculation. Addition is a pure function; it's *deterministic*. If you know the inputs, you can always repeat the calculation to get the output. Two plus two is always four.

The more your code is composed from pure functions, the less you need to log [103]. This is one of the many reasons that referential transparency is so desirable, and why you should favour the *functional core, imperative shell* style of architecture.

> Log all impure actions, but no more.

Log everything that you can't reproduce. That includes all nondeterministic code such as getting the current date, time of day, generating a random number, reading from a file or database, et cetera. It also includes everything that has side effects. All else you don't need to log.

Of course, if your code base doesn't separate pure functions from impure actions, you'll have to log everything.

13.3 CONCLUSION

Separate unrelated concerns. Changes to the user interface shouldn't involve editing the database code, or vice versa.

Separation of concerns imply that you should separate – that is, decompose – the various parts of your code base. Decomposition is only valuable if you can recompose the disparate parts.

This sounds like a job for object-oriented design, but despite its original promise, it has turned out to be ill-suited to the task. While you *can* achieve object-oriented decomposition, you have to jump through various hoops to make it work. Most developers don't know how to do this, so instead tend to compose objects by nesting them.

When you do that, you tend to sweep important behaviour under the rug. That makes it harder to fit the code in your head.

Sequential composition, where pure functions return data that can be used as input for other pure functions, offers a saner alternative; one that does fit in your head.

While I don't expect organisations to throw their so-called object-oriented code bases overboard for Haskell, I do recommend moving towards *functional core, imperative shell*.

This makes it easier to isolate those parts of the code base that implement impure actions. These are typically also the parts where you need to apply cross-cutting concerns, which is best done with Decorators.

RHYTHM

I've visited and worked with many software development organisations. Some follow one process, and others a different one. Multiple organisations tell me that they follow a certain process, but what they actually do differs.

Some teams do daily stand-ups, except that they really only do them every other day when they feel like it.

I've worked in a team where we *did* do a daily stand-up every morning. One team member, however, always managed to centre the meeting around his desk, where he'd remain sitting. He was also the sort of person who'd completely disregard the *what-I-did-yesterday, what-I-am-going-to-do-today, any-blockers* format and instead ramble on for fifteen minutes while my feet hurt more and more from standing.

I've worked in a team with a nice Kanban board, except that they'd spend significant time firefighting. Those nice work items provided poor insight to the work that was actually being done.

One of the best teams I've worked with had almost no process. It didn't matter because they'd implemented Continuous Deployment. That team delivered features faster than stakeholders could absorb. Instead of the incessant *is-it-done-yet?* questions, team members would sometimes ask stakeholders if they had had time to admire the features they'd asked for. Most commonly, the answer was that they hadn't had time to do that.

I don't intend to tell you how to organise. Whether you follow Scrum, XP [5], PRINCE2, or daily chaos, I hope this book contains ideas that you can use. While I don't wish to dictate any particular software development process, I've come to realise that having a loose rhythm or structure to the day can be beneficial. This applies to how you work, personally, and how a team might work.

14.1 PERSONAL RHYTHM

Every day may be different, but I find it useful to have a loose structure as a default. No daily activity should be mandatory, because that only causes stress if you miss it one day, but structure can help you get something done.

Although my wife would probably tell you that I'm one of the most disciplined people she knows, I, too, tend to procrastinate. Having a rhythm to my day helps me minimise wasting my time.

14.1.1 TIME-BOXING

Work in time-boxed intervals, like 25 minutes. Then take a five-minute break. You probably know this as the Pomodoro technique, but it's not. The Pomodoro technique is more involved [18], and I find the extra activities irrelevant.

Working for 25 minutes, however, has some benefits. Some of these may seem obvious, but others are less evident.

In the obvious department, 25 minutes of uninterrupted work makes a big task seem more manageable. Even if a work item seems daunting or unappealing, it's easier to tell yourself that you 'can at least look at it for 25 minutes'. My experience is that the hardest part of most tasks is to get started.

Be sure to keep a countdown visible. You can use a physical kitchen timer, such as the one shown in figure 14.1, or a piece of software. I use a program that always shows the remaining number of minutes in the system tray[1] of my screen. The advantage of a visible countdown is that it counters the need to 'just' check Twitter, email, or similar. Whenever I get such an urge, I glance at the countdown and think to myself: "*Okay, I've 16 more minutes left of this time box. I can do that, and* then *I'll have a break.*"

Figure 14.1 You probably call it *the Pomodoro technique* when you work in 25-minute time boxes. It's probably not, but here's a pomodoro kitchen timer from which that technique takes its name.

Breaks offer a less obvious advantage. When you take a break, make it a proper break. Get out of your chair, walk around, leave the room. Do yourself the favour and get away from your computer. Subsection 12.1.3 already discussed this particular benefit. It's striking how often a change of scenery gives you a new perspective.

Even if you don't feel stuck, taking a break could make you realise that you've just wasted the last fifteen minutes. That doesn't sound nice, but I'd rather waste fifteen minutes than three hours.

More than once, I've been *in the zone* when the timer goes off. When everything just flows, having to stop and get away from the computer is almost

---

1. On Windows the system tray is usually placed on the lower right of the screen. It's also called the *notification area.*

painful. I've found, however, that if I do, I sometimes come back and realise that what I've just been doing *can never work*, because of some problem that'll manifest itself later.

Had I just stayed in the zone, I could have wasted hours instead of minutes.

Programmers love being in the zone because it *feels* so productive, but there's no guarantee that it is. It's not a contemplative state of mind. You may be writing many lines of code, but there's no guarantee they'll be useful.

The most curious aspect is this: If what you're doing in the zone actually *is* useful, a five-minute break doesn't matter. I've often found that even after a couple of minutes away from the computer, I can drop right back into the zone if I feel that I'm on the right track.

14.1.2 Take Breaks

I once developed a piece of open-source software that became moderately popular. It became popular enough that users started to suggest various features and capabilities that I hadn't originally planned for. The first version worked adequately, but I understood that I had to rewrite most of the code so that it would be more flexible.

The new design required much contemplation. Fortunately, at that time, I was working in a job where I had half an hour of commute each way. I did most of the design work for that new version biking[2] back and forth.

Being away from the computer is remarkably productive. I've had most of my good ideas doing something else. I regularly exercise, and many an insight has come to me while running, or in the shower, or doing the dishes. I recall many a Eureka! moment being on my feet. I don't recall having had a single revelation while in front of the computer.

---

2. Copenhagen is a bicycle city, and I bike if possible. It's faster and provides a bit of exercise. While sometimes lost in thought, I wasn't a danger to other people.

I think this happens because my System 1 [51] (or some other subconscious process) keeps churning away at a problem even when I'm not aware of it. That only works, though, if I've already spent time in front of the computer, working on the problem. You can't just lie on your sofa and expect a steady stream of enlightenment to flow through you. It's the alternation that seems to do the trick.

If you're working in an office setting, going for a walk may be difficult. Still, I think it may be more productive than sitting in front of the computer all day.

If possible, take breaks away from your computer. Do something else for twenty minutes or half an hour. Try to combine it with physical activity if you can. It doesn't have to be hard physical exercise; it could be just going for a walk. For example, if you have a grocery store nearby, you could go shopping. I do that every other day. Not only do I get a break in my work day, shopping is efficient because there's few other people when I go.

Keep in mind that intellectual work is different from physical work. You can't measure productivity by how long you work. In fact, the longer you work, the less productive you become. Long hours may even lead to negative productivity, because you'll make mistakes that you'll then have to waste time correcting. Don't work long hours.

14.1.3 Use Time Deliberately

Don't just let the day happen to you. I don't intend to turn this book into a personal productivity lecture. There are plenty of such books available already. At a minimum, though, I'll advise you to use your time deliberately. For inspiration, I'll tell you about some routines that work for me.

The Pragmatic Programmer suggests that you should learn a new programming language every year [50]. I'm not sure that I agree with that particular rule. Knowing more than one language is a good idea, but one every year seems excessive. There are other things to learn as well: test-driven development, algorithms, specific libraries or frameworks, design patterns, property-based testing, et cetera.

I don't try to learn a new language every year, but I do try to expand my knowledge. Unless I have appointments, I start my day with two 25-minute time boxes where I try to educate myself. These days, I usually read a textbook and do the exercises. Earlier in my career, I started each morning answering questions on Usenet[3] and later on Stack Overflow. You learn a lot by teaching. I've also done programming katas.

Another productivity tip is to limit the amount of meetings you go to. I once consulted a company that held meetings all the time. For a while, I held a central role, so I'd get many meeting requests.

I noticed that many of the meetings were actually requests for information. Stakeholders would hear that I'd been in a meeting without them, so they'd request one to learn what had been discussed. That's understandable, but inefficient, so I started to write things down.

When people would request a meeting with me, I'd ask them for an agenda. This was often enough to make them cancel the meeting. In other cases, once I saw the agenda, I'd send them what I'd already written down. They'd immediately get the information they needed, instead of waiting hours or days for a meeting. Meetings don't scale; documentation does.

14.1.4 TOUCH TYPE

In 2013 a conflict between the Danish teachers' union and their public employers erupted and schools closed for an indefinite time. The conflict lasted 25 days, but no one knew how long it'd be when it started.

My daughter was ten years old at the time. I didn't want her lounging around at home, so I put together a curriculum. One of the things I had her do was to follow an online touch-typing tutorial one hour a day. When the conflict was over she was touch-typing, and she's been typing like that since.

---

3. Yes, that was a long time ago!

When Covid-19 locked down the schools in 2020, my thirteen-year-old son got the same assignment. He, too, now touch-types. It takes a few weeks, one hour a day, to learn.

I've worked with programmers who can't touch type, and I've noticed how inefficient it makes them. Not because they don't type fast enough; after all, typing isn't the bottleneck in software development. You spend more time reading code than typing it, so productivity strongly correlates to code readability.

Still, it's not the typing speed, or lack thereof, which makes *hunt-and-peck typing* inefficient. The problem is that when you're always searching the keyboard for the next key to hit, you don't notice what's happening on the screen.

Modern IDEs come with many bells and whistles. They tell you when you make mistakes. I've been touch-typing since my single-digit years, but I'm not a particularly accurate typist. I use the delete key quite a bit.

While I tend to mistype when writing a text like this one, I make fewer typing mistakes when coding. This is because statement completion and other IDE features 'do the typing' for me.

I've seen programmers who are so busy hunting for the next key that they miss all the help that the IDE offers. Worse, if they mistype, they don't see the mistake until they try to compile or run the code. When they finally look at the screen, they're baffled that something doesn't work.

When I pair with such programmers, I've been looking at a typo for tens of seconds, so it's painfully clear to me what's wrong, but for the hunt-and-peck typist it's a new context, and it takes time to reorient.

Learn to touch type. IDE is an acronym for *Integrated Development Environment*, but for modern tools, perhaps *Interactive Development Environment* would be more descriptive. If, however, you don't look at it, little interaction can take place.

14.2 TEAM RHYTHM

When you work in a team, you'll have to align your personal rhythm with the team's. Most likely the team has recurring activities. You may do a daily stand-up, hold sprint retrospectives every other week, or go to lunch at a particular time of day.

As already stated, I'm not going to dictate any particular process, but there are some activities I think you should schedule. You could even make a checklist out of them.

14.2.1 REGULARLY UPDATE DEPENDENCIES

Code bases have dependencies. When you read from a database, you use an SDK for that particular brand of database. When you write a unit test, you use a unit testing framework. When you want to authenticate users with a JSON Web Token, you use a library for that.

Such dependencies typically come in packages, delivered via a package manager. .NET has NuGet, JavaScript has NPM, Ruby has RubyGems, and so on. That type of distribution means that packages may frequently be updated. A package author can easily do Continuous Deployment, so every time there's a bug fix or a new feature, you may get a new version of the package.

You don't have to update to the newest version *every* time one comes out. If you don't need the new feature, you can skip that version.

On the other hand, it's dangerous to fall too far behind. Some package authors are conscientious about breaking changes while others are more cavalier. The longer you wait between updates, the more breaking changes will pile up. It'll get harder and harder to move forward, and you could end up in a situation where you no longer dare upgrade the dependencies.

This goes for language and platform versions as well. Ultimately, you could be stuck on such an old version of your language that it becomes difficult to hire new employees. This happens.

The irony is that if you update regularly, it's painless. In the Git log of the example code repository, you can see that I've updated the dependencies once in a while. Listing 14.1 shows a excerpt of the log.

Listing 14.1 Git log excerpt showing package updates, plus a few surrounding commits for good measure.

```
0964099 (HEAD) Add a schedule link to each day
2295752 Rename test classes
fdf2a2f Update Microsoft.CodeAnalysis.FxCopAnalyzers NuGet
9e5d33a Update Microsoft.AspNetCore.Mvc.Testing NuGet pkg
f04e6eb Update coverlet.collector NuGet package
3bfc64f Update Microsoft.NET.Test.Sdk NuGet package
a2bebea Update System.Data.SqlClient NuGet package
34b818f Update xunit.runner.visualstudio NuGet package
ff5314f Add cache header on year calendar
df8652f Delete calendar flag
```

How often should you update dependencies? That depends on the number, and how stable those dependencies are. For the example code base, I felt that it was fine to check for updates every other month or so. A larger code base might have an order of magnitude more packages, and that alone could justify a more frequent schedule.

Another factor is how often particular dependencies change. Some only change rarely while others blow through revisions. You'll have to experiment to find the best frequency for your code base, but until you know what it is, pick an arbitrary rhythm. It might make sense to attach this work item to another regular activity. If, for example, you're using Scrum with two-week sprints, you could schedule the package update activity to be the first thing you do in a new sprint[4].

14.2.2 SCHEDULE OTHER THINGS

The reason you should schedule dependency updates is that this is something that's easy to forget. It doesn't make sense to check for updates every day, so it's unlikely to become part of anyone's work rhythm.

---

4. Don't make it the last thing in a sprint, because then it'll be sacrificed for something more urgent.

It's also the type of problem that once you start noticing it, it's too late. There are other problems that fall in that category.

Certificates[5] expire, but they typically have lifetimes measured in years. It's easy to forget to renew them, but if you forget it, the software will stop working. When that happens, perhaps none of the original developers are left on the team. It's better to proactively renew certificates, so schedule this activity.

The same goes for domain names. They expire after several years. Make sure someone renews them.

Another example is database backups. It's easy to automate backups, but do you know whether they work? Can you actually restore the system from a backup? Consider doing that as a regular exercise. It's a disappointment to discover that the backups don't work when you need them for real.

14.2.3 CONWAY'S LAW

I had my own office in the first job I had. This was in 1994 when open office landscapes weren't as common as they are today. I've never had my own office since then[6]. Employers have learned that open offices are less expensive, and agile processes like XP recommend sitting together [5].

To be clear, I don't like open office spaces. I find them noisy and distracting. On the other hand, I grant that face-to-face communication fosters cooperation. If you've ever tried having a written discussion in a chat forum, about a GitHub issue, or about a feature specification, you know that they can drag on for days or weeks. You can often resolve what looks like a conflict by *talking* to the other person for fifteen minutes.

Even if a technical discussion doesn't 'feel personal', there's something about face-to-face discussions that helps resolve misunderstandings.

---

5. X.509 certificates, for example.
6. This isn't entirely true; I've been self-employed for years, and when I'm not at a client, I work from home. I'm writing this book in my home office.

On the other hand, if you rely entirely on talking and sitting together, you risk instituting an oral culture. Nothing gets written down, you must have the same discussions over and over, and repeatedly answer the same questions. Knowledge is lost when people move on.

Consider this through the lens of Conway's law:

> *"Any organization that designs a system [...] will inevitably produce a design whose structure is a copy of the organization's communication structure."* [21]

If everybody sits together and can arbitrarily communicate with anyone else, the result could be a system with no discernable architecture, but plenty of ad hoc communication. Spaghetti code [15], in other words.

Consider how the way you organise the work impacts the code base.

While I dislike open offices and ad hoc chatter, I don't recommend the other extreme either. Rigid hierarchies and chains of command are hardly conducive to productivity. Personally, I like to organise work (even corporate work) the way open-source software is typically organised, with pull requests, reviews, and mostly written communication. I like this because it enables asynchronous software development [96].

You don't have to do it like that, but organise your team in a way that fosters both communication and the software architecture you prefer. The point is to be aware that team organisation and architecture are connected.

14.3 CONCLUSION

You can find plenty of books about personal productivity, so I wanted to avoid most of the topics that such books normally discuss. How you work is personal, and how a team is organised displays much variety.

I did, however, want to discuss a few things that have taken me many years to realise. Take breaks; get away from the computer. I get my best ideas when I'm doing something else. Perhaps so will you.

THE USUAL SUSPECTS

What about performance? What about security? Dependency analysis? Algorithms? Architecture? Computer science?

All of these subjects are relevant for software engineering. They're probably the topics that occur to you when you hear the term *software engineering*. They are the usual suspects. Until now, I've pretended that they don't exist. It's not because I consider them irrelevant, but because I find that comprehensive treatments already exist.

When I consult with development teams, I rarely find that I have to teach them about performance. Often, I encounter a team member who knows more about algorithms and computer science than I do. And it's not that hard to find someone who knows more about security than me.

I wrote this book because it's my experience that the topics it covers are the practices that I *do* need to teach. The book, I hope, fills a hole (the exclamation point in figure 15.1), even if it's just an amalgamation of wisdom I've picked up from pioneers who came before me.

Just because I wanted to focus on those other things, it doesn't mean that I've been ignoring the usual suspects. As the penultimate chapter, I want to discuss how I approach performance, security, and a few other things.

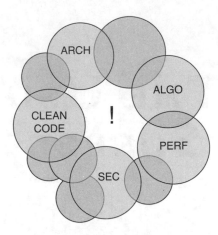

Figure 15.1 The usual suspects of software engineering: architecture, algorithms, performance, security, and the approach to code exemplified by such books as *Clean Code* [61] and *Code Complete* [65]. You can find great treatments of such topics elsewhere, but I felt that there was a knowledge gap without comprehensive treatment. This book is an attempt at filling that gap.

15.1 PERFORMANCE

I've noticed a common pattern when I introduce an idea that someone doesn't like. Sometimes, I can tell from their facial expressions that they're struggling to come up with a counter-argument to ward off the anathema. A little while goes by, and then it comes:

"But what about performance?"

Indeed, what about performance? I admit that the narrow focus on performance that some people exhibit annoys me, but I think I understand where it comes from. I think that it's part legacy, and part apotropaic deflection.

15.1.1 LEGACY

For decades, computers were slow. They could calculate faster than a person could, but compared to modern computers, they were glacial. At the time the industry started to organise itself into the academic discipline of computer science, performance was a ubiquitous concern. If you used inefficient algorithms it could make a program unusable.

No wonder that a typical computer science curriculum would include algorithms, computational complexity theory with its big O notation, and a focus on memory footprint. The problem is that this curriculum seems to have ossified.

Performance still matters to a degree, but modern computers are so fast that you often can't tell the difference. Does it matter that a particular method returns in 10 or 100 nanoseconds? Well, if you call it in a tight loop, it might, but often, it doesn't matter.

I've met plenty of developers who will waste hours shaving a few microseconds off a method call, only to then query a database with the result[1]. There's little reason to optimise an operation if you then combine it with another operation that's orders of magnitudes slower. If you must focus on performance, at least optimise the bottlenecks.

Performance should never be the primary centre of attention; *correctness* should. Gerald Weinberg tells a story "to drive home this point to those whose minds are tangled in questions of efficiency and other secondary matters" [115]. It involves a derailed software project and a programmer brought in to fix it. The software in question is hopelessly complicated, has tons of bugs, and is on the brink of being cancelled. Our hero comes up with a rewrite that works and presents it to the original developers.

The main developer of the original software asks how long it takes to run the program. When hearing the answer, he dismisses the new idea because the defective program runs ten times faster. To which our protagonist answers:

> *"But your program doesn't work. If the program doesn't have to work, I can write one that takes one millisecond per card[2]" [115]*

---

1. In case the folly of this is lost on the reader: querying a database typically takes time measured in milliseconds. To be fair, everything gets faster all the time, so this may not be true when you read this.
2. This was back in the days of punch cards.

Make it work first, and then you can think about performance. Maybe. Perhaps security is also more important. Perhaps you should ask other stakeholders how to prioritise.

And if it turns out that stakeholders prioritise performance, *measure!* Modern compilers are sophisticated; they may inline method calls, optimise poorly structured loops of yours, et cetera. The machine code that they generate may look nothing like you imagine it looks. Additionally, performance is highly sensitive to things such as what hardware you are using, what software you have installed, what other processes are doing, and a host of other factors [59]. You can't reason about performance. If you think it's important, measure.

15.1.2 LEGIBILITY

Another reason some people focus on performance is harder to explain. I think it has to do with legibility. I picked up this idea from a book on a completely different topic called *Seeing Like a State* [90].

It argues that some schemes are instituted to make the obscure intelligible. As an example, it explains how the introduction of cadastral maps (figure 15.2) was a solution to that sort of problem. Medieval villages were organised in an oral culture where only the locals knew who had rights to use which plot of land when. This made it impossible for kings to directly levy taxes. Only the local nobles had enough local knowledge to tax the peasants [90].

As feudalism yielded to centralised states, kings needed ways to bypass their dependency on local nobles. A cadastral map was a way to introduce legibility to an opaque world [90].

When you do that, however, much may be lost in translation. For instance, in medieval villages the right to use a plot of land might be tied to other criteria than just who you were. You could, for example, have the right to grow a crop on a particular plot of land *during* the growing season. After harvest, all land would be converted into commons, with no individual rights associated until next growing season. Cadastral maps couldn't capture such complicated 'business rules', so they instituted and codified simplified ownership. Those maps didn't record the current state of affairs. They changed reality.

Figure 15.2 Cadastral maps were introduced by sovereign kings to bypass their dependency on local nobles. They introduce legibility at the expense of detail. Be careful that you don't mistake the map for the terrain.

There's a lot of that going on in software development. Since it's so intangible, we try to introduce all sorts of measurements and processes in attempts to be able to grasp it. Once we've introduced such devices, they shape our perception. As the adage goes, to one holding a hammer the world looks like a nail.

To one holding a hammer the world looks like a nail.

I once consulted a company to help them on their way towards Continuous Deployment. After I'd worked some weeks with various developers, one of the managers took me aside and asked me:

"Which of my developers are good?"

He wasn't a 'technical' manager. He'd never programmed. He couldn't tell.

I found the question unethical, since those developers had trusted me while I sat with them; I didn't answer.

Managers have a hard time managing software development, because how do you measure something as intangible as that? They usually institute proxy measurements like hours worked. If you've ever been billed by the hour, you know how perverse those incentives are.

I think that for some people, the fixation on performance is really an attempt to come to grips with the intangible nature of their profession. Being measurable, performance becomes the cadastral map of software engineering. For some, the art inherent in software engineering is a source of great discomfort. Making it a question of performance makes it legible.

15.2 SECURITY

Software security is like insurance. You don't really want to pay for it, but if you don't, you'll be sorry that you didn't.

As with so many other aspects of software engineering, security is about finding an appropriate balance. There's no such thing as a completely secure system. Even if you put it on a computer disconnected from the Internet, surrounded by armed guards, someone might bribe, force, or hustle their way to it.

You'll have to work with other stakeholders to identify security threats and appropriate mitigations.

15.2.1 STRIDE

You can use STRIDE threat modelling [48] to identify potential security issues. It's a thought exercise or workshop where you think of as many relevant threats to your system as you can. To help you think of potential issues, you can use the STRIDE acronym as a kind of checklist.

- Spoofing. Attackers try to pose as someone they're not in order to gain unauthorised access to the system.

- Tampering. Attackers try to tamper with data, for example through SQL injection.

- Repudiation. Attackers deny that they've performed an action, such as receiving an item they've paid for.

- Information disclosure. Attackers can read data they shouldn't be able to read. Examples include man-in-the-middle attacks and SQL injection.

- Denial of service. Attackers attempt to make the system unavailable to its regular users.

- Elevation of privilege. Attackers attempt to gain more permissions than they have.

Threat modelling occupies a space that involves both programmers, IT professionals, and other stakeholders such as 'business owners'. Some issues are best dealt with in code, others in network configuration, and some you really can't do much about.

Denial of service, for example, can't be entirely prevented for an online system. When Microsoft developed the STRIDE model, much of their network-facing code was written in C and C++. These languages are vulnerable to buffer overflows [4], so you could often make systems crash or hang by sending them malevolent input.

While managed code such as C# and Java prevent many such issues, you can't guarantee that a distributed denial of service attack can't bring your system to its knees. You can try to provision enough capacity to deal with a spike in traffic, but if the attack is sufficiently massive, there's little you can do.

Different systems have varying threat profiles. A mobile phone app or desktop application is susceptible to different kinds of attacks than a web service.

Let's threat-model the restaurant reservation system. As you may recall, it's a REST API that enables clients to make and edit reservations. Additionally, a restaurant's maître d' can make a GET request against a resource to see the schedule for a day, including all reservations and who arrives when. The schedule includes the names and emails of guests.

I'm going to go through each of the STRIDE items as if it was a checklist, but I'm only going to do it informally to give you an idea of the thought process. You might want to consider a more systematic execution.

15.2.2 SPOOFING

Is the system vulnerable to spoofing? Yes, when you make a reservation, you can claim to be whoever you like. You can just give *Keanu Reeves* as the name, and the system will accept that. Is that a problem? It could be, but we'll probably have to ask restaurant owners if that would give them problems.

After all, the current implementation of the system doesn't make any decisions based on the name, so spoofing isn't going to change its behaviour.

15.2.3 TAMPERING

Is the system vulnerable to tampering? It has a table of reservations in a SQL Server database. Could someone edit this data without being authorised to do so?

There's more than one scenario to consider.

The REST API itself enables you to edit your reservation via PUT and DELETE HTTP requests. Just as you can make a new reservation without authenticating yourself, you can edit one if you have the resource address (i.e. the URL). Should we be concerned?

Yes and no. Each resource address uniquely identifies one reservation. One part of the resource address is the reservation ID, which is a GUID. There's no way for an attacker to guess a GUID, so this should give us some comfort[3]. On the other hand, when you make a new reservation, the response to the POST

---

3. If you think that this sounds like *security by obscurity* I can see why. It isn't, though. A GUID is as difficult to guess as any other 128-bit cryptographic key. After all, it's just a 128-bit number.

request includes a `Location` header with the resource address. A man in the middle would be able to intercept the response and see the address.

There's a simple mitigation of this threat: require HTTPS. A secure connection shouldn't be optional; it should be mandatory. This is a good example of the sort of mitigation that's better handled by an IT professional. It's typically a question of configuring the service appropriately, rather than code that you have to write.

Another tampering scenario to consider is direct database access. Would it be possible to gain direct access to the database? A substantial answer to this question is to secure the deployment of the database, or trust that a cloud-based database is sufficiently protected. Again, the competencies required point to IT professionals rather than programmers.

An attacker could also gain access to the database via SQL injection. The responsibility for mitigating such a threat falls squarely on programmers. The restaurant reservation code base uses named parameters as shown in listing 15.1. When using ADO.NET, this is the recommended mitigation against SQL injection.

Listing 15.1 Use of named SQL parameter `@id`.
(Restaurant/e89b0c2/Restaurant.RestApi/SqlReservationsRepository.cs)

```
public async Task Delete(Guid id)
{
    const string deleteSql = @"
        DELETE [dbo].[Reservations]
        WHERE [PublicId] = @id";

    using var conn = new SqlConnection(ConnectionString);
    using var cmd = new SqlCommand(deleteSql, conn);
    cmd.Parameters.AddWithValue("@id", id);

    await conn.OpenAsync().ConfigureAwait(false);
    await cmd.ExecuteNonQueryAsync().ConfigureAwait(false);
}
```

Since protection against SQL injection attacks is the responsibility of developers, make sure to look for it during code reviews and when pair programming.

15.2.4 REPUDIATION

Can users of the system deny that they performed an action? Yes, even worse, users can make reservations and subsequently never show up. This is a problem that plagues not only restaurants, but also doctors, hairdressers, and many other places where reservations are made.

Can we mitigate this threat? We could require users to authenticate and perhaps even use a digital signature to record an audit trail. We could also ask users to pay a reservation fee with a credit card. We should, however, ask the restaurant owners what they think.

Most restaurants might be concerned that such draconian measures would scare customers away. This is another example where security involves finding a good balance. You can make a system so secure that it no longer fulfils its purpose.

15.2.5 INFORMATION DISCLOSURE

Is the reservation system vulnerable to information disclosure? It doesn't store passwords, but it does store guests' email addresses, which we should consider as personally identifiable information. They shouldn't fall into the wrong hands.

We should also consider each reservation's resource address (URL) sensitive. If you have such an address, you can DELETE the resource. You could use that to gain access to a sold-out restaurant by deleting someone else's reservation.

How could an attacker gain access to such information? Perhaps with a man-in-the-middle attack, but we've already decided to use HTTPS, so feel safe in that regard. SQL injection could be another attack vector, but we've also already decided to address that concern. I think that we don't have to worry too much about that.

There is, however, one remaining concern. A restaurant's maître d' can make a GET request against a resource to see the schedule for a day, including all reservations and who arrives when. The schedule includes the names and emails of guests, so that the guests can identify themselves when they arrive. Listing 15.2 shows such an interaction with the mitigation already in place.

Listing 15.2 An example schedule GET request and its corresponding response. Compared to what the actual example system produces, I've simplified both the request and the response to highlight the important bits.

```
GET /restaurants/2112/schedule/2021/2/23 HTTP/1.1
Authorization: Bearer eyJhbGciOiJIUzI1NiIsInCI6IkpXVCJ9.eyJ...

HTTP/1.1 200 OK
Content-Type: application/json; charset=utf-8
{
  "name": "Nono",
  "year": 2021,
  "month": 2,
  "day": 23,
  "days": [{
    "date": "2021-02-23",
    "entries": [{
      "time": "19:45:00",
      "reservations": [{
        "id": "2c7ace4bbee94553950afd60a86c530c",
        "at": "2021-02-23T19:45:00.0000000",
        "email": "anarchi@example.net",
        "name": "Ann Archie",
        "quantity": 2
      }]
    }]
  }]
}
```

The mitigation is to require the maître d' to authenticate. I've chosen JSON Web Token as the authentication mechanism. If the client doesn't present a valid token with a valid role claim, it receives a 403 Forbidden response.

You can even write integration tests like the one in listing 15.3 to verify correct behaviour.

Only the *schedule* resource requires authentication, because it's the only one that contains sensitive information. While the restaurants don't wish to scare customers away by requesting that they authenticate, it's reasonable to demand of employees that they do.

Listing 15.3 Test that verifies if the client doesn't present a valid JSON Web Token with the "MaitreD" role claim, the API rejects the request with a `403 Forbidden` response. In this test, the only role claims are `"Foo"` and `"Bar"`. *(Restaurant/0e649c4/Restaurant.RestApi.Tests/ScheduleTests.cs)*

```
[Theory]
[InlineData(    1, "Hipgnosta")]
[InlineData( 2112, "Nono")]
[InlineData(90125, "The Vatican Cellar")]
public async Task GetScheduleWithoutRequiredRole(
    int restaurantId,
    string name)
{
    using var api = new SelfHostedApi();
    var token =
        new JwtTokenGenerator(new[] { restaurantId }, "Foo", "Bar")
            .GenerateJwtToken();
    var client = api.CreateClient().Authorize(token);

    var actual = await client.GetSchedule(name, 2021, 12, 6);

    Assert.Equal(HttpStatusCode.Forbidden, actual.StatusCode);
}
```

15.2.6 DENIAL OF SERVICE

Can an attacker transmit a stream of bytes to the REST API to make it crash? If they can, I think that the issue is out of our hands.

An API written in a high-level language like C#, Java, or JavaScript doesn't work by manipulating pointers. The sort of buffer overflow that makes a system crash can't happen with managed code. Or rather, if it does, it's not a bug in the user code; it'd be a defect in the platform. There's nothing we can do to mitigate that sort of threat, apart from keeping the production system up to date.

Would a distributed denial of service attack be a problem? It probably would. We should talk to our IT professionals and ask if there's something they can do.

We might also consider if we could make the system more resilient to unexpected high volumes of traffic. For some systems, that's probably a good idea. A kind of system closely related to a restaurant reservation system would be a system that sells concert tickets. A popular artist giving a stadium concert could easily swamp a system with thousands of requests per second when the tickets are released.

One way to make such a system resilient to load spikes is to architect it accordingly. You could, for example, put all potential writes on a durable queue while reads are based off materialised views. This suggest a CQRS-like architecture, which is beyond the scope of this book.

Such an architecture is more complex than handling writes as they happen. It'd be possible to architect the restaurant reservation system like that, but we (my pretend stakeholders and I) decided that it didn't present a good return on investment.

In threat modelling, it's okay to identify a threat only to decide not to address it. Ultimately, it's a business decision. Just make sure that the rest of your organisation understands the risks.

15.2.7 ELEVATION OF PRIVILEGE

Would it be possible for an attacker to somehow start out as a regular user, but then through some clever trick give him- or herself administrator rights?

Once more, SQL injection is a common vulnerability also in this category. If attackers can execute arbitrary SQL commands on the database, they can also spawn external processes on the operating system[4].

An effective remedy is to run the database and all other services with as restricted permissions as possible. Don't run the database as administrator.

Since we've already decided to be aware of SQL injection attacks when we write code, I'm not so concerned about this kind of threat.

---

4. On SQL Server, for example, you can run the xp_cmdshell stored procedure. Starting with SQL Server 2005, however, it's disabled by default. Don't enable it.

This concludes the STRIDE threat model example for the restaurant reservation system.

Clearly, there's much more to security engineering than this, but as someone who's not a professional security expert, that's how I tend to approach it. If during threat modelling I identify an issue I'm not sure how to tackle, I have a friend I can call.

15.3   OTHER TECHNIQUES

Performance and security are perhaps the two largest aspects of 'traditional' software engineering, but there are oodles of other practices to consider. The topics I've chosen to present are based on my experience. These are the issues that tend to come up when I consult teams. By omitting other topics, I don't mean to imply that they aren't important.

Other practices you may find useful include canary releases and A/B testing [49], fault tolerance and resiliency [73], dependency analysis, leadership, distributed systems algorithms [55], architecture, finite state machines, design patterns [39][33][66][46], Continuous Delivery [49], the SOLID principles [60], and many other topics. Not only is the field vast; it keeps growing.

I do, however, want to briefly discuss two other practices.

15.3.1   PROPERTY-BASED TESTING

Programmers new to automated testing often struggle coming up with test values. One reason may be that sometimes certain values have to be included in the test, even if they have no bearing on the test case. As an example, consider listing 15.4, which verifies that the `Reservation` constructor throws an `ArgumentOutOfRangeException` if the supplied quantity isn't a natural number.

This parametrised test uses the values `0` and `-1` as examples of invalid quantities. `0` is a boundary value [66], so should be included, but the exact negative number is irrelevant. `-42` would have been just as useful as `-1`.

Listing 15.4 A parametrised test that verifies that the `Reservation` constructor throws an `ArgumentOutOfRangeException` on an invalid quantity.
(Restaurant/812b148/Restaurant.RestApi.Tests/ReservationTests.cs)

```
[Theory]
[InlineData( 0)]
[InlineData(-1)]
public void QuantityMustBePositive(int invalidQuantity)
{
    Assert.Throws<ArgumentOutOfRangeException>(
        () => new Reservation(
            Guid.NewGuid(),
            new DateTime(2024, 8, 19, 11, 30, 0),
            new Email("vandal@example.com"),
            new Name("Ann da Lucia"),
            invalidQuantity));
}
```

Why should you have to bother coming up with numbers when any negative number would do? What if there was a framework that could produce arbitrary negative numbers?

There are several such reusable software packages. This is the foundational idea behind *property-based testing*[5]. In the following, I'll use a library called *FsCheck*, but others exist[6]. FsCheck integrates with both xUnit.net and NUnit so that you can easily integrate your property-based tests with more 'traditional' tests. This also makes it easier to refactor existing tests to property-based tests, as listing 15.5 implies.

The `[Property]` attribute marks the method as a property-based test driven by FsCheck. It looks like a parametrised test, but all method arguments are now generated by FsCheck instead of being supplied by `[InlineData]` attributes.

The values are randomly generated, usually skewed towards 'typical' boundary values like *0, 1, -1*, and so on. By default, each property runs a

---

5. The term *property* here means 'trait', 'quality', or 'attribute'. Thus, property-based testing involves testing a property of the System Under Test, for example that the `Reservation` constructor throws an exception for all nonpositive quantities. In this context, *property* has nothing to do with C# or Visual Basic properties (getter or setter methods).

6. The original property-based testing library is the Haskell QuickCheck package. It was first released in 1999 and is still an active project. A plethora of ports exist, for many languages.

Listing 15.5 The test from listing 15.4 refactored to a property-based test.
(Restaurant/05e64f5/Restaurant.RestApi.Tests/ReservationTests.cs)

```
[Property]
public void QuantityMustBePositive(NonNegativeInt i)
{
    var invalidQuantity = -i?.Item ?? 0;
    Assert.Throws<ArgumentOutOfRangeException>(
        () => new Reservation(
            Guid.NewGuid(),
            new DateTime(2024, 8, 19, 11, 30, 0),
            new Email("vandal@example.com"),
            new Name("Ann da Lucia"),
            invalidQuantity));
}
```

hundred times. Think of it as 100 `[InlineData]` attributes adorning a single test, but each of the values randomly regenerated each time it executes.

FsCheck comes with some built-in wrapper types, such as `PositiveInt`, `NonNegativeInt`, and `NegativeInt`. These are just wrappers around integers, but come with the guarantee that FsCheck will only generate values that fit the description: only non-negative integers[7] for `NonNegativeInt`, and so on.

For the `QuantityMustBePositive` test, we really need arbitrary non-positive integers, but such a wrapper type doesn't exist. One way to produce values in the desired range, though, is to ask FsCheck to produce `NonNegativeInt` values and then negate them.

The `Item` property[8] returns the integer wrapped inside the `NonNegativeInt` value. One of the static language analysers I've turned on points out that the `i` parameter could be null. All those question marks is the C# way of dealing with possible null references, terminating in the fallback value `0`. I mostly consider it noise. The important operation is the unary minus operator in front of `i`. It inverts the non-negative integer to a non-positive integer.

---

7. That is, numbers greater than *or equal* to zero.
8. Here, a C# property; not a property-based testing property. Indeed, the overloaded terminology can be confusing.

Once you realise that you can let a library like FsCheck produce arbitrary test values, you may start to look at other test data in a new light. How about that `Guid.NewGuid()`? Couldn't you let FsCheck produce that value instead?

Indeed, as listing 15.6 shows, you can.

Listing 15.6 The property from listing 15.5 refactored to let FsCheck also produce the reservation ID. *(Restaurant/87fefaa/Restaurant.RestApi.Tests/ReservationTests.cs)*

```
[Property]
public void QuantityMustBePositive(Guid id, NonNegativeInt i)
{
    var invalidQuantity = -i?.Item ?? 0;
    Assert.Throws<ArgumentOutOfRangeException>(
        () => new Reservation(
            id,
            new DateTime(2024, 8, 19, 11, 30, 0),
            new Email("vandal@example.com"),
            new Name("Ann da Lucia"),
            invalidQuantity));
}
```

In fact, none of the hard-coded values have any impact on the outcome on the test. Instead of `"vandal@example.com"`, you could use any string for the email. Instead of `"Ann da Lucia"`, you could use any string for the name. FsCheck will happily produce such values for you, as shown in listing 15.7.

Listing 15.7 The property from listing 15.6 refactored to let FsCheck produce all parameters. *(Restaurant/af31e63/Restaurant.RestApi.Tests/ReservationTests.cs)*

```
[Property]
public void QuantityMustBePositive(
    Guid id,
    DateTime at,
    Email email,
    Name name,
    NonNegativeInt i)
{
    var invalidQuantity = -i?.Item ?? 0;
    Assert.Throws<ArgumentOutOfRangeException>(
        () => new Reservation(id, at, email, name, invalidQuantity));
}
```

You can take this concept surprisingly far. Sooner or later, you run into special requirements for input data that you can't just model with one of the built-in wrapper types like NonNegativeInt. A good property-based testing library like FsCheck has an API for such situations.

In fact, I often find that I have a harder time coming up with comprehensive test cases than I have describing the general properties of a System Under Test. This happened twice while I was developing the example restaurant system.

For the complex logic supporting the maître d's view of a day's schedule, I struggled to come up with specific test cases. When I realised the situation, I switched to defining the behaviour with a sequence of more and more specific properties[9]. Listing 15.8 shows the core of it.

Listing 15.8 Core implementation of an advanced property-based test. This test method is configured and called by the code in listing 15.9.
(Restaurant/af31e63/Restaurant.RestApi.Tests/MaitreDScheduleTests.cs)

```
private static void ScheduleImp(
    MaitreD sut,
    Reservation[] reservations)
{
    var actual = sut.Schedule(reservations);

    Assert.Equal(
        reservations.Select(r => r.At).Distinct().Count(),
        actual.Count());
    Assert.Equal(
        actual.Select(ts => ts.At).OrderBy(d => d),
        actual.Select(ts => ts.At));
    Assert.All(actual, ts => AssertTables(sut.Tables, ts.Tables));
    Assert.All(
        actual,
        ts => AssertRelevance(reservations, sut.SeatingDuration, ts));
}
```

This is actually the 'implementation' of the test. It receives a MaitreD argument and an array of reservations so that it can invoke the Schedule method.

---

9. You can see the progression of commits, as well as the final result, in the Git repository that accompanies the book. I consider this code example too specific to warrant a step-by-step walk through here, but I've described the example in details in a blog post [108].

There's another method that uses FsCheck's API to properly configure the sut and `reservation` arguments and call `ScheduleImp`. That's the test method that the unit testing framework actually runs. You can see it in listing 15.9.

Listing 15.9 Configuration and execution of the core property shown in listing 15.8. *(Restaurant/af31e63/Restaurant.RestApi.Tests/MaitreDScheduleTests.cs)*

```
[Property]
public Property Schedule()
{
    return Prop.ForAll(
        (from rs in Gens.Reservations
         from  m in Gens.MaitreD(rs)
         select (m, rs)).ToArbitrary(),
        t => ScheduleImp(t.m, t.rs));
}
```

This property uses advanced features of FsCheck, which are beyond the scope of this book. If you're not familiar with the FsCheck API, the details will make little sense to you. That's okay. I didn't show the code to teach you FsCheck. I included it to demonstrate that there's a wider world of software engineering than what's covered in this book.

15.3.2 BEHAVIOURAL CODE ANALYSIS

In this book, I've mostly taken a close look at code. You can, and should, consider the impact and cost of each line of code. This doesn't imply, though, that a bigger picture is irrelevant. In subsection 7.2.6 about fractal architecture, I also discussed the importance of the bigger picture.

That, still, is a static view of a code base. When you look at code, even high-level code, you see it as it currently is. On the other hand, you have a version control system. You can analyse it for additional insights. Which files change most frequently? Which files tend to change together? Do certain developers work only with certain files?

Analysis of version control data began as an academic discipline [44], but with two books [111][112] Adam Tornhill has done much work to make this practical. You could make behavioural code analysis part of your Continuous Delivery pipeline.

Behavioural code analysis extracts information from Git to identify patterns and problems that may only be visible over time. Even if a file may have low cyclomatic complexity and modest size, it could be problematic for other reasons. It could, for example, be coupled to other files that are more complex.

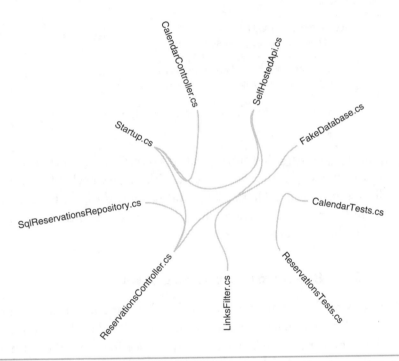

Figure 15.3 Change coupling map. The files linked by a line are the files that tend to change together. There are more files in the code base being analysed, but only those that change together above a certain threshold are included in the diagram.

Some coupling you can identify with dependency analysis, but other kinds of coupling can be harder to find. This is particularly the case with copy-and-paste code. By analysing which files, and which parts of the files, that change together, you can uncover dependencies that might otherwise have been invisible [112]. Figure 15.3 shows a change coupling map that highlights which files most often change together.

You can dive into such a change coupling map to see an 'X-ray' of a single file [112]. Which methods cause the most problems?

With the right tools, you can also produce maps of hotspots in your code, as shown in figure 15.4. Such interactive *enclosure diagrams* present each file as a circle. The size of each circle indicates its size or complexity, while the colour indicates change frequency. The more commits that contain the file, the more intense the colour [112].

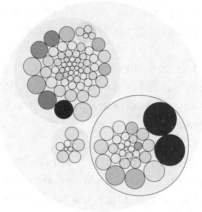

Figure 15.4 Hotspot enclosure diagram. The larger the circle, the more complex the file. The more intense the colour, the more frequently it changes. I find it suggestive that these diagrams tend to look like bacteria growths in a petri dish.

You can use behavioural code analysis as an active software engineering tool. Not only can you produce compelling diagrams, you can also quantify change coupling and hotspots in such a way that you can use the numbers as thresholds for further investigation.

Keep the discussion in subsection 7.1.1 in mind. Numerical thresholds are useful when they help direct your attention in a productive direction. Don't let thresholds become law.

You may want to keep an eye on trends as well. Trends are also actionable, and if you aren't starting with a greenfield code base, your numbers may not look good, but at least, you can immediately start to improve a trend.

If you're part of a larger team, you can also use behavioural code analysis to identify knowledge distribution and team coupling. A variant of the hotspot enclosure diagram is a knowledge map that shows the 'main author' of each file in different colours. This approaches a real quantification of a team's bus factor.

15.4 CONCLUSION

When you hear the term *software engineering*, you most likely think of 'classic' practices and disciplines such as performance and security engineering, formal code reviews, complexity analysis, formal processes, and so on.

Software engineering is all of those things, as well as the practices and heuristics I've presented in this book. Other books [48][55] discuss these more 'traditional' notions of software engineering, which is the reason I've given them cursory treatment.

Clearly, performance is important, but it's hardly the most important attribute of software. That the software works correctly is more important than whether it performs well. Once you've developed software that works as it's supposed to work, you may consider performance. Keep in mind, however, that you have finite resources.

What is most important? That the software performs better, or that it's secure? Is it more important that the code base is in a state that can support the organisation in years to come, or that it runs marginally faster?

As a programmer, you may have an opinion about this, but these are questions that should involve other stakeholders.

TOUR

I hope that if you follow the practices presented in this book, you'll have a better chance of producing code that fits in your head; code that will sustain your organisation. What does such a code base look like?

In this last chapter, I'll take you on a tour of the example code base that accompanies the book. I'll point out some highlights that I feel are particularly compelling.

16.1 NAVIGATION

You didn't write the code, so how should you find your way in it? That depends on your motivation for looking at it. If you're a maintenance programmer and you've been asked to fix a defect with an attached stack trace, you may immediately go to the top frame in the trace.

On the other hand, if you have no immediate goal and you just want to get a sense for the application, it'd be most natural to start at the program's entry point. In a .NET code base, that's the `Main` method.

In general, I find it reasonable to assume that a code reader will be familiar with the basic workings of the language, platform, and framework in use.

To be clear, I don't assume that *you*, the reader of this book, is familiar with .NET or ASP.NET, but when I program, I expect a team member to know the ground rules. For example, I expect that a team member knows the special significance of the Main method in .NET.

Listing 16.1 shows the Main method that meets you in the code base. It hasn't changed since listing 2.4.

Listing 16.1 Entry point for the restaurant reservation system. This listing is identical to listing 2.4. *(Restaurant/af31e63/Restaurant.RestApi/Program.cs)*

```
public static class Program
{
    public static void Main(string[] args)
    {
        CreateHostBuilder(args).Build().Run();
    }

    public static IHostBuilder CreateHostBuilder(string[] args) =>
        Host.CreateDefaultBuilder(args)
            .ConfigureWebHostDefaults(webBuilder =>
            {
                webBuilder.UseStartup<Startup>();
            });
}
```

In ASP.NET Core code bases, the Main method is a piece of boiler plate that rarely changes. Since I expect other programmers who are going to work with this code base to know the basics of the framework, I find it best to keep code as unsurprising as possible. On the other hand, there's little informational content in listing 16.1.

Developers with a glancing knowledge of ASP.NET will know that the webBuilder.UseStartup<Startup>() statement identifies the Startup class as the place where the real action is. That's where you should go look to understand the code base.

16.1.1 SEEING THE BIG PICTURE

Use your IDE to navigate to the Startup class. Listing 16.2 show the class declaration and constructor. It uses Constructor Injection [25] to receive an

IConfiguration object from the ASP.NET framework. This is the conventional way to do things and should be familiar to anyone with experience with the framework. While unsurprising, little information is so far gained.

By convention, the Startup class should define two methods: Configure and ConfigureServices. These follow immediately after listing 16.2. Listing 16.3 shows the Configure method.

Listing 16.2 Startup declaration and constructor. Listing 16.3 follows immediately after. *(Restaurant/af31e63/Restaurant.RestApi/Startup.cs)*

```
public sealed class Startup
{
    public IConfiguration Configuration { get; }

    public Startup(IConfiguration configuration)
    {
        Configuration = configuration;
    }
```

Listing 16.3 Configure method on the Startup class declared in listing 16.2. *(Restaurant/af31e63/Restaurant.RestApi/Startup.cs)*

```
public static void Configure(
    IApplicationBuilder app,
    IWebHostEnvironment env)
{
    if (env.IsDevelopment())
        app.UseDeveloperExceptionPage();

    app.UseAuthentication();
    app.UseRouting();
    app.UseAuthorization();
    app.UseEndpoints(endpoints => { endpoints.MapControllers(); });
}
```

Here we learn that the system uses authentication, routing, authorisation, and the framework's default implementation of the Model View Controller [33] (MVC) pattern. The abstraction level is high, but the code fits in your head; the cyclomatic complexity is 2, there are only 3 activated objects, and 12 lines of code. Figure 16.1 shows one way to plot it to a hex flower diagram. This illustrates how the code fits into the conceptual model of fractal architecture.

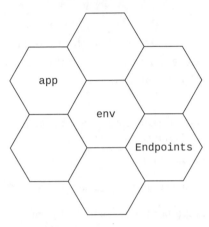

Figure 16.1 Hex flower diagram of the `Configure` method in listing 16.3. There's more than one way to fill out a hex flower. The examples in chapter 7 fill each cell with a branch according to cyclomatic complexity analysis. This one instead fills each cell with an activated object.

This is essentially just a laundry list. All the methods invoked in listing 16.3 are framework methods. The `Configure` method's sole purpose is to enable those particular built-in features. Reading it, you know a little about what to expect from the code. For example, you should expect each HTTP request to be handled by a method on a Controller class.

Perhaps there's more information to be gathered from the `ConfigureServices` method in listing 16.4?

There's a bit more information here, but it's still at a high level of abstraction. It also fits in your head: the cyclomatic complexity is *1*, there are 6 activated objects (`services`, `urlSigningKey`, a new `UrlIntegrityFilter` object, two variables both called `opts`, and the object's `Configuration` property), and 21 lines of code. Again, you can plot the method to a hex flower diagram like figure 16.2 to illustrate how the method fits the concept of fractal architecture. As long as you can map each chunk of a method into a cell in a hex flower diagram, the code is likely to fit in your head.

Listing 16.4 ConfigureServices method on the Startup class declared in listing 16.2. *(Restaurant/af31e63/Restaurant.RestApi/Startup.cs)*

```
public void ConfigureServices(IServiceCollection services)
{
    var urlSigningKey = Encoding.ASCII.GetBytes(
        Configuration.GetValue<string>("UrlSigningKey"));

    services
        .AddControllers(opts =>
        {
            opts.Filters.Add<LinksFilter>();
            opts.Filters.Add(new UrlIntegrityFilter(urlSigningKey));
        })
        .AddJsonOptions(opts =>
            opts.JsonSerializerOptions.IgnoreNullValues = true);

    ConfigureUrSigning(services, urlSigningKey);
    ConfigureAuthorization(services);
    ConfigureRepository(services);
    ConfigureRestaurants(services);
    ConfigureClock(services);
    ConfigurePostOffice(services);
}
```

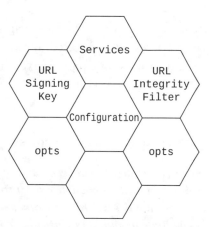

Figure 16.2 Hex flower diagram of the ConfigureServices method in listing 16.4. Like figure 16.1 this diagram fills each cell with an activated object.

There are few details in the method; it works more like a table of contents for the code base. Would you like to know about authorisation? Navigate to the `ConfigureAuthorization` method to learn more. Would you like to investigate the code base's data access implementation? Navigate to the `ConfigureRepository` method.

When you navigate to learn more, you zoom in on that detail. This is an example of the fractal architecture discussed in subsection 7.2.6. At each level, the code fits in your head. When you zoom in on a detail, the higher level shouldn't be required to understand the code at the new level.

Before we zoom in on a detail, I'd like to discuss how to navigate a code base.

16.1.2 FILE ORGANISATION

A question that I frequently get is how to organise the files in a code base. Should you create a subdirectory for Controllers, another for Models, one for Filters, and so on? Or should you create a subdirectory for each feature?

Few people like my answer: *Just put all files in one directory*. Be wary of creating subdirectories just for the sake of 'organising' the code.

File systems are *hierarchies*; they are trees: a specialised kind of acyclic graph in which any two vertices are connected by exactly one path. Put another way, each vertex can have at most one parent. Even more bluntly: If you put a file in a hypothetical `Controllers` directory, you can't *also* put it in a `Calendar` directory.

As an analysis of the Firefox code base notes:

> *"the system architects realized there were multiple ways in which the system could be sliced-and-diced, indicating possible crosscutting concerns, and that choosing one separation into modules would cause other cohesive parts of the system to be split up across multiple modules. In particular, choosing to divide the* browser *and* toolkit *components of Firefox has caused the* places *and* themes *components to become split."* [110]

This is the problem with hierarchies. Any attempt at organisation automatically excludes all other ways to organise things. You have the same problem with inheritance hierarchies in single-inheritance languages such as C# and Java. If you decide to derive from one base class, you've excluded all other classes as potential bases.

"Favor object composition over class inheritance." [39]

Just as you should avoid inheritance, you should eschew the use of directory structure to organise the code.

As with all advice, exceptions do exist. Consider the sample code base. The `Restaurant.RestApi` directory contains 65 code files: Controllers, Data Transfer Objects, Domain Models, filters, SQL scripts, interfaces, Adapters, et cetera. These files implement various features such as reservations and the calendar, as well as cross-cutting concerns such as logging.

The only exception to the rule is a subdirectory called `Options`. Its four files exist only to bridge the gap from JSON-based configuration files to code. The classes in these files are specialised to adapt to the ASP.NET *options* system. They're Data Transfer Objects and exist only for that singular purpose. I feel quite confident that they shouldn't be used for any other purpose, so I decided to put them out of sight.

When I tell people that organising code files in elaborate hierarchies is a bad idea, they incredulously counter: *How will we find files?*

Use your IDE. It has navigation features. When, earlier, I wrote that you should use your IDE to navigate to the `Startup` class, I didn't mean *'locate the* `Startup.cs` *file in the* `Restaurant.RestApi` *directory and open it.'*

I meant, *use your IDE to go to the definition of a symbol.* In Visual Studio, for example, this command is called *Go To Definition* and by default bound to F12. Other commands enable you to go to implementations of interfaces, find all references, or search for a symbol.

Your editor has *tabs*, and you can switch between them using standard keyboard shortcuts[1].

---

1. On Windows, that would be Ctrl + Tab.

I've mob-programmed with developers to teach them test-driven development. We'd be looking at a test, and I'd say something like *"Okay, could we switch to the System Under Test, please?"*

The driver would then think about the name of that class, go to the file view, scroll through it to find the file, and double-click to open it.

All the while, the file was open in another tab. We worked with it three minutes ago, and it was just a keyboard shortcut away.

As an exercise, hide your IDE's file view. Learn to navigate code bases using the rich code integration offered by the IDE.

16.1.3 FINDING DETAILS

A method like listing 16.4 gives you the big picture, but sometimes you need to see implementation details. If, for example, you want to learn how data access works, you should navigate to the `ConfigureRepository` method in listing 16.5.

Listing 16.5 `ConfigureRepository` method. Here you can learn how the data access components are composed. *(Restaurant/af31e63/Restaurant.RestApi/Startup.cs)*

```
private void ConfigureRepository(IServiceCollection services)
{
    var connStr = Configuration.GetConnectionString("Restaurant");
    services.AddSingleton<IReservationsRepository>(sp =>
    {
        var logger =
            sp.GetService<ILogger<LoggingReservationsRepository>>();
        var postOffice = sp.GetService<IPostOffice>();
        return new EmailingReservationsRepository(
            postOffice,
            new LoggingReservationsRepository(
                logger,
                new SqlReservationsRepository(connStr)));
    });
}
```

From the `ConfigureRepository` method you can learn that it registers an `IReservationsRepository` instance with the built-in Dependency

Injection Container. Again, the code fits in your head: the cyclomatic complexity is *1*, it activates 6 objects, and there are 15 lines of code. Figure 16.3 shows a possible hex flower mapping.

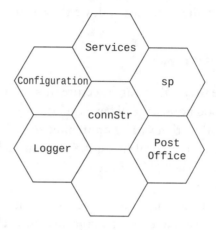

Figure 16.3 Hex flower diagram of the `ConfigureRepository` method in listing 16.5. Like figure 16.1 this diagram fills each cell with an activated object.

Since you've zoomed in on a detail, the surrounding context shouldn't matter. What you need to keep track of in your head is the `services` parameter, the `Configuration` property, and the variables that the method creates.

You can learn a few things from this code:

- If you want to edit the application's connection string you should use the standard ASP.NET configuration system.
- The `IReservationsRepository` service is actually a three-levels-deep Decorator that also involves logging and emailing.
- The innermost implementation is the `SqlReservationsRepository` class.

Depending on what interests you, you can navigate to the relevant type. If you want to know more about the `IPostOffice` interface, you can *Go To Definition* or *Go To Implementation*. If you want to look at `SqlReservationsRepository`, navigate to it. When you do that, you zoom in on an even deeper level of detail.

You can find code listings from `SqlReservationsRepository` throughout the book, for example listings 4.19, 12.2, and 15.1. They all fit in your brain as already discussed.

All the code in the code base follows these principles.

16.2 ARCHITECTURE

I've had little to say about architecture. It's not that I consider it unimportant, but again, good books already exist on the topic. Most of the practices I've presented work with a variety of architectures: layered [33]; monolithic; ports and adapters [19]; vertical slices; the actor model; micro-services; functional core, imperative shell [11]; et cetera.

Clearly, software architecture impacts how you organise code, so it's hardly irrelevant. You should explicitly consider the architecture for each code base you work in. There's no one-size-fits-all architecture, so you shouldn't consider any of the following as gospel. It's a description of a single architecture that works well for the task at hand. It's not suitable for all situations.

16.2.1 MONOLITH

If you've looked at the book's sample code base, you may have noticed that it looks disconcertingly monolithic. If you consider the full code base that includes the integration tests, as figure 16.4 illustrates, there are all of three packages[2]. Of those, only one is production code.

The entire production code compiles to a single executable file. That includes the database access, HTTP specifics, Domain Model, logging, email functionality, authentication, and authorisation. All in one package? Isn't that a monolith?

In a sense, you could argue that it is. From a deployment perspective, for example, you can't separate the various parts to put them on different

---

2. In Visual Studio these are called *projects*.

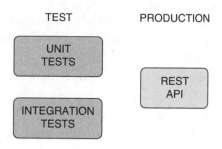

Figure 16.4 The packages that make up the sample code base. With only a single production package, it reeks of a monolith.

machines. For the purposes of this sample application, I decided that this wasn't a 'business' goal.

You also can't reuse parts of the code in new ways. What if we wanted to reuse the Domain Model to run a scheduled batch job? If you tried to do that, you would find that the HTTP-specific code would tag along, as would the email functionality.

That, however, is only an artefact of how I chose to package the code. One package is simpler than, say, four.

Internally in that single package, I've applied the *functional core, imperative shell* [11] architecture, which tends to lead towards a ports-and-adapters-style architecture [102].

I'm not that worried whether it'd be possible to separate that code base into multiple packages, should it become necessary.

16.2.2 Cycles

Monoliths tend to have a bad reputation because they so easily devolve into spaghetti code. A major reason is that inside a single package, all code can easily[3] call all other code.

---

3. To be fair, in a language like C#, you can use the `private` access modifier to prevent other classes from calling a method. That's not much of a barrier to a developer in a hurry: Just change the access modifier to `internal` and move on.

This often leads to one piece of code that depends on another part, that again depends on the first. An example I often see is illustrated by figure 16.5: data access interfaces that return or take as parameters objects defined by an object-relational mapper. The interface may be defined as part of the code base's Domain Model, so the implementation is coupled to that. So far, so good, but the interface is defined in terms of the object-relational mapper classes, so the abstraction also depends on implementation details. This violates the Dependency Inversion Principle [60] and leads to coupling.

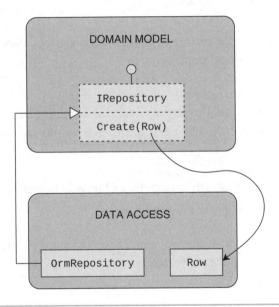

Figure 16.5 A typical data access cycle. The Domain Model defines a data access interface, here called IRepository. Members are defined with return types or parameters taken from the data access layer. For example, the Row class could be defined by an object-relational mapper (ORM). Thus, the Domain Model depends on the data access layer. On the other hand, the OrmRepository class is an ORM-based implementation of the IRepository interface. It can't implement the interface without referencing it, so the data access layer also depends on the Domain Model. In other words, the dependencies form a cycle.

In such cases, coupling manifests as cycles. As illustrated by figure 16.6, *A* depends on *B*, which depends on *C*, which again depends on *A*. No mainstream languages prevent cycles, so you have to be eternally vigilant to avoid them.

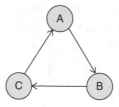

Figure 16.6 A simple cycle. A depends on B, which depends on C, which again depends on A.

There is, however, a hack that you can use. While mainstream languages allow cycles in code, they do prohibit them in package dependencies. If, for example, you try to define a data access interface in a Domain Model package and you want to use some object-relational mapper classes for parameters or return values, you'll have to add a dependency to your data access package.

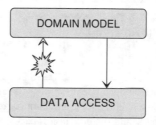

Figure 16.7 A cycle foiled. If the Domain Model package already references the data access package, the data access package can't reference the Domain Model package. You can't create a dependency cycle between packages.

Figure 16.7 illustrates what happens next. Once you want to implement the interface in the data access package, you'll need to add a dependency to the Domain Model package. Your IDE, however, refuses to break the Acyclic Dependency Principle [60], so you can't do that.

This should be motivation to break a code base into multiple packages. You get your IDE to enforce an architectural principle, even if it's only at a coarse-grained level. It's poka-yoke applied to architecture. It passively prevents large-scale cycles.

The familiar way to separate a system into smaller components is to distribute the behaviour over Domain Model, data access, ports or user interface, and a Composition Root [25] package to compose the other three together.

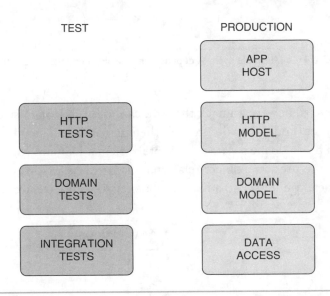

Figure 16.8 Hypothetical decomposition of the example restaurant reservation code base. The *HTTP model* would contain all the logic and configuration related to HTTP and REST, the *Domain Model* the 'business logic', and the *data access* package the code that talks to the database. The *app host* package would contain the Composition Root [25] that composes the three other packages. Three test packages would target the three production packages that contain complex logic.

As figure 16.8 implies, you may also want to unit test each package separately. Now, instead of three packages, you have seven.

The passive prevention of cycles is worth the extra complexity. Unless team members have extensive experience with a language that prevents cycles, I recommend this style of architecture.

Such languages do exist, though. F# famously prevents cycles. In it, you can't use a piece of code unless it's already defined above. Newcomers to the language see this as a terrible flaw, but it's actually one of its best features [117][37].

Haskell takes a different approach, but ultimately, its explicit treatment of side effects at the type level steers you towards a ports-and-adapters-style architecture. Your code simply doesn't compile otherwise [102]!

I've been writing F# and Haskell for enough years that I naturally follow the beneficial rules that they enforce. I'm confident that the sample code is nicely decoupled, even though it's packaged as a monolith. But unless you have a similar experience, I recommend that you separate your code base into multiple packages.

16.3 USAGE

If you're looking at an unfamiliar code base, you'd like to see it in action. A REST API doesn't have a user interface, so you can't just launch it and start clicking on buttons.

Or, to a certain degree, you can. If you run the application, you can view its 'home' resource in a browser. The JSON representations served by the API contain links that you can follow in your browser. It's a limited way to interact with the system, though.

Using your browser, you can only issue GET requests. To make a new reservation, however, you'll have to make a POST request.

16.3.1 LEARNING FROM TESTS

When a code base has a comprehensive test suite, you can often learn about intended usage from the tests. For example, you might want to learn how to make a new reservation in the system.

Listing 16.6 shows a test I wrote as I was expanding the code base to a multi-tenant system. It's representative of the way these tests are written.

As usual, this is code that fits in your head: it has a cyclomatic complexity of *1*, 6 activated objects, and 14 lines of code. The abstraction level is high, in the sense that it doesn't tell you the details of how it makes assertions, or how PostReservation is implemented.

Listing 16.6 Unit test that makes a reservation at the restaurant *Nono*.
(Restaurant/af31e63/Restaurant.RestApi.Tests/ReservationsTests.cs)

```
[Fact]
public async Task ReserveTableAtNono()
{
    using var api = new SelfHostedApi();
    var client = api.CreateClient();
    var dto = Some.Reservation.ToDto();
    dto.Quantity = 6;

    var response = await client.PostReservation("Nono", dto);

    var at = Some.Reservation.At;
    await AssertRemainingCapacity(client, at, "Nono", 4);
    await AssertRemainingCapacity(client, at, "Hipgnosta", 10);
}
```

If you're curious about that, you may decide to navigate to the
PostReservation implementation to see listing 16.7.

Listing 16.7 Test Utility Method [66] that makes a reservation.
(Restaurant/af31e63/Restaurant.RestApi.Tests/RestaurantApiClient.cs)

```
internal static async Task<HttpResponseMessage> PostReservation(
    this HttpClient client,
    string name,
    object reservation)
{
    string json = JsonSerializer.Serialize(reservation);
    using var content = new StringContent(json);
    content.Headers.ContentType.MediaType = "application/json";

    var resp = await client.GetRestaurant(name);
    resp.EnsureSuccessStatusCode();
    var rest = await resp.ParseJsonContent<RestaurantDto>();
    var address = rest.Links.FindAddress("urn:reservations");

    return await client.PostAsync(address, content);
}
```

This Test Utility Method [66] uses an HttpClient to interact with the REST
API. You may recall from listing 16.6 that the client in question communicates
with a self-hosted instance of the service. When you zoom in on the

PostReservation method, however, you no longer need to keep track of that. The only thing you need to know is that you have a working client.

This is another example of how the fractal architecture works. When you zoom in on a detail, the surrounding context becomes irrelevant. You don't have to keep it in your head.

Specifically, you can see that the helper method serialises the reservation to JSON. It then finds the appropriate address to use for making the POST request.

That's more detailed than before. Perhaps that taught you what you wanted to know. If you were curious about how to format the POST request, which HTTP headers to use, et cetera, then you need look no further. If, on the other hand, you'd like to know how to navigate to a particular restaurant, you'd have to zoom in on the GetRestaurant method. Or if you want to learn how to find a particular address in a JSON representation, you could zoom in on FindAddress.

Well-written tests can be a great learning resource.

16.3.2 LISTEN TO YOUR TESTS

If the book *Growing Object-Oriented Software, Guided by Tests* [36] had a motto, it'd be *listen to your tests*. Good tests can teach you more than how to interact with the System Under Test.

Keep in mind that test code is code too. You'll have to maintain it just like you must maintain the production code. You should refactor test code when it starts to rot, just like production code.

You may introduce Test Utility Methods [66] like listings 16.7 or 16.8. It turns out that the GetRestaurant method in listing 16.8 serves as a general-purpose entry point for any HttpClient that wants to interact with this particular REST API. Since it's a multi-tenant system, the first step for any client is to navigate to the desired restaurant.

If you look closer at listings 16.7 or 16.8, there's nothing test-specific about them. Might they be useful in other contexts?

Listing 16.8 Test Utility Method [66] that finds a restaurant resource based on its name. *(Restaurant/af31e63/Restaurant.RestApi.Tests/RestaurantApiClient.cs)*

```
internal static async Task<HttpResponseMessage> GetRestaurant(
    this HttpClient client,
    string name)
{
    var homeResponse =
        await client.GetAsync(new Uri("", UriKind.Relative));
    homeResponse.EnsureSuccessStatusCode();
    var homeRepresentation =
        await homeResponse.ParseJsonContent<HomeDto>();
    var restaurant =
        homeRepresentation.Restaurants.First(r => r.Name == name);
    var address = restaurant.Links.FindAddress("urn:restaurant");

    return await client.GetAsync(address);
}
```

The benefit of a REST API is that it supports any client that 'speaks' HTTP and can parse JSON[4]. Still, if the only thing you do is to publish the API, all third-party programmers will have to develop their own client code. If a substantial segment of your clients are on the same platform as your test code, you could promote those Test Utility Methods to an 'official' client SDK.

Situations like that regularly happen to me. As I refactor test code, I realise that some of it would also be useful as production code. That's always a happy discovery. When that happens, move the code over. Profit.

16.4   CONCLUSION

'Real' engineering is a mix of deterministic processes and human judgment. If you need to build a bridge, you have formulas to calculate load-bearing strength, but you still need to involve people to deal with the myriad complexities related to the task. What sort of traffic should the bridge support? What is the desired throughput? What are the temperature extremes? What is the underground like? Are there environmental concerns?

---

4. Or XML, if you're in that mood.

If engineering was an entirely deterministic process, you wouldn't need people. All it would require would be computers and industrial robots.

It's possible that some engineering disciplines may move into that realm in the future, but if that happens, it stops being engineering; it becomes manufacturing.

You might consider this distinction merely ontological, but I believe that it pertains to the art of software engineering. There are quantitative methodologies that you can adopt. That doesn't discharge you from an obligation to use your brain.

The task is to combine skill with appropriate processes, heuristics, and technologies to make development more likely to succeed. In this book, I've presented multiple techniques you can adopt *today*. An early reader considered some of these ideas *advanced*. That may be so, but they are *possible*.

"The future is already here—it's just not very evenly distributed" – *William Gibson*

Likewise, the techniques presented here are no pie in the sky. Some organisations already use them. You could, too.

A LIST OF PRACTICES

This appendix contains a list of various methods and heuristics that are described throughout the book, including where to find them.

A.1 THE 50/72 RULE

Write conventional Git commit messages.

- Write a summary in the imperative, no wider than 50 characters.
- If you add more text, leave the next line blank.
- You can add as much extra text as you'd like, but format it no wider than 72 characters.

Apart from the summary, focus on explaining *why* a change was made, since *what* constitutes the change is already visible via Git's diff view. See subsection 9.1.1.

A.2   THE 80/24 RULE

Write small blocks of code.

In C-based languages like C#, Java, C++, or JavaScript, consider staying within a 80 × 24 character box. That corresponds to an old terminal window.

Don't take the threshold values *80* and *24* too literally. I picked them for three reasons:

* They work well in practice
* Continuity with tradition
* Mnemonically, it sounds like the Pareto principle, also known as the *80/20 rule*

You can decide on other threshold values. I think the most important part of this rule is to pick a set of thresholds and consistently stay within those limits.

Read more in subsection 7.1.3.

A.3   ARRANGE ACT ASSERT

Structure automated tests according to the Arrange Act Assert pattern. Make it clear to readers where one section ends and the next begins. See subsection 4.2.2 for the main idea, and 4.3.3 for additional details.

A.4   BISECTION

When you're struggling to understand the cause of a problem, bisection can be a useful technique. Remove half of your code and check if the problem is still present. Either way, you know in which half you can find the cause.

Keep halving the code until you've reduced it so much that you have a minimal working example. At that point, you may have removed so much irrelevant context to reproduce the problem that it's clear what the problem is. Read more in section 12.3.

A.5 CHECKLIST FOR A NEW CODE BASE

When you create a new code base, or add a new 'project' to an existing code base, consider following a checklist. Here's a suggestion:

- Use Git
- Automate the build
- Turn on all error messages

You can modify this checklist to suit your particular context, but keep it short and simple. Read more in section 2.2.

A.6 COMMAND QUERY SEPARATION

Separate Commands from Queries. Commands are procedures that have side effects. Queries are functions that return data. Every method should be either a Command or a Query, but not both. See more in subsection 8.1.6.

A.7 COUNT THE VARIABLES

Count all the variables involved in a method implementation. Include both local variables, method parameters, and class fields. Make sure to keep the number low. See subsection 7.2.7.

A.8 CYCLOMATIC COMPLEXITY

Cyclomatic complexity is one of few actually useful code metrics. It measures the number of pathways through a piece of code, thereby giving you an indication about the complexity of a method.

I find that instituting a threshold of seven works well in practice. You can accomplish useful work with a cyclomatic complexity of seven, so the threshold is big enough that you don't have to refactor all the time. On the other hand, it's still low enough that you can easily fit such a method in your brain. Read more in subsection 7.1.2.

The metric also gives you the minimum number of test cases you have to write to fully cover a method.

A.9 DECORATORS FOR CROSS-CUTTING CONCERNS

Don't inject logging dependencies into your business logic. That's not separation of concerns; that's jumbling them together. The same goes for caching, fault tolerance, and most other cross-cutting concerns.

Instead, use the Decorator design pattern, as described in section 13.2.

A.10 DEVIL'S ADVOCATE

The Devil's Advocate technique is a heuristic you can use to evaluate whether more test cases would improve confidence in the test suite. You can use it to review existing (test) code, but you can also use it as inspiration for new test cases that you should consider adding.

The technique is to deliberately implement the System Under Test incorrectly. The more incorrect you can make it, the more test cases you should consider adding. Read more in subsection 6.2.2.

A.11 FEATURE FLAG

If you can't complete a coherent set of changes in half a day's work, hide the feature behind a feature flag, and continue to integrate your changes with other peoples' work.

Read more in section 10.1.

A.12 FUNCTIONAL CORE, IMPERATIVE SHELL

Favour pure functions.

Referential transparency means that you can replace a function call with its result, with no change of program behaviour. This is the ultimate abstraction. The output encapsulates the essence of the function, while all implementation details remain hidden (unless you need them).

Pure functions also compose well, and they're easy to unit test.

See subsection 13.1.3 for more details.

A.13 HIERARCHY OF COMMUNICATION

Write code for future readers; it may be yourself. Favour communicating behaviour and intent according to this prioritised list:

1. Guide the reader by giving APIs distinct types.
2. Guide the reader by giving methods helpful names.
3. Guide the reader by writing good comments.
4. Guide the reader by providing illustrative examples as automated tests.
5. Guide the reader by writing helpful commit messages in Git.
6. Guide the reader by writing good documentation.

The items on the top of the list are more important than the items at the bottom. See subsection 8.1.7.

A.14 JUSTIFY EXCEPTIONS FROM THE RULE

Good rules work well most of the time, but there are always occasions where a rule is in the way. It's okay to deviate from a rule when circumstances require it, but justify and document the reason. See subsection 4.2.3 for a discussion.

It's a good idea to get a second opinion before you decide to deviate from a rule. Sometimes, you may not be able to see a good way to get what you want *and* follow the rule, but a co-worker can.

A.15   PARSE, DON'T VALIDATE

Your code interacts with the rest of the world, and the rest of the world isn't object-oriented. Instead, you receive data as JSON, XML, comma-separated values, protocol buffers, or in other formats that carry few guarantees as to the integrity of the data.

Convert less-structured data to more-structured data as soon as possible. You can think of this as *parsing*, even if you don't parse plain text. Read more in subsection 7.2.5.

A.16   POSTEL'S LAW

Keep Postel's law in mind for pre- and postconditions.

> *Be conservative in what you send, be liberal in what you accept.*

Methods should accept input as long as they can make sense of it, but no further. Return values should be as trustworthy as possible. Read more in subsection 5.2.4.

A.17   RED GREEN REFACTOR

When engaging in test-driven development, follow the Red Green Refactor process. You can think of it as a checklist [93]:

1. Write a failing test.
   - Did you run the test?
   - Did it fail?
   - Did it fail because of an assertion?
   - Did it fail because of the *last* assertion?
2. Make all tests pass by doing the simplest thing that could possibly work.
3. Consider the resulting code. Can it be improved? If so, do it, but make sure that all tests still pass.
4. Repeat.

Read more in subsection 5.2.2.

A.18 REGULARLY UPDATE DEPENDENCIES

Don't let your code base fall behind its dependencies. Check for updates at a regular schedule. It's easy to forget, but if you fall too far behind, it could be difficult to catch up. See subsection 14.2.1.

A.19 REPRODUCE DEFECTS AS TESTS

If at all possible, reproduce bugs as one or more automated tests. See subsection 12.2.1.

A.20 REVIEW CODE

It's easy to make mistakes when you write code. Have another person perform a code review. It doesn't capture all mistakes, but it's one of the most effective quality assurance techniques we know of.

You can perform code reviews in many ways: continually, when pair or mob programming, or asynchronously as pull request reviews.

Reviews should be constructive, but rejection should be a real option. If you can't reject a change, then a review is worth little.

Make code reviews part of your daily rhythm. See section 9.2.

A.21 SEMANTIC VERSIONING

Consider using Semantic Versioning. Read more in section 10.3.

A.22 SEPARATE REFACTORING OF TEST AND PRODUCTION CODE

Automated tests give you confidence when you need to refactor your production code. Refactoring test code, on the other hand, is more dangerous because you have no automated tests of the tests.

This doesn't mean that you can't refactor your test code at all, but you should be careful when you do. Particularly, don't refactor *both* test and production code at the same time.

When you refactor production code, leave the test code alone. When you refactor test code, leave the production code alone. Read more in subsection 11.1.3.

A.23 SLICE

Work in small increments. Each increment should improve a running, working system. Start with a vertical slice, and add functionality to it. Read more in chapter 4.

Don't consider this process exclusive. I find that it works as my main process for moving forward, but sometimes, you need to stop and do other things. Fixing bugs, for example, or working on cross-cutting concerns.

A.24 STRANGLER

Some refactorings are quickly done. Renaming a variable, method, or class is built into most IDEs and is just a button click away. Other changes require a few minutes, or perhaps hours. As long as you can go from one consistent state of the code base to another consistent state in less than half a day, you may not need to do anything special.

Other changes have a greater potential impact. I've done refactorings that took days, even more than a week, to implement. That's not a good way to work.

When you detect that this may be the case, use the Strangler process to implement the changes. Establish the new way of doing things side-by-side with the old way, and gradually migrate code from the old to the new way.

This can take hours, days, or even weeks, but during the migration process, the system is always consistent and integrable. When no code calls the original API, you can delete it.

Read more in section 10.2.

A.25 THREAT-MODEL

Take deliberate security decisions.

For people who aren't security experts, the STRIDE model is easy enough to get your head around that you can do a decent job of it.

- Spoofing
- Tampering
- Repudiation
- Information disclosure
- Denial of service
- Elevation of privilege

Threat modelling should involve IT professionals and other stakeholders, since proper mitigation typically involves weighing business concerns against security risks.

Read more in subsection 15.2.1.

A.26 TRANSFORMATION PRIORITY PREMISE

Try to work in a way so that your code is in a valid state most of the time. Transforming one valid state into another valid state typically involves a phase where the code is invalid, for example where it may not compile.

The Transformation Priority Premise suggests a series of small transformations that minimises the invalid phases. Try to edit your code by moving through a series of these small changes. Read more in subsection 5.1.1.

A.27 X-DRIVEN DEVELOPMENT

Use a *driver* for the code that you write. It could be static code analysis, a unit test, built-in refactoring tools, et cetera. See section 4.2 for more details.

It's okay to deviate from this rule, but the closer you adhere to it, the less you tend to go astray.

A.28   X Out Names

Replace method names with Xs to examine how much information a method's signature communicates. You can do it in your head; you don't actually have to do it in your editor. The point is that in a statically typed language, types can carry much information, if you let them. Read more in subsection 8.1.5.

BIBLIOGRAPHY

[1] Adzic, Gojko, *The Poka-Yoke principle and how to write better software*, blog post at https://gojko.net/2007/05/09/the-poka-yoke-principle-and-how-to-write-better-software, 2007.

[2] Allamaraju, Subbu, *RESTful Web Services Cookbook*, O'Reilly, published 2010.

[3] Atwood, Jeff, *New Programming Jargon*, blog post at https://blog.codinghorror.com/new-programming-jargon, 2012.

[4] Barr, Adam, *The Problem with Software. Why Smart Engineers Write Bad Code*, MIT Press, 2018.

[5] Beck, Kent, and Cynthia Andres, *Extreme Programming Explained: Embrace Change*, Addison-Wesley, published 2004.

[6] Beck, Kent, tweet at https://twitter.com/KentBeck/status/250733358307500032, 2012.

[7] Beck, Kent, *Implementation Patterns*, Addison-Wesley, published 2007.

[8] Beck, Kent, *Naming From the Outside In*, Facebook note at https://www.facebook.com/notes/kent-beck/naming-from-the-outside-in/464270190272517 (accessible without a Facebook account), 2012.

[9] Beck, Kent, *Test-Driven Development By Example*, Addison-Wesley, published 2002.

[10] Beck, Kent, tweet at https://twitter.com/KentBeck/status/1354418068869398538, 2021.

[11] Bernhardt, Gary, *Functional Core, Imperative Shell*, online presentation at www.destroyallsoftware.com/screencasts/catalog/functional-core-imperative-shell, 2012.

[12] Böckeler, Birgitta, and Nina Siessegger, *On Pair Programming*, blog post at https://martinfowler.com/articles/on-pair-programming.html, 2020.

[13] Bossavit, Laurent, *The Leprechauns of Software Engineering*, Laurent Bossavit, 2015.

[14] Brooks, Frederick P., Jr., *No Silver Bullet – Essence and Accident in Software Engineering*, 1986. This essay can be found in various sources, and is easily located on the Internet. In writing this book, I referred to my copy of *The Mythical Man-Month: Essays on Software Engineering. Anniversary Edition*, Addison-Wesley, published 1995, in which the essay constitutes chapter 16.

[15] Brown, William J., Raphael C. Malveau, Hays W. "Skip" McCormick III, and Thomas J. Mowbray, *AntiPatterns: Refactoring Software, Architectures, and Projects in Crisis*, Wiley Computer Publishing, 1998.

[16] Cain, Susan, *Quiet: The Power of Introverts in a World That Can't Stop Talking*, Crown, 2012.

[17] Campidoglio, Enrico, tweet at https://twitter.com/ecampidoglio/status/1194597766128963584, 2019.

[18] Cirillo, Francesco, *The Pomodoro Technique: The Life-Changing Time-Management System*, Virgin Books, 2018.

[19] Cockburn, Alistair, *Hexagonal architecture*, online article at https://alistair.cockburn.us/hexagonal-architecture/, 2005.

[20] Cohen, Jason, *Modern Code Review* in [75], 2010.

[21] Conway, Melvin E., *How Do Committees Invent?*, *Datamation*, 1968. I admit that I don't own a copy of the April 1968 issue of *Datamation* magazine.

Instead, I've used the online reprint that Melvin Conway hosts at http://www
.melconway.com/Home/Committees_Paper.html.

[22] Cunningham, Ward, and Bill Venners, *The Simplest Thing that Could Possibly Work. A Conversation with Ward Cunningham, Part V*, interview at www.artima.com/intv/simplest.html, 2004.

[23] Cwalina, Krzysztof, and Brad Abrams, *Framework Design Guidelines, Conventions, Idioms, and Patterns for Reusable .NET Libraries*, Addison-Wesley, published 2005.

[24] DeLine, Robert, *Code Talkers* in [75], 2010.

[25] Deursen, Steven van, and Mark Seemann, *Dependency Injection Principles, Practices, and Patterns*, Manning, 2019.

[26] Evans, Eric, *Domain-Driven Design: Tackling Complexity in the Heart of Software*, Addison-Wesley, published 2003.

[27] Feathers, Michael C., *Working Effectively with Legacy Code*, Prentice Hall, published 2004.

[28] Foote, Brian, and Joseph Yoder, *The Selfish Class* in [62], 1998.

[29] Forsgren, Nicole, Jez Humble, and Gen Kim, *Accelerate*, IT Revolution Press, 2018.

[30] Fowler, Martin, *CodeOwnership*, blog post at https://martinfowler.com/bliki/CodeOwnership.html, 2006.

[31] Fowler, Martin, *Eradicating Non-Determinism in Tests*, blog post at https://martinfowler.com/articles/nonDeterminism.html, 2011.

[32] Fowler, Martin, *Is High Quality Software Worth the Cost?*, blog post at https://martinfowler.com/articles/is-quality-worth-cost.html, 2019.

[33] Fowler, Martin, David Rice, Matthew Foemmel, Edward Hieatt, Robert Mee, and Randy Stafford, *Patterns of Enterprise Application Architecture*, Addison-Wesley, 2003.

[34] Fowler, Martin, Kent Beck, John Brant, William Opdyke, and Don Roberts, *Refactoring: Improving the Design of Existing Code*, Addison-Wesley, 1999.

[35] Fowler, Martin, *StranglerFigApplication*, blog post at https://martinfowler.com/bliki/StranglerFigApplication.html, 2004.

[36] Freeman, Steve, and Nat Pryce, *Growing Object-Oriented Software, Guided by Tests*, Addison-Wesley, published 2009.

[37] Gabasova, Evelina, *Comparing F# and C# with dependency networks*, blog post at http://evelinag.com/blog/2014/06-09-comparing-dependency-networks, 2014.

[38] Gabriel, Richard P., *Patterns of Software. Tales from the Software Community*, Oxford University Press, 1996.

[39] Gamma, Erich, Richard Helm, Ralph Johnson, and John Vlissides, *Design Patterns: Elements of Reusable Object-Oriented Software*, Addison-Wesley, published 1994.

[40] Gawande, Atul, *The Checklist Manifesto: How to Get Things Right*, Metropolitan Books, 2009.

[41] Haack, Phil, *I Knew How To Validate An Email Address Until I Read The RFC*, blog post at https://haacked.com/archive/2007/08/21/i-knew-how-to-validate-an-email-address-until-i.aspx, 2007.

[42] Henney, Kevlin, tweet at https://twitter.com/KevlinHenney/status/3361631527, 2009.

[43] Herraiz, Israel, and Ahmed E. Hassan, *Beyond Lines of Code: Do We Need More Complexity Metrics?* in [75], 2010.

[44] Herzig, Kim Sebastian, and Andreas Zeller, *Mining Your Own Evidence* in [75], 2010.

[45] Hickey, Rich, *Simple Made Easy*, Strange Loop conference talk, 2011. A recording is available at www.infoq.com/presentations/Simple-Made-Easy.

[46] Hohpe, Gregor, and Bobby Woolf, *Enterprise Integration Patterns: Designing, Building, and Deploying Messaging Solutions*, Addison-Wesley, published 2003.

[47] House, Cory, tweet at https://twitter.com/housecor/status/1115959687332159490, 2019.

[48] Howard, Michael, and David LeBlanc, *Writing Secure Code, Second Edition*, Microsoft Press, 2003.

[49] Humble, Jez, and David Farley, *Continuous Delivery: Reliable Software Releases Through Build, Test, and Deployment Automation*, Addison-Wesley, published 2010.

[50] Hunt, Andy, and Dave Thomas, *The Pragmatic Programmer: From Journeyman to Master*, Addison-Wesley, 1999.

[51] Kahneman, Daniel, *Thinking, fast and slow*, Farrar, Straus and Giroux, 2011.

[52] Kay, Alan, and Andrew Binstock, *Interview with Alan Kay*, Dr. Dobb's, www.drdobbs.com/architecture-and-design/interview-with-alan-kay/240003442, July 10, 2012.

[53] Kerievsky, Joshua, *Refactoring to Patterns*, Addison-Wesley, published 2004.

[54] King, Alexis, *Parse, don't validate*, blog post at https://lexi-lambda.github.io/blog/2019/11/05/parse-don-t-validate, 2019.

[55] Kleppmann, Martin, *Designing Data-Intensive Applications: The Big Ideas Behind Reliable, Scalable, and Maintainable Systems*, O'Reilly, 2017.

[56] Lanza, Michele, and Radu Marinescu, *Object-Oriented Metrics in Practice: Using Software Metrics to Characterize, Evaluate, and Improve the Design of Object-Oriented Systems*, Springer, 2006.

[57] Levitt, Steven D., and Stephen J. Dubner, *Freakonomics—A Rogue Economist Explores The Hidden Side Of Everything*, William Morrow & Company, Revised and Expanded Edition 2006.

[58] Levitt, Steven D., and Stephen J. Dubner, *SuperFreakonomics: Global Cooling, Patriotic Prostitutes And Why Suicide Bombers Should Buy Life Insurance*, William Morrow & Company, 2009.

[59] Lippert, Eric, *Which is faster?*, blog post at https://ericlippert.com/2012/12/17/performance-rant, 2012.

[60] Martin, Robert C., and Micah Martin, *Agile Principles, Patterns, and Practices in C#*, Prentice Hall, published 2006.

[61] Martin, Robert C., *Clean Code: A Handbook of Agile Software Craftsmanship*, Prentice Hall, 2009.

[62] Martin, Robert C., Dirk Riehle, and Frank Buschmann (editors), *Pattern Languages of Program Design 3*, Addison-Wesley, 1998.

[63] Martin, Robert C., *The Sensitivity Problem*, blog post at http://butunclebob .com/ArticleS.UncleBob.TheSensitivityProblem, 2005?

[64] Martin, Robert C., *The Transformation Priority Premise*, blog post at https:// blog.cleancoder.com/uncle-bob/2013/05/27/TheTransformationPriorityPremise .html, 2013.

[65] McConnell, Steve, *Code Complete, Second Edition*, Microsoft Press, 2004.

[66] Meszaros, Gerard, *xUnit Test Patterns: Refactoring Test Code*, Addison-Wesley, 2007.

[67] Meyer, Bertrand, *Object-oriented Software Construction*, Prentice Hall, 1988.

[68] Milewski, Bartosz, *Category Theory for Programmers*, originally a series of blog posts at https://bartoszmilewski.com/2014/10/28/category-theory-for-programmers-the-preface, 2014–2017. Also available as a print book, Blurb, 2019.

[69] Minsky, Yaron, *Effective ML*, recording of a lecture given at Harvard. The recording itself is available on YouTube at https://youtu.be/-J8YyfrSwTk, but you may instead prefer Yaron Minsky's web page that includes a bit of context: https://blog.janestreet.com/effective-ml-video, 2010.

[70] Neward, Ted, *The Vietnam of Computer Science*, blog post at http://blogs .tedneward.com/post/the-vietnam-of-computer-science, 2006.

[71] Norman, Donald A., *The Design of Everyday Things. Revised and Expanded Edition*, MIT Press, 2013.

[72] North, Dan, *Patterns of Effective Delivery*, Roots opening keynote, 2011. A recording is available at https://vimeo.com/24681032.

[73] Nygard, Michael T., *Release It! Design and Deploy Production-Ready Software*, Pragmatic Bookshelf, 2007.

[74] Nygard, Michael T., *DevOps: Tempo, Maneuverability, and Initiative*, DevOps Enterprise Summit conference talk, 2016. A recording is available at https://youtu.be/0rRWvsb8JOo.

[75] Oram, Andy, and Greg Wilson (editors), *Making Software: What Really Works, and Why We Believe It*, O'Reilly, 2010.

[76] O'Toole, Garson, *The Future Has Arrived – It's Just Not Evenly Distributed Yet*, online article on https://quoteinvestigator.com/2012/01/24/future-has-arrived, 2012.

[77] Ottinger, Tim, *Code is a Liability*, 2007. This was originally a blog post, but the original domain has since lapsed and been taken over by another entity. The blog post is still available via the Internet Archive at http://web.archive.org/web/20070420113817/http://blog.objectmentor.com/articles/2007/04/16/code-is-a-liability.

[78] Ottinger, Tim, *What's this about Micro-commits?*, blog post at https://www.industriallogic.com/blog/whats-this-about-micro-commits, 2021.

[79] Peters, Tim, *The Zen of Python*, 1999. Originally a mailing list post, it's long been available at www.python.org/dev/peps/pep-0020.

[80] Pinker, Steven, *How the Mind Works*, The Folio Society, 2013. I'm referring to my Folio Society edition, which, according to the colophon, "follows the text of the 1998 Penguin edition, with minor emendations." It was "first published by W.W. Norton in 1997."

[81] Pope, Tim, *A Note About Git Commit Messages*, blog post at https://tbaggery.com/2008/04/19/a-note-about-git-commit-messages.html, 2008.

[82] Poppendieck, Mary, and Tom Poppendieck, *Implementing Lean Software Development: From Concept to Cash*, Addison-Wesley, published 2006.

[83] Preston-Werner, Tom, *Semantic Versioning*, specification at https://semver.org. The root of the web site shows the latest version. As I'm writing in October 2020, the latest version is Semantic Versioning 2.0.0, which was published in 2013.

[84] Pyhäjärvi, Maaret, *Five Years of Mob Testing, Hello to Ensemble Testing*, blog post at https://visible-quality.blogspot.com/2020/05/five-years-of-mob-testing-hello-to.html, 2020.

[85] Rainsberger, J.B., *Integration Tests Are a Scam*, Agile 2009 conference talk, 2009. A recording is available at www.infoq.com/presentations/integration-tests-scam.

[86] Rainsberger, J.B., tweet at https://twitter.com/jbrains/status/167297606698008576, 2012.

[87] Reeves, Jack, *What Is Software Design?*, *C++ Journal*, 1992. If, like me, you don't have a copy of the *C++ Journal* lying around, you can find the article online. www.developerdotstar.com/mag/articles/reeves_design.html seems to have been stable for years. Also available as an appendix in [60].

[88] Ries, Eric, *The Lean Startup: How Constant Innovation Creates Radically Successful Businesses*, Portfolio Penguin, 2011.

[89] Robinson, Ian, Jim Webber and Emil Eifrem, *Graph Databases: New Opportunities for Connected Data. Second Edition*, O'Reilly, 2015.

[90] Scott, James C., *Seeing Like a State: How Certain Schemes to Improve the Human Condition Have Failed*, Yale University Press, 1998.

[91] Seemann, Mark, *10 tips for better Pull Requests*, blog post at https://blog.ploeh.dk/2015/01/15/10-tips-for-better-pull-requests, 2015.

[92] Seemann, Mark, *A heuristic for formatting code according to the AAA pattern*, blog post at https://blog.ploeh.dk/2013/06/24/a-heuristic-for-formatting-code-according-to-the-aaa-pattern, 2013.

[93] Seemann, Mark, *A red-green-refactor checklist*, blog post at https://blog.ploeh.dk/2019/10/21/a-red-green-refactor-checklist, 2019.

[94] Seemann, Mark, *Church-encoded Maybe*, blog post at https://blog.ploeh.dk/2018/06/04/church-encoded-maybe, 2018.

[95] Seemann, Mark, *CQS versus server generated IDs*, blog post at https://blog.ploeh.dk/2014/08/11/cqs-versus-server-generated-ids, 2014.

[96] Seemann, Mark, *Conway's Law: latency versus throughput*, blog post at https://blog.ploeh.dk/2020/03/16/conways-law-latency-versus-throughput, 2020.

[97] Seemann, Mark, *Curb code rot with thresholds*, blog post at https://blog.ploeh.dk/2020/04/13/curb-code-rot-with-thresholds, 2020.

[98] Seemann, Mark, *Devil's advocate*, blog post at https://blog.ploeh.dk/2019/10/07/ devils-advocate, 2019.

[99] Seemann, Mark, *Feedback mechanisms and tradeoffs*, blog post at https://blog .ploeh.dk/2011/04/29/Feedbackmechanismsandtradeoffs, 2011.

[100] Seemann, Mark, *From interaction-based to state-based testing*, blog post at https://blog.ploeh.dk/2019/02/18/from-interaction-based-to-state-based-testing, 2019.

[101] Seemann, Mark, *Fortunately, I don't squash my commits*, blog post at https:// blog.ploeh.dk/2020/10/05/fortunately-i-dont-squash-my-commits, 2020.

[102] Seemann, Mark, *Functional architecture is Ports and Adapters*, blog post at https://blog.ploeh.dk/2016/03/18/functional-architecture-is-ports-and-adapters, 2016.

[103] Seemann, Mark, *Repeatable execution*, blog post at https://blog.ploeh.dk/2020/ 03/23/repeatable-execution, 2020.

[104] Seemann, Mark, *Structural equality for better tests*, blog post at https://blog .ploeh.dk/2021/05/03/structural-equality-for-better-tests, 2021.

[105] Seemann, Mark, *Tautological assertion*, blog post at https://blog.ploeh.dk/2019/ 10/14/tautological-assertion, 2019.

[106] Seemann, Mark, *Towards better abstractions*, blog post at https://blog.ploeh .dk/2010/12/03/Towardsbetterabstractions, 2010.

[107] Seemann, Mark, *Visitor as a sum type*, blog post at https://blog.ploeh.dk/2018/ 06/25/visitor-as-a-sum-type, 2018.

[108] Seemann, Mark, *When properties are easier than examples*, blog post at https:// blog.ploeh.dk/2021/02/15/when-properties-are-easier-than-examples, 2021.

[109] Shaw, Julia, *The Memory Illusion: Remembering, Forgetting, and the Science of False Memory*, Random House, 2017 (paperback edition; original published in 2016).

[110] Thomas, Neil, and Gail Murphy, *How Effective Is Modularization?* in [75], 2010.

[111] Tornhill, Adam, *Your Code as a Crime Scene: Use Forensic Techniques to Arrest Defects, Bottlenecks, and Bad Design in Your Programs*, Pragmatic Bookshelf, 2015.

[112] Tornhill, Adam, *Software Design X-Rays: Fix Technical Debt with Behavioral Code Analysis*, Pragmatic Bookshelf, 2018.

[113] Troy, Chelsea, *Reviewing Pull Requests*, blog post at https://chelseatroy.com/2019/12/18/reviewing-pull-requests, 2019.

[114] Webber, Jim, Savas Parastatidis, and Ian Robinson, *REST in Practice: Hypermedia and Systems Architecture*, O'Reilly, 2010.

[115] Weinberg, Gerald M., *The psychology of computer programming. Silver anniversary edition*, Dorset House Publishing, 1998.

[116] Williams, Laurie, *Pair Programming* in [75], 2010.

[117] Wlaschin, Scott, *Cycles and modularity in the wild*, blog post at https://fsharpforfunandprofit.com/posts/cycles-and-modularity-in-the-wild, 2013.

[118] Woolf, Bobby, *Null Object* in [62], 1997.

INDEX